THE HERMENEUTIC NATURE OF
ANALYTIC PHILOSOPHY

SANTIAGO ZABALA

THE HERMENEUTIC NATURE OF ANALYTIC PHILOSOPHY

A STUDY OF ERNST TUGENDHAT

FOREWORD BY GIANNI VATTIMO

*TRANSLATED BY THE AUTHOR WITH
MICHAEL HASKELL*

COLUMBIA UNIVERSITY PRESS   NEW YORK

COLUMBIA UNIVERSITY PRESS
Publishers Since 1893
New York   Chichester, West Sussex

Originally published in Italian as *Filosofare con Ernst Tugendhat*.
Copyright © 2004 Franco Angeli Editore S.p.A.
Copyright © 2008 Columbia University Press
All rights reserved

Library of Congress Cataloging-in-Publication Data

Zabala, Santiago, 1975–
The hermeneutic nature of analytic philosophy : a study of
Ernst Tugendhat / Santiago Zabala; foreword by Gianni Vattimo ;
translated by the author with Michael Haskell.
p. cm.
Includes bibliographical references and index.
ISBN 978-0-231-14388-2 (cloth : alk. paper)—
ISBN 978-0-231-51297-8 (e-book : alk. paper)
1. Tugendhat, Ernst. 2. Analysis (Philosophy) 3. Hermeneutics.
I. Title.

B3349.T834Z3313 2008
149'.94—DC22   2007043667

Columbia University Press books are
printed on permanent and durable acid-free paper.
This book is printed on paper with recycled content.

Printed in the United States of America

c 10 9 8 7 6 5 4 3 2 1

BOOK & JACKET DESIGNED BY VIN DANG

FOR MY MOM

CONTENTS

The Italian edition of this book appeared in 2004. Although this English translation is virtually unaltered, new secondary literature has been added and two paragraphs were rewritten and expanded in order to introduce the thought of Ernst Tugendhat to the Anglo-Saxon public. When quoting from works originally published in German and other languages, we have substituted quotations from and references to published English translations whenever possible, or, when it was not, to published editions of the original works in whatever language they were written.

We would like to thank Professor Ernst Tugendhat for having revised the English translation of the dialogue, which can be found in the epilogue. For offering valuable suggestions along the way, many thanks are due to Floriano von Arx, Pablo Cardoso, Robert Fellman, Jean Grondin, Alberto Martinengo, Ana Messuti, Richard Palmer, Richard Rorty, James Scott, Thomas Sheehan, Andrea Torrisi, Ugo Ugazio, and Gianni Vattimo.

Ernst Tugendhat came to my attention for the first time in the 1960s when I was studying in Heidelberg, through his phenomenological investigations of Aristotle, Husserl, and Heidegger (especially *TI KATA TINOS. Eine Untersuchung zu Struktur und Ursprung aristotelischer Grundbegriffe* [1958] and *Der Wahrheitsbegriff bei Husserl und Heidegger* [1967], which became indispensable books for anyone interested in continental philosophy). However, it is through my friend Richard Rorty's 1985 review of Tugendhat's *Traditional and Analytical Philosophy* (1976) for the *Journal of Philosophy* that I realized that Tugendhat, Jürgen Habermas, and Karl-Otto Apel were going to become the most distinguished German philosophers after the death of Hans-Georg Gadamer. This is now confirmed by Santiago Zabala's book, which offers the first presentation of the significance of Tugendhat's philosophy not only for the continental and analytical traditions, but also for the tradition to come. Unlike Habermas and Apel, who were born and raised in devastated postwar Germany, Tugendhat, who is Jewish, was born on March 8, 1930, in the former Czechoslovakia, in Brünn. He emigrated to Switzerland in 1938 and Venezuela in 1941, earned his undergraduate degree at Stanford in 1949, and returned to Germany as a graduate student in 1950 to participate in Heidegger's seminars in Fribourg. After having taught philosophy at Tubingen, Michigan, Heidelberg, Berlin, Vienna, and Prague, and working alongside Habermas at the Max Planck Institute of Starnberg, Tugendhat received numerous awards, including the 2006 Meister Eckhart Prize for his profound influence in German culture. Although today he is a recognized and distinguished world philosopher, the low level of recognition he has garnered outside Germany in the Anglo-Saxon world is quite amazing. His two books translated so far (*Traditional and Analytical Philosophy* and *Self-Consciousness and Self-Determination*) were discussed shortly after their publication only by those intellectuals that themselves overcame the continental-analytic divide (Rorty, Robert B. Pippin, Charles Taylor, and Charles Larmore) and who recognized in Tugendhat one of the first philosophers to fuse analytical philosophy and Heidegger's history of ontology.

If one believes that in order to enter into dialogue with both philosophical traditions one must also be fluent in the vocabularies of each, then it is not surprising that, first, Tugendhat could merge both traditions, and second, that the first book on his philosophy comes from Santiago Zabala, who shares Tugendhat's international upbringing, being multilingual and having lived in Rome, Vienna, Turin, Berlin and Geneva.

From my continental angle, analytic philosophy was a synonym for the so-called linguistic turn, an expression first used by Gustav Bergmann in his essay *Logic and Reality* (1964) and canonized by Rorty in *The Linguistic Turn*. Rorty's volume, which came out at the same time as Tugendhat's *Der Wahrheitsbegriff bei Husserl und Heidegger*, was one of the first attempts to trace the history of the analytic movement. The linguistic turn to which Rorty and Tugendhat refer is a phase of the fusion of traditions and the start not only of the historical self-understanding of the analytic tradition but also of the end of metaphysics. When Zabala, following Tugendhat's and Rorty's early indications, uses "the linguistic turn" interchangeably with "the end of metaphysics," he engages a specific moment in the history of contemporary philosophy that some analytical philosophers, such as Kevin Mulligan or Barry Smith, still do not take seriously enough. These are the philosophers who still believe that analytic philosophy should be scientific and who agree with Quine's dictum that the "philosophy of science is philosophy enough." Instead, Tugendhat belongs to those philosophers that began reading Wittgenstein's *Philosophical Investigations* side by side with Hegel's *Phenomenology of Spirit* and Freud's *Interpretation of Dreams* and who believe that analytic philosophy should have a deeper historical self-understanding of its own tradition. This is one of the be-liefs that Tugendhat, together with Rorty and other prominent American philosophers such as Michael Williams, Arthur Danto, Robert Brandom, Bas C. van Fraassen, and Barry Allen, agree upon. Tugendhat is a promi-nent promoter of this belief because, apart from being formed within the framework of Heidegger's thinking, he was always an attentive reader of Ludwig Wittgenstein, Gottlob Frege, John Searle, and Peter Strawson, who all played significant roles in his fusion of analytic and continental philosophy. According to Tugendhat, it is only by acquiring the herme-neutical dimension that analytic philosophy can legitimize its place within the history of philosophy from Plato through Aquinas to Donald David-son. For a continental reader such as myself, the fact that Tugendhat, as Zabala rightly shows, used his own critical interpretation of Heidegger to put forward an analytical position, just as Gadamer used it to put for-ward a hermeneutical one, demonstrates the enormous consequences that Heidegger's philosophy continues to have.

Although Zabala does not engage Tugendhat's later works on ethics, social philosophy, antinuclear activism, and pacifism (see *Probleme der Ethik* [1984], *Nachdenken über die Atomkriegsgefahr und warum man sie nicht sieht* [1987], *Ethik und Politik* [1992], *Vorlesungen über Ethic* [1993], *Egozentrizität und Mystik* [2003], *Über den Tod* [2006], and *Anthropologie statt Metaphysik* [2007]), his book deserves the same amount of atten-tion that the first full-length text on Heidegger by William J. Richardson, *Heidegger: Through Phenomenology to Thought* (1963) received—not only because it is the first study of his philosophy but because both works in-clude observations by Heidegger and Tugendhat that make their own in-vestigations part of these authors' works. Both philosophers—Heidegger through a letter published in the foreword and Tugendhat through a dia-logue published in the epilogue—respond in general to their interpret-ers, suggesting not only theoretical confirmations but also objections that perhaps would never have come to light if these two studies had not been brought forth.

The main thesis of this book is that the theoretical challenge of Tugend-hat is not really directed against hermeneutics and its Heideggerian bases but rather against analytical philosophy, to which the German philosopher seems closer for his concerns in defending method, logic, and a rigorous notion of truth. A parallel thesis to this one, or better, a slightly different formulation of the same thesis, is Zabala's argument that Tugendhat is, together with Gadamer, one of the most original disciples and interpreters of Heidegger. If Gadamer represents a hermeneutical Heideggerianism, then Tugendhat represents an "analytical" one. In these terms, this book's thesis seems quite audacious and shocking, but its meaning, even if one does not share its exaggerated aspects (such as "Gadamerians" like myself), is quite solidly discussed in Zabala's study. Driven by analytical concerns, Tugendhat studies Heidegger and discusses hermeneutics. He discusses the problem of truth not only as the general revelation of Being but also as the truth of statements. His conclusions are in fact a confirmation of Heidegger's thesis, with all the problematics that they do not dissolve. However, even Tugendhat's analytical struggle shows the impossibility of overcoming this aporia, or even the nonsense of the matter.

Neither Heidegger in *Being and Time* nor Gadamer in *Truth and Method* (this last one explicitly and consciously) provides a logical-methodical foundation for the truth of statements. One can observe that Kant also did not respond to this demand; he held only that Pure Reason was assumed as an acquired element (of statements) of Newton's physics and individuated the possible conditions in the a priori forms of the faculty of knowledge. Since neither Heidegger nor Gadamer has an analogous confidence in experimental sciences, they refused to take up the formulation of a method that would guarantee the truth of statements. This seems like a serious flaw that exposes them to the risk of relativism. It is from this observation that Tugendhat begins his exploration of Heidegger's doctrine of truth as revealing. As we all know, *Being and Time* opposes, to the idea of truth as conformity of the proposition to the thing, that of an original disclosure—the disclosure, *aletheia*—that renders possible any access to beings and therefore also any eventual conformity or deformity. False statements also move inside this original disclosure, and there are no explicit methodological criteria to distinguish them from true ones. Tugendhat also suggests that such absence of criteria is the same in ethics, or better, in Heidegger's nonethic. As far as Gadamer is concerned, it is clear that the title of his inaugural work, *Truth and Method*, has a polemical sense, although it is not implicit: the experience of truth is given also where no method is present and, better still, outside or before the sphere of verified and verifiable statements. The call to ethics and the problem of good and evil, which Heidegger rigorously avoids facing, may not only be an indication of a parallel problem but also a way to solve it. The theme of truth as the concrete validity of the statement (con)fuses itself in *Being and Time* with that of the authenticity of existence. If there isn't an objective criterion of comparison between the proposition and the thing, since beings are always revealed in the project that Da-sein is, then criteria for the truth of statements can only be found in the authenticity of the same project. Tugendhat does not follow this path, but the conclusions he arrives at—which Zabala calls the "semantization" of Heidegger's ontology—aren't that far away from it. If for hermeneutics, at least in its radical version, there are no facts, only interpretations (the expression, as we all know, is Nietzsche's), for Tugendhat's semantics—Zabala claims—there are no facts, only true propositions. But their truth does not consist of reflecting the object as a prelinguistic element but rather consists of their formulation according to a series of rules, which are those of the language in which they are enunciated. The object is never accessible extralinguistically. This does not mean we can stand on a basis of absolute linguistic idealism. The rules of language are as coercive or more than the evidence of the thing in the flesh. This coercion, according to me, has to do with Heidegger's authenticity; better still, it is a "semanticized" reformulation. In fact, if one searches in *Being and Time* and also in Heidegger's later work for a clarification of the notion of authenticity, one can certainly find his famous theory of the "decision to anticipate death." But the understandable sense of such anticipation is, we believe, only the assumption of one's own radical historicity. We originate from mortals and we are mortals; in other words, our destiny is in happenings, in eventualities. Truth, says *Being and Time*, "is only because and so long as Da-sein is." And for Da-sein to exist means it has been thrown in a concrete historical community, which, since being is mortal, becomes the only possible horizon. The explicit assumption—which can also be defined in opposition to every claim to grasp the ultimate foundation, or to pick the thing as it is "in itself"—takes away also to its specific thrownness the insuperable nature: this is also the difference between the assumption of the past as *Vergangenheit* (the stone of the past against which one is recalcitrant without being able to free oneself, the *es war* of Nietzsche) and its comprehension as *Gewesen*—as Da-sein that enters new interpretations and declinations into a disclosed project.

We know that in Tugendhat's original version (the semantization) and in this formula, which we rightly think we can derive from Heidegger, the answer we can advance to the problem of truth of statements is not satisfactory. But is there any answer that does not imply the dogmatic assumption of the immediate and prelinguistic evidence of the object? Descartes solved the problem only in terms of quality typical of the idea: what is given to me as a clear and distinct idea is true—in other words, it is the evidence of my own existence of a thinking being—but only given the condition that God excludes the hypothesis of the malicious genius. There is no evil as bad as the appeal to the "immediate" data. In Tugendhat, the Heideggerian identification of Being and language is valid. And precisely by seeking to avoid the "relativistic" outcome of this identification, one may also discover the other "identification" in Heidegger, that of Being with the event. Truth is only because and so long as Da-sein is, but Da-sein is historical and eventual and experiences truth only in the sphere of a historical horizon in which only every specific sentence gains sense. "Every," therefore, "any" sentence? An elegant response by Paul Ricouer to an interviewer for *Le Monde* (*Le Monde des livres*, January 30, 2004) may rescue us:

QUESTION. You refuse relativism then?

ANSWER. If I had to lay out my vision of the world, above all in its "practical commitments" aspects, I would say: given the place where I was born, the culture I received, what I read, learned and what I thought about, there exists for me a result that constitutes, here and now, the best thing to do. I call it "the action that suits." Here is a practical model that I extend also to the theoretical life. [This result,] in relation to others, constitutes for me an absolute. It is the thing to do or to think "for me." To my eyes, the serenity, the modesty of thought, as of action, consists in saying as Luther did: "Here I stand" (*Ici je me tiens, Hier stehe ich*).

It is no surprise that Ricouer was one of the greatest theoreticians of contemporary hermeneutics and also one who always worried, as did Tugendhat, about the criteria of truth and falsehood, of good and evil. The only possible escape from relativism (supposing it is a real risk, since only God, who looks "from nowhere," could truly be a relativist) is in this explicit assumption of our own historicity in the form of an "authentic" faithfulness to the rules of language and the form of life in which it expresses itself. Authenticity means, from a Heideggerian point of view, a conscious understanding of eventuality and finitude; true authenticity therefore knows also how to make itself a problem, not to take itself as an *es war* of which we would only be a determinational expression, in all and for all, foreseen. Even the idea of Being-event given to us in sentences and not only in the form of generic revealing may help explain the difference that Tugendhat invites us to recognize between the multiplicity of the works of art, which do not necessarily relate to one another but coexist as disclosures of truth. Scientific and ethical sentences on good and evil, which cannot be peacefully together, come forward as alternatives (see page ooo). Perhaps an important path opens up here to move beyond Heidegger and even beyond Tugendhat in the comprehension of what distinguishes the aesthetic experience and the truth that is announced in it (the setting-into-work) from the truth of statements. The key to all of this is in the radicalization of historicity. This is even more essential in a time when everybody talks more and more often about the "clash of civilizations," which it does not seem we are able to overcome either through an impossible relativism (everybody is inside a thrown project and cannot see the other projects "from the top") nor through an absolute recovery of truth either on the theoretical platform or in ethical decisions, which hide only a pretense of domination from the holders of truth. Tugendhat, like Gadamer, Ricouer, and—if more remotely—Heidegger, responds only with the formula of Luther: "Here I stand." This actually is already a response and therefore an explicit free and open assumption of one's own thrownness, to which only a possible experience of truth is given.

THE HERMENEUTIC NATURE OF
ANALYTIC PHILOSOPHY

CONTEMPORARY ANGLO-SAXON PHILOSOPHY EXHIBITS THE SAME SORT OF FRUIT-
FUL METAPHILOSOPHICAL CHAOS WHICH GERMAN IDEALISM EXHIBITED EARLY
IN THE NINETEENTH CENTURY. AS IN THOSE DAYS, EVERYBODY IS CERTAIN
THAT SOMETHING IMPORTANT HAPPENED WHEN PHILOSOPHY TOOK ITS LATEST
TURN, BUT NOBODY QUITE KNOWS WHAT. THE ONLY WAY WE SHALL FIND OUT IS
THROUGH SUCH ATTEMPTS AS ERNST TUGENDHAT'S—ATTEMPTS TO SPECIFY THE
NATURE OF PHILOSOPHY-AS-SEMANTICS BY SPECIFYING ITS SIMILARITIES WITH
AND DIFFERENCES FROM OTHER SORTS OF PHILOSOPHY.

— RICHARD RORTY —

Richard Rorty once described the culture of the future as one in which
human beings would want to live up to one another and where the relationship between master and disciple would be conceived not as "a power-
laden relation of 'overcoming' (*Überwindung*) but as a gentler relation
of turning to new 'purposes' (*Verwindung*)"—a "Gadamerian culture."[1]
The Gadamerian culture to which Richard Rorty alludes is represented
by the philosophy of Ernst Tugendhat. This book seeks not only to be
a historical account of Tugendhat's so-called linguistic turn, his passage
from phenomenology to analytical philosophy, but also a clarification
of his postmetaphysical position. Tugendhat, as Rüdiger Bubner has explained, "is one of Heidegger's last pupils" and "at the same time one
of the least subservient to his master. If the lesson which can be learned
from Heidegger is, as many proclaim, that the ethos of philosophy is

open and relentless questioning, then Tugendhat has taken this lesson to heart and applied it not least to against his teacher."[2] Tugendhat represents an "eccentric case" within the philosophical community because he is one of the few disciples of Heidegger—if not the only one—of his generation in Germany who continued Heidegger's work with analytic methods.[3] In today's contemporary philosophical culture, continental as well as analytical philosophers feel discomfort toward this philosopher because, on the one hand, he has shifted to the analytical field and, on the other, he continues to pose the question of the meaning of Being in a Heideggerian style. Tugendhat may be considered one of the first philosophers to pursue the attitude of his master, Heidegger, toward metaphysics not as a power-laden relation, capable of determining an *Überwindung*, but rather as distortion (*Verwindung*), which establishes a relationship of conformity. This distortion occurs through a "semantization" of Heidegger's ontology.[4] For Tugendhat, only formal semantics can answer Heidegger's open questions. Tugendhat's "eccentric case" is actually caused simply by his original interpretation and continuation of Heidegger's ontology in analytical philosophy—and this because Tugendhat's points of reference are as continental as they are analytical: Aristotle, Hegel, Husserl, Heidegger, Davidson, Habermas, Pothast, Wittgenstein, Fichte, Kant, Frege, Quine, Dummett, Strawson, Searle. This presence of thinkers from both traditions makes his philosophy a concentration of postmodern intuitions. The justifications for placing Tugendhat in the future Gadamerian culture can only be found in his linguistic turn. According to Rorty, "philosophers in the year 2100 . . . will read Gadamer and Putnam, Kuhn and Heidegger, Davidson and Derrida, Habermas and Vattimo, Theunissen and Brandom, side by side. If they do, it will be because they . . . will have substituted a conversational model, one in which philosophical success is measured by horizons fused rather than problems solved, or even by problems dissolved."[5] In the year 2100, Tugendhat will be remembered more for his passage from phenomenology to analytical philosophy than for his specific positions in analytical philosophy—in other words, for having fused philosophical horizons and styles. In contemporary philosophy, the marked division between analytical and continental philosophy has ended up creating an atmosphere where the impossibility of metaphysics and of overcoming it are seen only as an introduction to a philosophical culture of dialogue, of fusions.[6] Tugendhat should be considered one of the first examples of this culture, though he himself is unaware of this even as he helps lay the foundation for a culture that prefers philosophers who engage in dialogue with their predecessors while maintaining the proper distance for overcoming them in terms of *Verwindung*.[7]

The renewal of philosophy through the *Verwindung* of metaphysics is mostly determined by the outcome of the linguistic turn and, therefore, by the outcome of the idea that the linguistic a priori is the structural form of experience. Tugendhat, by maintaining in an open Gadamerian way the dialogue between the analytic philosophy of language and traditional European philosophy, is by all means the paradigmatic example of this turn. Vattimo believes:

> By now it has become a banality to say that the division between "analytical" (followers of the Vienna circle and of Wittgenstein) and "continentals" (phenomenologist, existentialist, and hermeneutics) does not subsist anymore, if one even considers it to have ever existed. . . . Both sides have been distancing themselves from the rationalistic motivations of modern philosophy, from the exclusive predilection of it for the problem of knowledge, and, in general, from Descartes' doubts. . . . Hegel already objected to Descartes' idea that each critical reflection happens within a historical condition that renders it possible and furnishes its substratum and framework. It is just on the basis of this awareness of the historicity of knowledge that the division between analytics and continentals has progressively dissolved, even if on both fields, a lot is still to be done in order to develop all the consequences.[8]

Philosophy then enters a condition in which it has no more "discoveries" to make. Instead, it only engages the "analysis" of the linguistic-analytic program. As Rorty noticed, this move raises the question of whether the result of making philosophy linguistic—of replacing Aristotle's and Descartes' problematics with Frege's—might not move philosophy away from "the secure path of a science" toward something more like the later Heidegger's historico-practico-existential meditations. "For the further one gets in the direction Tugendhat points the more philosophy will become a matter of therapy rather than discovery."[9]

According to Rüdiger Bubner, one of Gadamer's most distinguished disciples, "instead of following the aesthetic line followed by Heidegger's essay on *The Essence of the Work of Art* and largely taken over by Gadamer's hermeneutics, Tugendhat chooses the logical direction, seeking in formal semantics a differentiated and precise answer to the ontological question of Being."[10] Tugendhat basically asks himself: what is called "thinking" after the linguistic turn? The work undertaken toward such a turn, first by Frege and Peirce and then by Wittgenstein and Heidegger, has made possible not only the removal of metaphysics from the theory of truth as coherence but also the end of the dispute between subject and object, which has caused so much harm to philosophical and scientific investigations, in order to finally discuss "how assertions are justified."[11] Thanks to this linguistic turn, according to Tugendhat, the methodological reference can only be linguistic, and ontology becomes a formal semantic; in other words, it becomes a theory of meanings of singular terms capable of overcoming the metaphysics of presence. If we accept Rorty's "suggestion that nominalism can best be summarized in Gadamer's doctrine that only language can be understood,"[12] then Tugendhat is by all means a nominalist who tries to push philosophy toward a linguistic recognition of understanding. In him there is no trace of the resistance many analytical philosophers have always demonstrated toward any historical origin of theory; on the contrary, in order to show the linguisticity of the ontological problem, Tugendhat has reconstructed that history. According to Jürgen Habermas, Tugendhat is one of those philosophers who found that the "ontological shift of hermeneutics guided by language offered a movable viewpoint from which others could perceive the convergence of the later philosophies of Heidegger and Wittgenstein."[13] Tugendhat, together with Derrida, Rorty, Nancy, Vattimo, Apel, Sellars, Badiou, and Brandom, is a philosopher of the linguistic turn and the end of metaphysics[14] heralded by Heidegger. All these thinkers recognize the "third realm" announced by Frege.[15] Asking what the meaning of thinking is after the linguistic turn is not only the main theme explored by these philosophers but also the starting point for understanding them. Tugendhat is the paradigmatic example of this passage from phenomenology to analytic philosophy, where the fusion between analytic and continental ontology allows one not only to see the phenomenological origins of the linguistic turn but also its Austrian and Bretanian sources.[16] To the continental public, Tugendhat is seen as the "lawyer" of analytical philosophy, because he believes that philosophy has always been, without being aware of it, linguistic analysis; to the analytical public he is seen instead as a "traditionalist," because his investigations are a constant struggle not to ignore the metaphysics of presence (as most analytical philosophers have) in order to overcome it. Tugendhat has insisted upon problems that metaphysics has not questioned correctly, since metaphysics never grasped the linguistic sphere on which those problems were supposed to be questioned.

> This aim is a reflection of my own development, which started out from Heidegger and led to language-analytical philosophy. I became convinced that Heidegger's question about the understanding of "Being" can only acquire a concrete and realizable meaning within the framework of a language-analytical philosophy. Although there is hardly any mention of Heidegger in these lectures I owe to him the specific mode of access with which I approach the problems of analytical philosophy. For this reason the book is dedicated to him.[17]

With these words, in the preface to *Traditional and Analytical Philosophy*,[18] Tugendhat not only dedicates his most important book to Heidegger but also distances himself from his master in order to try to develop and carry out further the investigations into "the understanding of 'Being'" in analytical philosophy. According to Tugendhat, philosophy is primarily ontology, a study of beings as such, but contrary to traditional ontology, the transfer of ontology to the sphere of language means that the problem of objects as such is actually investigated only when one questions how to refer to them. This transfer of ontology to the sphere of language takes us beyond the ontology of presence toward an analytical philosophy of language that "contains in itself the idea of a semantic ontology capable of taking on inherited ontology and transcendental philosophy."[19] If Being that can be understood is language, then analytical philosophy's goal, according to Tugendhat, is not to denounce the traditional philosophical problems as false (this is his original insight within the context of analytical philosophy), nor to clarify them through the explanation of their correspondence to expressive rules, but to understand them better. Philosophy, according to Tugendhat, "is not the explanation of something that is not yet understood, but the clarification of what is already understood."[20] In other words, it is a matter of "elimination of a metaphorical mode of speaking in philosophy, and above all the removal of the metaphor of seeing that dominates all traditional thinking, since this is the fundamental metaphor to which one can appeal in using any other metaphor."[21]

One of the greatest flaws of analytic philosophy is its inability to think about history and to enter into dialogue with other philosophical positions. Bubner considers "rare the exceptions in which the stimuli from the analytical school are taken back in a productive form, and, for example, as in Tugendhat's and others' cases, combined with historical knowledge, avoiding in this way mere imitation."[22] It is on just this point that Tugendhat insists in his work, which becomes the first tentative attempt to frame analytical philosophy as the inheritor of ontology and transcendental philosophy, creating, perhaps for the first time, a genuine bridge between the traditional problems of continental philosophy and the method of linguistic analysis of analytical philosophy.[23] Tugendhat's theoretical challenge is more a revolt against analytical philosophy than against continental philosophy. His investigations are not a critique of continental philosophy but rather an exposition of the problems that the continental tradition was not able to see or has ignored.[24] The semantic program Tugendhat proposes turns out to be a development of phenomenological and hermeneutical understanding; in other words, it always refers to Husserl and Heidegger, who are at the heart of his linguistic turn.

Rorty observed that "Tugendhat shares with both Putnam and Heidegger a distaste for the idea of a 'God's-eye view' which will let us see the relation between our language and the world from some standpoint 'outside' our language."[25] This problem is at the center of the investigations of the problem of self-consciousness in *Self-Consciousness and Self-Determination*, Tugendhat's last book on analytical philosophy, written in the late 1970s, before he dedicated himself wholly to ethics and human rights.[26] This book was tremendously successful not only in the Anglo-

Saxon community but also in Germany and France. Written in the analytical tradition, it is certainly one of that tradition's historically richest books, as it analyzes theories of self-consciousness from Aristotle, Fichte, Hegel, and Kierkegaard to Wittgenstein, Heidegger, and Mead. Through a sharp criticism of Cartesian and idealistic subjectivism, Tugendhat establishes a reformulation of self-consciousness on the basis of the linguistic turn. According to him, theories of self-consciousness have always followed the metaphysical model of presence, which uses the subject-object model, constructing consciousness as a simple relation with an object. In this way, self-consciousness is configured as the relationship of an object in front of a subject, and it becomes in this way an object as any other is. Instead, according to Tugendhat, each intentional consciousness is a propositional consciousness; in other words, mental states, acknowledged by all theories of self-consciousness, are *propositional attitudes*. This proposal has opened a vast debate[27] with the so-called school of Heidelberg, Dieter Henrich, Konrad Cramer, Ulrich Pothast, and Manfred Frank, who work toward the rehabilitation of Cartesian subjectivity.

Tugendhat is certain that ontology is fundamental for analytical philosophy, since the formal semantics outlined by Frege becomes the inheritor of Aristotelian ontology. The dissolution of ontology in semantics is the inevitable consequence of the end of metaphysics and therefore of the "predicative" point of view that Tugendhat defends against any form of Platonism. The metaphysical nature of the history of philosophy, according to Tugendhat, is that each nominalization of an expression is equivalent to an objectification: the "blue" becomes the "blueness." The meaning of linguistic expressions has been conceived in terms of objects. In other words, all decisive steps in ontology are a result of an "objectual reinterpretation" that hides the linguistic dimension of thought. To understand a sentence does not mean to represent the object that it refers to but to understand the rules that determine its correct application. The primary unit of comprehension is not the object but the sentence. Analytical philosophy and hermeneutics, according to Tugendhat, share the same program, since both consider language relative and limited, excluding the possibility of a metalanguage. Human understanding is neither a transcendental consciousness nor an overworldly consciousness but a linguistic, empirical, existential community. The hermeneutical nature of analytical philosophy consists in questioning not only the arrangement centered on subjects but also the one centered on objects, because the intersubjective understanding of language becomes the new system of a universal point of reference. If for hermeneutics "there are no facts, only interpretations," then for analytical philosophy, "there are no facts, only true propositions."[28]

Every time a philosopher changes his position, people talk about a "turn" and a succession of periods before and after the turn, as has happened with Heidegger and Wittgenstein. A preference is always given to one of these periods, rather than there being an attempt to understand the intrinsic nature of the thinker. If it is true that a philosopher always thinks the same thought, this same thought will reveal itself more through the intrinsic nature of the philosopher than through the different phases of his chronological path. Heidegger gives an example of this in his famous letter to William J. Richardson, author of *Heidegger: Through Phenomenology to Thought*,[29] when he tells him that the "distinction you make between Heidegger I and II is justified only on the condition that this is kept constantly in mind: only by way of what [Heidegger] I has thought does one gain access to what is to-be-thought by [Heidegger] II. But the thought of [Heidegger] I becomes possible only if it is contained in [Heidegger] II."[30]

Tugendhat's analytical philosophy became possible thanks to phenomenology, a system of thought characterized by both positions. One must remember that Tugendhat is neither the first nor the only thinker to have fused Heidegger and Wittgenstein and framed analytical philosophy inside the metaphysical tradition. Apel, Sellars, Brandom, Cavell, and Dreyfus are as much exceptions to the rule as Tugendhat is. It is true that Tugendhat is the only one to have framed analytical philosophy as an explicit heir to ontology and transcendental philosophy.

Among Tugendhat's books, I should mention *TI KATA TINOS. Eine Untersuchung zu Struktur und Ursprung aristotelischer Grundbegriffe* (1958), *Der Wahrheitsbegriff bei Husserl und Heidegger* (1967), *Traditional and Analytical Philosophy: Lectures on the Philosophy of Language* (1976), *Self-Consciousness and Self-Determination* (1979), *Logisch-semantische Propädeutik* (with U. Wolf, 1983), *Probleme der Ethik* (1984), *Philosophische Aufsätze* (1992), *Ethik und Politik* (1992), *Vorlesungen über Ethik* (1993), *Dialog in Leticia* (1997), *Wie sollen wir handeln?* (with C. López and A. M. Vicuña, 2000), the collection of essays *Aufsätze, 1992–2000* (2001), *Egozentrizität und Mystik* (2003), *Über den Tod* (2006), and, recently, *Anthropologie statt Metaphysik* (2007). The preface to *Philosophische Aufsätze*[31] is important for this investigation since it is the only text where Tugendhat outlines the various phases of his thought, which we can divide into four periods: (1) the overcoming of Husserl through analytic philosophy, (2) the correction of Heidegger's concept of truth, (3) the analytical critique of traditional ontology, and (4) the introduction to analytical philosophy. These four moments are the four parts of this book. Few studies[32] have been published on Tugendhat, to the point that he has been completely ignored in many histories of contemporary philosophy.[33] The division between analytic and continental philosophy has created this condition. Only now that this division seems less accentuated[34] can Tugendhat become an example of a philosopher who has "attempted to build bridges between continents and centuries."[35] If, as Rorty believes, in the year 2100 philosophers will be mostly recognized by the capacity they have demonstrated to fuse horizons rather than for the problems they have solved or even dissolved, Tugendhat will be the paradigmatic example of such a philosopher. Hence already today, in contemporary philosophy Tugendhat is mostly known for his linguistic turn rather than for his position inside analytical philosophy.[36]

OVERCOMING HUSSERL

THE METAPHYSICS OF PHENOMENOLOGY

TUGENDHAT IS VERY CERTAIN OF THE KIND OF CONSTRUAL OF SELF-CONSCIOUS-NESS HE CANNOT ACCEPT. HE CALLS IT THE SUBJECT-OBJECT MODEL, AND ITS BASIC ERROR IS TO CONSTRUE CONSCIOUSNESS AS A RELATION TO AN OBJECT.
— CHARLES TAYLOR —

If, as Gadamer says, the ground of language is itself to be interpreted, then "the subject as starting point, just as orientation to the object, is contested by making the intersubjective communication in language the new universal system of reference. Formulated so generally, this is the same as the hermeneutic program, but in linguistic analysis it is carried through in a more elementary fashion."[1] After the end of metaphysics, according to Tugendhat, two possibilities open up: hermeneutics and analytical philosophy. Both find themselves on the ground of language and interpret themselves as postmetaphysical. One may consider analytical philosophy "as a reduced hermeneutic, as a first-floor hermeneutics. What linguistic analysis still lacks is a historical dimension and a comprehensive concept of understanding."[2] In this first chapter, I will show how the parallels between analytical philosophy, hermeneutics, and phenomenology all come down to the ground of metaphysics, hence, to the metaphysical remainders that characterize phenomenology. Tugendhat, in his famous study *Der Wahrheitsbegriff bei Husserl und Heidegger*,[3] investigates the Husserlian notions of *kategoriale Anschauung* and *Wesensschau* in an attempt to capture their meaning, but he is forced to recognize that the effort is useless because of the still metaphysical nature of the phenomenological method. This consists of presupposing that all things can be considered from a pure and isolated subjectivity, as to allow us, with a mental eye, to see essences and universals.[4] This so-called mental eye is common to all metaphysical traditions from Plato to Husserl, who with the doctrine of eidetic intuition confers upon it a theoretic foundation.[5] But at the beginning of the twentieth century, Wittgenstein not only demonstrated that this is impossible, but also that it is useless, since philosophy is nothing but communication. Wittgenstein's solution only corrects an incorrect approach, one that pushed the Western tradition to consider the immediate knowledge founded upon a perception comparable to the external intuition. To clarify a concept in the intersubjective perspective means, according to Tugendhat, to explain the (semantic and grammatical) use of the words that correspond to that same concept.[6] The meaning of a word is its use in language.

The impossibility of the mental eye means the end of any pure subjectivity, the end of Cartesian subjectivity, which implies objects that can be seen "objectively" or "scientifically." The end that this metaphysical tradition reaches with phenomenology does not mean the end of philosophy: "it is not, as some have feared and others hoped, the end of philosophy, but the beginning of a new one."[7] If the old philosophy only referred to what could be seen clearly, the new philosophy refers only to what can be clearly communicated. The difference lies all in the different point of view: pure and isolated subjectivity on the one hand and intersubjective communication as the original and genuine *medium* of our understanding on the other.

The major merit of phenomenology, according to Tugendhat, consists of its restricting the goal of philosophy to mere description, and certainly not of Husserl's introduction of the *noema*. This introduction "appears, rather, as the last attempt to construe what is not an object as quasi-objective and thereby to make oneself immune to everything which does not fit into the intentional subject-object schema."[8] Tugendhat distinguishes in the phenomenological movement[9] two different points of embarkation: that which considers the mental eye essential to grasp phenomena as the slave of metaphysics, and that which does not consider it essential. This second form of phenomenology includes also the attitude of nonmetaphysical philosophers such as Heidegger, Wittgenstein, and Austin, for whom philosophy is essentially a descriptive enterprise concentrating on illuminating and clarifying "our inexplicit knowledge of the structure of our experience and of the different types of our experience."[10]

MAKING THE NONEXPLICIT EXPLICIT

According to Tugendhat, the problem of philosophy consists in making explicit the nonexplicit, that is, the a priori. He explains:

> Wittgenstein uses St. Augustine's Statement to point out a special characteristic by which this *a priori* concept differs from empirical concepts. St. Augustine says: "What then is time? If nobody asks me, I know it; if when asked I wish to explain it, I don't know it." The point of this sentence is missed if it is taken to contain a paradox—that somebody knows something and at the same does not know it. St. Augustine refers to two kinds of knowledge, the knowledge which we have of a concept when we merely use it and the knowledge which is contained in the ability to explain it. The surprising point is that there are concepts where we have the one kind of knowledge and not the other. This is surprising because this difference is not to be found in the case of empirical concepts.[11]

This problem, which traditionally is the problem of the clarification of concepts, has accompanied the history of philosophy from Plato's dialogues to Hegel and Husserl. While the sciences investigate hypotheses and empirical concepts, philosophy must clarify and render explicit those concepts that belong to the totality of our understanding. Husserl calls this totality the *Lebenswelt*, the life-world, and the concept of time falls in this totality. We must switch from the transcendental conditions of any possible experience to the linguistic clarification of such experience, and the tool we have to do that with is philosophy. But the problem as it emerges from the famous words of St. Augustine is precisely making explicit nonexplicit knowledge. Implicit knowledge is always, contrary to a posteriori knowledge, resistant to further illumination or interpretation. Tugendhat believes that the concepts that condition our (a priori) understanding may be clarified only by means of reflection on what is already given. Husserl and phenomenology think instead that this reflection is only intuitive, that a priori concepts may be understood as inwardly perceived essences. Actually, the "only alternative seems to be that of language analysis, especially as it has been developed by Wittgenstein. This approach begins with the assumption that every concept consists in the way a linguistic expression is used."[12] Being unable to understand the concept of time means being unable to govern the grammatical rules that express such a concept. The meaning of an expression is explained through the explanation of the form in which the expression is used.

When St. Augustine sought to explain the concept of time, he actually wanted to learn how to use that concept correctly. This is the real goal of philosophy: to show how to use a concept correctly. Tugendhat believes that philosophy should be understood as reflective, because the concepts in its domain are a priori such that in order to understand them, some way must be found inside of ourselves instead of outside, as happens in empirical investigations. Of what does this internal reflection consist? According to Husserl, the "a priori concepts, like all concepts, are understood as essences that must be inwardly perceived."[13] In other words, inward reflection is only possible through "intuition" and "intention." This intuition is not the reception of empirical facts to which the intention would then add a meaning; it is only the fulfillment (*Erfüllung*) of the intention. When we direct our attention to the meaning of a word but we do not grasp it immediately, we have the simple intention, while understanding such a meaning, grasping it, would be the fulfillment of the intention. The intention and its fulfillment are simply terms for the beginning and the conclusion of the process of clarification. The methodological goal of phenomenology is: Never be satisfied with mere intentions; always fulfill them. Obviously, this is valid for any descriptive research.

Since Husserl starts from the assumption of the mental eye, it is obvious in his thinking that this fulfillment should be the intuition. Instead, according to Tugendhat, the fulfillment of the intention to grasp a meaning should be, at least potentially, an intersubjective process. This process is the intersubjective methodical introduction of the meaning. The meaning of a term is methodologically introduced when all the necessary points that must be taken into consideration to teach or show someone the use of the term in question are exposed. From this point of view, the idea that the fulfillment of the intuition of a meaning, such as the meaning of time, consists of an intuition seems a tentative way to avoid the introduction of methodology. It is much simpler to imagine an intuition of the meaning of time than to expose the methodological introduction of it.

For Husserl, the goal of philosophy is to clarify the nonexplicit knowledge of the structure of experience; this conception of philosophy works also for analytical philosophers because for them, investigating the meaning of words is also at the same time an investigation of the general structure of linguistic understanding.

> It is important to notice that the step from the analysis of word meaning to the analysis of the structure of linguistic understanding is not just a step from less to more general. The structure being analyzed is, although linguistic, not given in words at all. On the contrary, philosophers have to invent new words (or new meanings for old words) in order to describe the structural aspects they are interested in.[14]

This means that describing the structure of linguistic understanding takes us to aspects of understanding that are not linguistic. Philosophy is occupied with that aspect of our understanding that contains the a priori, and it is just here that some form of illumination is possible. Illumination consists of transforming the nonexplicit knowledge into explicit knowledge, making our confused knowledge into clear knowledge.[15] "The kind of knowledge that is susceptible to, and may call for, explanation is synthetic. . . . The knowledge with which philosophy is concerned is analytic."[16] For this reason, philosophy for Tugendhat is not the explanation of something that is not yet understood but the clarification of what has already been understood.[17]

THE HERMENEUTIC NATURE OF ANALYTIC PHILOSOPHY

If, as hermeneutics posits, it is the *origin*[18] that calls for argumentation, analytical philosophy and hermeneutics share the same nature[19] and program.[20] Of what does this program consist? According to Tugendhat, the hermeneutic nature of analytical philosophy consists of (1) recognizing our "own language as relative and limited,"[21] (2) considering useless the appeal to a "metalanguage," and (3) the impossibility of observing our understanding through some mental eye. This understanding may be only "reflectively explained" without ever having been observed: it is "not a transcendental or somehow preworldly consciousness but an empirically available language community."[22] These characteristics all belong to a philosophical approach that recognizes its own hermeneutic trait and is therefore postmetaphysical.[23] Philosophy must not be exclusively critical, concerned only with analyzing "mere words," but, to put it in Husserl's terms, "with the things in themselves."[24] The regression from the clarification of things to the clarification of words does not mean that from now on words take the place of things, but that concepts must be clarified by means of the corresponding linguistic expression.[25]

The concepts that philosophy deals with are interdependent because, more than just being constitutive of our understanding as a whole, they constitute a network for understanding new linguistic horizons. Philosophy therefore has the function of clarifying this network; establishing which relations interfere among these concepts means constructing artificial expressions—in other words, creating new words. It is this last aspect that distinguishes the philosophy of language from linguistics, and thus philosophical semantics from linguistic semantics. Linguistic semantics is imprisoned in objectivity because it remains essentially concerned with constructing a metalanguage (which is always its own) capable of determining the importance of each linguistic expression. This metalanguage functions in the same way as the mental eye of phenomenology; it does not need to create new words because it already possesses an artificial language capable of seeing instead of clarifying, adapting instead of making explicit:

> Hence the above-required move from the explanation of concepts back to that of words does not mean that the explanation (and consequently any explanation) of words now takes the *place* of concept clarification. Rather, it is always the concept that must be clarified by means of the ways of

using the word. . . . To be precise, it means that the use of a metalanguage is ruled out and the clarification of the meaning of a word of one's own language can no longer take place in a manner analogous to the clarification of foreign terms but merely amounts to making what one "already" understands explicable and thereby explicit.[26]

To the question of why philosophical semantics must create new words, Tugendhat answers that the constitutive concepts of our linguistic understanding, such as *time*, cannot be contained in single words but demand entire linguistic structures. When Aristotle, for example, created the words "subject" and "object," which were *"philosophische Erfindungen,"* he needed "to thematize the predicative structure of our understanding."[27]

It is not possible to supply a definition of words that reveal philosophical determinations. Tugendhat insists on the idea that philosophy supplies description but no definitions; each new clarification demands the renewed recognition of the fundamental concept of philosophy. If "one wants to give an adequate explanation of 'morality,' one must consider a range of word groups such as 'good'/'bad,' 'ought'/'must,' 'guilt'/ 'indignation,' and so on. On the one hand, these groups display certain interrelationships with each other; on the other hand, they are part of yet further interrelationships."[28] Philosophical definitions are useless because some concepts cannot be clarified by means of language. One arrives at a point where language actually becomes the house of Being, and one must turn to linguistic games. "Only if an explanation is adequate can it serve as a clarification. Adequacy [*Angemessenheit*] concerns the character of the truth we demand of philosophical clarifications."[29] The philosophical clarification cannot be a phenomenal trait of its own because there cannot be an adequate clarification of, for example, moral phenomena that does not move itself from the language that constitutes it. It is not possible to postulate an extralinguistic morality. Moral phenomena are not things that have a prelinguistic status.

Rather, we get hold of it only by grasping other words that make up the environment for understanding the word "morality." This, however, implies that what we have to measure [*anzumessen*] our philosophical clarification against is not necessarily the corresponding word but is indeed the given linguistic understanding. A philosophical clarification of a word is fruitful if it succeeds in elucidating a feature (or aspect) of our actual understanding.[30]

The "we" in this passage from Tugendhat, as we have already seen, is not a "transcendental or preworldly consciousness" but rather an "empirically existential linguistic community" determined by the fact that our understanding tends primarily to communicate rather than define. Confronting new linguistic communities is the best way to keep the "we" as open as possible: "it now makes positive sense to leave open the range of 'we': by being confronted with the understanding of other language communities, we can learn new possibilities for understanding, which we can then incorporate into an expanded 'We.'"[31] The end of metaphysics also means the end of modernity, and hence of any possible cultural metalanguage.[32] The fact that our language is essentially predicative does not mean that all other languages must also be predicative. It is certainly possible that

> a human language should be found that had no semantic predicative structure, hence one in which conclusions according to predicative logic would be impossible. But if such a language should nonetheless turn up, that would not mean that something formerly asserted would prove false. Rather, our comprehension [*Verständnis*] of the possibilities of human understanding [*Verstehens*] would expand, similarly to how our understanding of "space" has expanded through the discovery of non-Euclidean spaces.[33]

According to Tugendhat, a foreign language is mostly a potential expansion of our own language; it must be thematized in the second person, not in the third, as happens in the objectivating methods of linguistics. Therefore linguistics, instead of entering into dialogue with foreign languages, limits itself by speaking about them. If philosophy is "communication," one must deal with foreign languages as one deals with one's own, speaking with them and never about them. Instead, the metaphysical philosopher deals in the third person with foreign languages because he remains attached to the metalanguage of the mental eye. "The potential expansion of horizons that can result from the encounter with other language communities shows the latently hermeneutical nature of the analytic method."[34]

THERE ARE NO FACTS, ONLY TRUE PROPOSITIONS

As we have seen, the hermeneutical nature of analytical philosophy consists of questioning not only the subject-centered structure but also the one centered on objects, since the intersubjective understanding in language becomes the new universal system of reference.

> For phenomenology as well as for linguistic analysis, both our understanding of the *meaning* (sense) of linguistic expressions and our reference [*Meinen*] to *objects* belong at the center of philosophical consideration, but with opposing proprieties. For Husserl, the intentional "act" that "refers to" [*meint*] an object is the primary unit of consciousness. The intentional act and the correlative object make up, to use Heidegger's expression, the basic relationship of human "awareness" [*Erschlossenheit*]. On the other hand, for linguistic analysis the primary unit of awareness is understanding the meaning of a sentence. While Husserl attempted to build the understanding of meanings—somehow—into the intentional relation to objects, linguistic analysis conceived the reference to objects as a *factor* in understanding the meanings of sentences. Here, then, we have a clear confrontation, as a *chassé croisé*, which bears on the starting point of both positions.[35]

Phenomenology, instead, being linked to the "seen" model, reaches the conclusion that the fundamental phenomenon of consciousness is intentionality: being consciously directed toward an object. This "act" was introduced as a technical term in order to indicate the intentional experience. "Just as seen has a visual image 'before' it, philosophers have thought of the 'object' as an analogous correlate of intentional consciousness which is interpreted as 'representation.'"[36] Phenomenology, adapting itself to the model according to which an object is thought about in analogy to a visual image, believes not only that facts exist but, most of all, that these facts may be intentionally experienced. This structure is supported independently of language, in other words, without considering the problem of linguistic meanings.[37]

In this essentially *gegenstandstheoretisch* structure, the meaning of a sentence depends from the intentional relation with the object in such a way that the understanding of a sentence is founded upon the representation of this object. Although Husserl does not make the mistake of conceiving of meanings as objects, according to Tugendhat, he still establishes the relation between expressions and objects exclusively by means of their meanings.[38] If the "meaning-conferring" meanings are acts and the function of names is that of designating an object in the act of naming, Husserl is obliged by his approach to extend to all the other expressions this particular characteristic of names: every expression is also related to some object.[39] This is the particular metaphysical characteristic that results from Husserl's theory of meanings, from his focus on intentionality: nominal expressions become the model of expressions in general.[40] "According to Wittgenstein, traditional thinking essentially consists in assimilating the unlike and in leveling differences; thus, one assimilates all the other words of language to names, the knowledge of the inner domain to knowledge of the external world, and thinking and understanding to seen." This is why Husserl believes one can always refer to the meaning "in a reflective act of thinking" and at the same time convert the meaning into an object; this is because he believes that something has meaning when it is understood as an object. The linguistic expression with which we then signify the meaning is not the original but a name: objectification is expressed linguistically in a nominalization. According to this conception, "we can nominalize a predicate like 'is green' and speak of 'the greenness.'"[41] Tugendhat's objection is that the object referred to by a nominalized expression is neither a synthetic objectivity nor, as it has been assumed up to now with Husserl, the meaning itself, but rather it is the *what-is-said* (*das Gesagte*), following specific rules of meanings. The *what-is-said* "is defined in such a way that all possible utterances which have the same truth-conditions stand for an identical what-is-said. Defined in this way, what-is-said is, as for Husserl, an 'ideal' object which, however, is not built up from syntheses of objects but is the result of an abstraction based on linguistic utterances in accordance with their conditions of use."[42] The meaning of a nominal expression may only be understood as the rule for the use of the expression that identifies the referenced object.

The Husserlian theory of categorical acts was tentative to comprehend, on the basis of an inadequate metaphysical approach, the meaning of composed expressions. Husserl does not fail because he started from the consciousness of objects but because he based his thought on an untenable concept of object, an object seized from an isolated, presemiotic consciousness,[43] in other words, from the mental eye. This concept of object is responsible, according to Tugendhat, of much confusion in the history of philosophy:

> The lack of clarity and the ambiguity in the expression "object" has had an irritating effect throughout German philosophy. Besides the two concepts I have discussed, a third concept plays a less important role in Husserl but, on the other hand, was decisive for Kant: *gegenständlich*, in the sense of "objectivity." It is not an accident that this concept can be more easily expressed by an adverb than by a noun, for in reality it stands for a modal-like determination of a *statement* ("It not only appears to be the case that . . . but it is objectively so"). Even in Kant, however, this concept was combined with the other two (in this case without great damage) because of the lack of familiarity with sentences (cf., e.g., *Critique of Pure Reason*, A104). The same ambiguity is also operative in the talk of an "objectification" [*Vergegenständlichung*]. Heidegger's thesis about the objectification of Being in modern philosophy is based on the third concept of "object." Hence his "de-objectification" may lead to a conception (particularly in talk of "beings") which in turn is guilty of objectification in the sense of the first definition of "object."[44]

An object is essentially denoted by an expression of a subject and is made out of a definite logicolinguistic form that permits it to appear in a sentence in certain positions and not in others. All this is based on the idea that the understanding of sentences is primary in comparison with the reference of objects: a sentence is the primary unit of meaning because it is based on the fact that it is the smallest unit for intersubjective understanding. A name can be understood also if no object is given to stand with it. "This fact seems to indicate that while the conception of the subject-object schema was based on the individual subject, from the outset the under-standing of sentences belongs to intersubjective communication." In this context the fundamental question becomes: how can a predicative sentence be understood? The metaphysical idea based upon the synthesis is absolutely unusable for the elucidation of predicative sentences. One has to ask: if a person who utters a sentence does not connect with the object for which the subject of the sentence stands, what does he do with it? "The most natural answer," says Tugendhat, "seems to be: He character-izes it in a certain way, and he does this by classifying and distinguishing it by means of the predicate."[45] In other words, a predicative sentence does not have the function of expressing an intentional act and representing something, but rather of characterizing it in a certain way. "The analytic approach is no less realistic; it is only less inward oriented, and necessar-ily so, because the inwardness of the 'representation' is quasi-sensual and therefore loses touch with what has to be clarified, the linguistic structure of awareness."[46]

According to Tugendhat, the manipulation of linguistic signs is the primary element of understanding, even before a means of expression. The manipulation of linguistic signs guided by rules (semantics) takes the place, at least for predicates, of that which in Husserl intentionality had. In this situation, it seems that when an object is characterized by means of a predicate, one must not represent the thing the predicate stands for. So when we say "the meadow is green" we understand the predicate "is green" without perception of the green or representation of the meadow. The predicate is general:

> If it must stand for something and if this something must be capable of being represented, it cannot be a matter of sensory intuition. We would have to represent something which corresponds to the entire scope of the predicate. The non-sensible representation that is needed on this account is what Plato and Aristotle named *noein*. And in his theory of "eidetic ab-straction" Husserl has tried to give a foundation to the existence of an "in-tuition of essences" in an analysis which he takes to be a phenomenologi-cal description but which, perhaps, is only a remarkable reconstruction of something which does not exist.[47]

Either way, we do not need a representation to understand the understanding of predicates. This understanding does not take place by pointing to a general essence but by applying the predicate to different objects; understanding the meaning of the predicate does not consist of seeing something but of "mastering the rule which determines the application of the predicate. The generality of the predicate is a rule—generality, not a 'general object.' "[48]

One may ask now how, in more general and elevated levels, this senseless understanding is determined in declarative forms. Regarding the conjunctions "and" and "or," Tugendhat talks about "the conjunctive connections of names or statements." In analytical philosophy, each specific rule linking statements that contain these words to definite truth conditions are represented in the truth tables. Tugendhat explains that the meaning of "and" is determined by the fact that a phrase, "p and q," is true only if both clauses of which it is composed are true and that it is false in all other cases:

> In this form the explanation is circular, since the definiendum reappears in the definiens in the word "both." It is impossible to introduce the sense of the word "and" by means of other words without circularity. Nevertheless, we are able to explain to someone who knows neither the word "and" nor an equivalent expression (and in this way we can reconstruct our own understanding) by exhibiting—analogously to what happened in the case of predicates—under what conditions a sentence ("p and q") is true and under what conditions it is false.[49]

The explanation of a fact starts from the corresponding sentence and meaning; the meaning of the predicate is the rule that determines its application. This is why there are not facts but only true or false propositions;[50] "we do not *represent* objects to ourselves, we *mean* objects."[51] In other words, "in the perspective of language itself, the universal dimension in which we live with understanding is not primarily a world of objects, entities, or facts, but a world of sentences, of unities of meaning."[52]

> An assertion that *a* is *F* is true not when the predicate *F* is merely applied or is applicable but when the predicate can *legitimately* be applied to it. This

relation of the legitimate applicability of a predicate to an object is what is denoted by the word "applies" [*Zutreffen*]. Thus we arrive at the following truth-definition for predicative assertions: *the assertion that* a *is* F *is true if and only if the predicate* F *applies* [zutrifft] *to the object for which the singular term* a *stands.*[53]

CORRECTING HEIDEGGER

VERIFYING HEIDEGGER'S PHILOSOPHY FROM WITHIN

THE TRUTHS (EMERGING IN THE PLURAL) OF THIS TEMPORALIZED *URSPRUNGS-PHILOSOPHIE* ARE IN EACH CASE PROVINCIAL AND YET TOTAL; THEY ARE MORE LIKE THE COMMANDING EXPRESSION OF SOME SACRAL FORCE FITTED OUT WITH THE AURA OF TRUTH. AS FOR THE APOPHANTIC CONCEPT OF TRUTH DEVELOPED IN *BEING AND TIME* (SECTION 44), ERNST TUGENDHAT SHOWS HOW HEIDEGGER "PRECISELY BY THE FACT THAT HE TURNS THE WORD 'TRUTH' INTO A BASIC TERM . . . PASSES OVER THE PROBLEM OF TRUTH."

— JÜRGEN HABERMAS —

John Lloyd Ackrill noted that the whole discussion of Tugendhat's study on Aristotle, *TI KATA TINOS. Eine Untersuchung zu Struktur und Ursprung aristotelischer Grundbegriffe*,[1] "is conducted in the framework of ideas of Heidegger and with terminology derived from him."[2] Pierre Aubenque believes that Tugendhat's work is inspired primarily by Heidegger's exegetical works, in other words, by the significance Heidegger attributes to language. Language, says Aubenque, is no longer considered an instrument of thought,

> but on the contrary, as the place of a philosophical revelation of which the philosopher is nothing else than semi-conscious instrument. Tugendhat does not base his analysis on the concept but on a fundamental structure in the Greek language which expresses itself in Aristotelian philosophy,

namely the predicative structure, which Aristotle calls *chategorein*; hence, *ti kata tinos leigen*, or "Why is this attribute inherent in that subject?"[3]

Tugendhat believes this structure to be at the base of all Western logic and further believes that it should not be considered as a simple logical structure but as the ontological structure that produces a fundamental duplicity in Being. Being is divided in two; if it articulates its presence by splitting, then *chategorein* is "the complete adequate designation of the new essence of presence."[4] This *Zweifältigkeit*—twofoldness or bifurcation or the double character of reality—is the logical distinction of the subject and predicate. As a consequence of this splitting, each question is necessarily formulated as *ti kata tinos*. "Being, in accordance with its essence, has become duplicate. And of each of its parts we can say it is only as long as it is joined with the other."[5]

This structure is the basis of the fundamental concepts of Aristotle's metaphysics. But, according to Tugendhat, Aristotle assumes it as such without ever discussing the nature of this basis. The metaphysical tradition has inherited and established these concepts as the foundation of all its investigations.[6] The first to investigate and find this specific foundation was Heidegger: the sense of Being that Greek ontology was not capable of expressing can be conveyed in German by *Anwesenheit* (presence that duplicates). Being, then, is not *selbständige Präsenz* (*ti*) but rather *Präsenz des Vorliegenden* (*ti kata tinos*). The fact that the *-ousia* of the Greeks could be understood as *parousia* (as presence) justifies the exclusion of temporality in the Platonic and Aristotelian conceptions of Being. Since in Aristotle each presence is the presence of something, the Platonic ideal here becomes the category. The coupling of "subject" and "predicate"—in other words, the relation between two terms where one refers to the other—is not only a simple logical or verbal structure but the description of this duplication, in which both parts are connected. This, according to Tugendhat's analysis, is the birthplace of Aristotle's fundamental concepts.[7]

In this way, Tugendhat not only limits himself to individuating and indirectly justifying the Heideggerian notion of "ontological difference"[8] in Aristotle's ontology but insists also on confronting the conception of truth put forward in *Being and Time*,[9] with its Greek and phenomenological origins.[10] There is a connection between the concept of *aletheia*[11] in Greek philosophy, the *Selbstgegebenheit* coined by Husserl in his phenomenology, and truth as *Unverborgenheit*. Tugendhat analyzes this last concept in *Der Wahrheitsbegriff bei Husserl und Heidegger* (*The Concept of Truth in Husserl and Heidegger*),[12] which should be considered equally important for any critical examination of Husserl's and Heidegger's accounts of truth.[13] Not only Otto Pöggeler, Gerd Brand, Reiner Schürmann, Jürgen Habermas, Rainer Rochlitz, Karl-Otto Apel, and Carl Gethmann, but also Cristina Lafont, Daniel O. Dahlstrom, Hubert L. Dreyfus, Mark Wrathall, Taylor Carman, Joanna Hodge, Karsten Harries, Brice R. Wachterhauser, Richard Wolin, and Andrew Bowie have used this book and written extensively on it.[14] In the introduction, Tugendhat wants to "save philosophy" because today we tend to see the theoretical attitude conditioned by the practice attitude. On the one side is the reduction to the minimal of the concept of truth in logistics, and, on the other, is a conception of truth as disclosure, which remains too vague and large to allow philosophy to correspond to its original goal: "to organize the whole of human life around truth, in other words, around the idea of a life conducted with critical responsibility."[15] If in Husserl's approach it was all about the phenomenological sphere in which objects can be given according to different modalities, for Heidegger it is about truth as clearing, *Lichtung*; in other words, it is of a dimension that is not the arrangement of objects inside a transcendental subjectivity but rather the horizon that the subject already finds disclosed. The pair *Selbstgegebenheit-Intentionalität* is substituted by the pair *Lichtung-Erschlossenheit*.[16]

Tugendhat bases his entire analysis (or we could call it a "correction") of Heidegger's philosophy on a tight grasp of the specific Husserlian sense of truth in terms of a difference "between mere 'intention' and the matter 'itself.'" This presupposes the possibility of distinguishing between the manner in which something in fact appears and the manner in which it "itself" is, because the specific sense of truth consists of "identifying" (or, in Heideggerian terms, "uncovering") an entity precisely as it is in itself. Hence, a proposition is true only if it refers to things in ways that permit them to be seen as they are in themselves. But Heidegger, elaborating his concept of truth through the separation of evidence from the adequation formula and correspondence from the appearance formula, proposed a concept of truth that consists of the self-manifestation of Being in its unconcealment. Truth considered as "unconcealedness" or "disclosedness" (*Unverborgenheit*) does not have anything to do with sentences that declare something but consists only of the event of this unconcealment. According to Tugendhat, "Heidegger did not explain how in the horizon of the '*Erschlossenheit*' the specific concept of truth works, but directly thematized under the name of truth the same '*Erschlossenheit*.' "[17]

Tugendhat does not want to deny Heidegger's use of disclosedness but simply point out that it is being equated with a concept ("truth") that is usually used to designate for a specific purpose. The purpose of the concept of truth traditionally was not to show the fact that something reveals itself but rather how it reveals itself in opposition to its concealing, but Heidegger loses the sense of truth by transposing it "without further justification to all disclosedness of entities within-the-world."[18] According to Tugendhat, Heidegger in *Being and Time* does in fact demonstrate that a statement is true when it uncovers beings and false when it covers them, but by considering truth as the event of unconcealment, he indirectly renounces justifying the distinctions not only between true and false assertions but also between good and evil actions. Tugendhat specifies by explaining that

> the fact that the concept of the good—and correlatively both the concept of deliberation and that of the justification of evaluative and normative statements—cannot be found in Heidegger is a consequence of his concept of truth. . . . The concept of the good also falls under the concept of truth, since all statements contain a truth claim (and this means a claim to justification); and sentences that say that something is good or better are statements. Now Heidegger did not (as might have been expected) also jettison the concept of truth along with the concept of the good. The issue here is more complex. Heidegger began with the assumption that a statement "discloses" something, and he formalized the concept of truth in such a way that he ultimately grasped it as coextensive with the concept of disclosure (section 44). But the specific meaning of *true*—namely, the claim to justification and proof—thereby drops out of the account. Yet since the

word *truth* is retained, it simultaneously appears as if the concept of truth is preserved and even deepened; and on this basis a peculiarly illusive situation arises.[19]

Before analyzing the whole of Tugendhat's interpretation of Heidegger's thought, it is interesting to note how this criticism received the immediate approval of Habermas and Apel (who probably felt oppressed by the heavy heredity of Heidegger's importance in German philosophy), to the point of their considering it at the origin of a "self-correction"[20] done by Heidegger himself. Apel, in the first part of *Toward a Transformation of Philosophy*,[21] even went as far as to believe that Heidegger actually accepted this correction in this passage of his essay "The End of Philosophy and the Task of Thinking," included in *On Time and Being* (1969):

To raise the question of *aletheia*, of unconcealment as such, is not the same as raising the question of truth. For this reason, it was inadequate and misleading to call *aletheia* in the sense of opening, truth. . . . How the attempt to think a matter can at times stray from that which a decisive insight has already shown, is demonstrated by a passage from *Being and Time* (1927). To translate this word (*aletheia*) as "truth," and, above all, to define this expression conceptually in theoretical ways, is to cover up the meaning of what the Greeks made "self-evidently" basic for the terminological use of *aletheia* as a prephilosophical way of understanding it.[22]

According to Apel, this passage was written two months after Tugendhat delivered a lecture ("Heidegger's Idea of Truth")[23] in February 1964 at the University of Heidelberg, where he formulated, for the first time, his criticism of Heidegger's concept of truth as *aletheia*.[24] Although a long debate began among Apel, Pöggeler, Gethmann, Schürmann, Habermas, Rochlitz, and many others on whether Tugendhat's criticism can be considered the origin of a self-correction by Heidegger himself,[25] it is Pöggeler who first correctly observed that this could not be considered a "self-correction" by Heidegger. According to Pöggeler, if Heidegger in the 1930s assumed that truth could be understood as "unconcealedness" or "disclosedness," it is because he was looking for a "different conceptual platform. . . . Already in his first lectures Heidegger put forward the demand to take into account the practical and religious truth together with the theoretical one."[26] I believe that Tugendhat's criticism of Heidegger's concept of truth, more than simply being a "correction," is a "confirmation" that Heidegger was not looking for a mere concept of truth or a concept of truth to distinguish true from false, un-valid from valid, good from evil, but, on the contrary, a "different conceptual platform" or "locus."[27]

Although I do not wish to enter this debate, but rather wish to continue Tugendhat's "verification of Heideggerianism from within" (especially as it is not only concerned with the concept of truth), I note that in 1982, Apel, in a response to Pöggeler, said that although he continued to believe that Heidegger "corrected himself" after Tugendhat's criticism, he added that Heidegger

> made clear that he in fact did not discover the original meaning of truth but something different—viz. the "lighting of Being"—that must precede truth, viz. propositional truth, being the condition of its possibility. I think that, by this clarification, Heidegger has summarized the meaning of his contribution to philosophical thought in the sense of his 3rd and last period of thought.[28]

Although Apel does open up to the possibility (even if explained in neo-Kantian terms) that there was another "locus," "conceptual platform," or "theme," he still sees this from a metaphysical point of view. He belongs to those who think that Heidegger, even in *Being and Time*, was looking for a more adequate description of the meaning of Being and of the idea of truth when instead, as Pöggeler and Vattimo have emphasized in their work, he was looking for a new conceptuality.[29] If one thinks that Heidegger was searching for a more correct concept of truth, then Tugendhat's criticism will be valid; if one doesn't, Tugendhat's effort will be seen as a confirmation of Heidegger's search for a new thought beyond metaphysics.[30]

DISCLOSEDNESS BEYOND REPRESENTATION

For Tugendhat, the main characteristics of the philosophy of the classical tradition are (1) its universality, by questioning Being in general; and

(2) that it starts from some fundamental principle. In Aristotle, this first principle was an absolute Being and in Kant a standpoint of knowledge. Beings as such were investigated only with regard to the condition (or correspondence) of their possibility (or verifiability), insofar as this condition could be known to be true, until Husserl, in *Ideas* (1913), began to put forward the idea of the phenomenological clarification of everything posited as true. But this, as explained in chapter 1, could only be done with reference to a transcendental subjectivity or mental eye understood as the sphere of the absolutely evident and conclusive truthfulness.[31] It was Heidegger, according to Tugendhat, who finally made the big step forward by no longer considering subjectivity as an absolute principle but rather as one that is already mediated by the ecstatic temporality of Dasein through "a precursory openness—its world as history." Tugendhat explains that to this extent the transcendental thesis is surpassed.

> In order to have a word which describes both the continuity and the break, let us call this position "meta-transcendental." What is most originally given is no longer characterized by the evidence of an absolute subjectivity but by the disclosure of the finitude of Dasein and—insofar as this disclosure stands out in an open field of play—through the clearing of this very field itself.[32]

Tugendhat considers Heidegger to be the only philosopher of the past century to have tried to overcome the classical tradition of the ontologico-transcendental point of view in such a way that "philosophy is finally brought to a close."[33] The best example of this closing (or dissolution) of philosophy can be seen in how Heidegger "broadened," "conflated," or "discarded" the concept of truth, overcoming Husserl's self-conscious transcendental subjectivity—hence *representation*. For Heidegger, the theme of truth is not secondary to nor independent from the problem of the meaning of Being, because his criticism of truth as adequation is intrinsically connected to his criticism of the ontological concept of Being as presence. This statement, since antiquity, was considered the authentic "locus" of truth and its intrinsic linkage to Being; they are, as Heidegger says, related "equiprimordially."[34] In *Being and Time*, Heidegger clearly explains how every statement, whether affirmative or negative, true or false, valid or un-valid, good or evil, is equiprimordially *synthesis* and *di-airesis*. The truth that occurs in the statement is a derivative one because the "apophantic as" is only possible within the "hermeneutic as": there is no "presuppositionless" apprehension of something presented to us that could later be "objectified" by means of a predicative modality of the subject.

> The statement is not the primary "locus" of truth but the *other way around*: the statement as a mode of appropriation of discoveredness and as a way of being-in-the-world is based in discovering, or in the *disclosedness* of Dasein. The most primordial "truth" is the "locus" of the statement and the ontological condition of the possibility that statements can be true or false (discovering or covering over).[35]

Heidegger's project of putting forward a temporal interpretation of Being is at the core of his hermeneutic transformation of phenomenology. This transformation has the emancipatory goals of overcoming not only the metaphysical nature of Being—presencing—but also all the objectivist theories of truth, such as the well-known formula "*veritas est adaequatio rei et intellectus.*" Husserl had emphasized how the truth of statements (hence, bringing the thing into light "as it is in itself") was grounded in a preliminary structure: the truth of aesthetic intuition. Although Heidegger shares this general orientation, he substitutes Husserl's aesthetic intuition for interpretation, which, in this way, becomes the preliminary structure of the statement. Heidegger believes that this statement, the "apophantic as," must be grounded in interpretation, the "hermeneutic as." The truth of statements is derived because its roots reach back to the disclosedness of understanding that determines prelinguistic adequacy.[36] It is only on the grounds of interpretation that language is possible. True statements are explicit articulations of what we understand through disclosedness because, as Heidegger explains in *Logic: The Question of Truth*, "the proposition is not the locus of truth; rather, truth is the locus of the proposition."[37] On the level of the "hermeneutic as," there is neither error nor falseness, while at the level of the "apophantic as" there are both.[38]

Heidegger's characterization of truth as disclosure, according to Tugendhat, "leads to obfuscating the problem of truth."[39] Although Tugendhat is certain that in this way truth receives another meaning, losing its natural one, he notes how Heidegger's thought is not as homogeneous as it makes itself out to be, and that today we seem to have gradually gained the ability to "differentiate what does not appear to lead further from what should not be abandoned."[40] In order to determine a word philosophically, it is necessary to start out from our natural understanding of language: the ordinary understanding of truth is the truth of the proposition. The concept of truth must coincide with the truth of the proposition. Heidegger, in *Being and Time*, not only starts from the natural understanding of truth but also holds to the already mentioned traditional philosophical conception of truth *"veritas est adaequatio rei et intellectus"*[41] and asks himself how this correspondence should really be interpreted. At first, Heidegger found a response in the sixth section of Husserl's *Logical Investigations*: the specific phenomenological thematic, according to the adequation formula, requires that finding a correspondence with the facts is neither the subject nor the statement but "the same thing in other modes of givenness." Tugendhat explains that, on the one hand, we find the state of affairs as it is intended is "signifying givenness, on the other, precisely this state of affairs, as it is itself. This 'being itself' of the state of affairs is not something transcendental to experience, but is only the correlate of a distinctive mode of givenness. The state of affairs as it is itself is the state of affairs as it manifests itself when it is itself given to us."[42] But Heidegger distances himself from Husserl because the act of expression in phenomenology is understood statically, as a static mode of intentionality that holds before oneself a specific objectivity. Tugendhat believes that Heidegger surpasses Husserl's intentionality through the concept of "disclosure," where the assertion is not understood statically but dynamically, hence where

> disclosure is to be understood as an occurrence that is actively related to its opposite—closedness or concealment. In the special case of the assertion, it becomes clear that wherever it arises in a concrete connection with life and with science it is not to be understood in a functionless fashion as the rigid positing of an objectivity, but dynamically as a letting be seen in which we point out something as something, in which we lift it out of

concealment, both for ourselves and for others so that, as Heidegger says, it is "unconcealed."[43]

If this statement is no longer understood as the representation of static entities but in its derivation from the *Unverborgenheit*, which does not depend on the distinction between true and false, then "uncovering" and "covering" are not the final determinations required by philosophy. Tugendhat notes that although Heidegger has revolutionized philosophy, his conclusion regarding the problem of truth, consisting of uncoveredness, is inappropriate, because he does not consider that the false assertion also uncovers. Truth as uncovering would be enlightening only if Heidegger explained that false assertions do not uncover. But this was not the case in *Being and Time*, where Heidegger specifically explains how in a false assertion entities are in a certain sense already uncovered and still not represented. Tugendhat sees that in his later essays "On the Essence of Truth" (1930), "On the Essences of Ground" (1929), and "On the Origin of the Work of Art" (1935) Heidegger also continues to put forward the same idea: in order that the assertion should be in accord with the entity, this same entity must "show itself" because its truth is grounded in the truth of entities as unconcealment.

Broadening the concept of truth from the truth of assertions to all modes of disclosing becomes useless, says Tugendhat, "if one sees the truth of assertion as consisting simply in the fact that it is in general disclosive."[44] But Tugendhat forgets that one of the goals of *Being and Time*, through the word "uncover" or the concept of unconcealment, was to stand not only for the disclosive assertion that points out, but also for any disclosure of inner-worldly beings. Truths of assertions are connected to the circumspective disclosure of concerns. But what is gained by broadening disclosure beyond intentionality and objective representations? It is the possibility of drawing distinctions between truth and falsehood even in modes of disclosure that lie outside of the traditional theoretical realm: disclosing new worlds and their horizons.[45] With disclosiveness, the metaphysical orientation toward a self-conscious subjectivity—which thought to find itself in possession of a god's-eye view, an ahistorical, absolute evidence—would be, as Tugendhat rightly concludes, "discarded."[46] In other words, the most important and original factor here is neither the substance nor the subject but the open field of play of Dasein. Heidegger not only gives transcendental philosophy a historical dimension but also opens it in order to finally give "up the idea of anchoring itself upon a last ground." It "became possible to radicalize and to build up anew the idea of a critical consciousness. But, by the same token, it also became possible to give it up in preference for a new immediacy."[47]

Thanks to his concept of truth as unconcealment, according to Tugendhat, Heidegger goes beyond every theory of truth as representation; in other words, he goes beyond the fatal limit marked by the visual metaphor. If to uncover stands for pointing out, *apophainesdai*, then every assertion must uncover (the false just as much as the true). At the same time, however, Heidegger employs the word in a narrow and pregnant sense in accordance with which the false assertion is not so much an uncovering as a covering over. Truth lies in uncoveredness. But at this point Tugendhat asks a crucial question: what does uncovering mean when it no longer signifies a pointing out in general? How is *aletheuein* to be differentiated from *apophainesdai*?

DISCLOSEDNESS BEYOND TRUTH

Tugendhat notes that Heidegger does not answer this question and also that he cannot answer it, because Heidegger never distinguished the broad from the narrow meaning of truth as uncovering. Although the uncovering thesis could have become revolutionary if he had maintained that the false assertion does not uncover, Heidegger specifically said that in the false assertion, the entity is "in a certain sense already uncovered and still not represented."[48] True assertions, for Heidegger, are the means of thematizing the disclosedness as the original truth underlying the uncovering and concealing of entities and therefore the truth and falsity of assertions.

Tugendhat's general objection to Heidegger lies in his designating truth *as disclosedness* when he should have designated it *disclosure beyond truth*, because he limited himself to the two concepts of concealing and unconcealing. When truth is limited within these boundaries, it is impossible to determine the specific sense of falsehood, and therefore also of truth. The characterization of falsehood as covering is not a subspecies of that concealment from which the apophansis receives its pointing out, nor a simple mixture of such a concealment with unconcealment, but rather it "covers the entity as it is itself and indeed in such a way that it uncovers it in another way, namely not in the way in which it is itself."[49] The core of the problem is that Heidegger, according to Tugendhat, never considered the difference between an "immediate and obtrusive givenness" and "the thing in itself" within the self-showing:

> So although, with his concepts of uncovering and unconcealment, he deep-ens Husserl's intentionality and givenness, the difference between given-ness in general and self-givenness escapes him. Heidegger has quite rightly seen that the distinguishing characteristic of Husserl's concept of truth as well as, in another sense, that of the Plato and Aristotle lay in this, that truth must here be understood in a circuit of self-manifestation and given-ness. He then went straight on to broaden this givenness in and for itself by inquiring into the condition of its possibility, without noticing that truth, for Husserl as also for Greek philosophy, in no way resided in givenness as such but in the possibility of a distinctive mode of givenness.[50]

With Heidegger, the specific sense of truth is reduced to the notion of uncovering as apophasis; hence, interpreting the truth of the statement is mere uncovering. In this way the specific problem of truth is overlooked and deformed to the point of broadening it beyond truth. Since in *Being and Time* the term "uncover" stands terminologically for any discourse of inner-worldly beings and the truth of assertions lies in uncovering, then it must follow that all allowing-to-be encountered of inner-worldly beings is true because the truth of an assertion does not lie in the *way* in which it uncovers but only in *that* it uncovers. Heidegger transferred truth to any form of disclosure. All uncovering of inner-worldly beings is grounded in the disclosure of the world. And since the disclosure of Dasein is un-derstood as being-in-the-world,[51] the disclosure of its world is "the most original truth." This original disclosure, explains Tugendhat, is the prod-uct of "a temporal field which first makes possible any self-manifestation of beings; any self-manifestation and not just the specifically true. That Heidegger speaks here of truth is due simply to the fact that he already calls self-manifestation itself truth."[52] The most originally given—the disclosedness of Dasein or the clearing of Being—becomes for Heidegger the meaning of truth. This is why Tugendhat thinks that it is important to try to establish (he uses the term "place") what is most originally given in relation to truth. The most originally given in the sense of the clearing of Being is not whatever is contained within the horizons—hence the world of this moment (present)—but rather the open field of play of this horizon itself. It is within this horizon that Tugendhat believes that Heidegger "deflates" the sense of truth from the "self-showing of the entity thus as it is in itself" to the mere "uncovering" of it.[53]

Since, according to Heidegger, truth-assertions about inner-worldly beings are inevitably linked to the historical horizon of our understanding, the problem of truth must now concentrate upon this horizon. The decisive question becomes: in what manner can one inquire into the truth of this horizon? Tugendhat believes it is pointless to inquire into this truth because "that would only mean inquiring into the truth of a truth."[54] If truth as disclosedness means an unconcealment that occurs with an understanding of the world in general, then the possibilities for testing truth are minimal. But Tugendhat asks himself why this conception seems so liberating: "Without denying the relativity and the opaqueness of our historical world, it made possible an immediate and positive truth relation, an explicit truth relation which no longer made any claim to certainty and so could not be disturbed by uncertainty either. Therewith, however, what is specific to the truth relation is not only overlooked but is converted into its opposite."[55]

Tugendhat does not neglect the possibility that disclosure is essentially directed toward the truth, but he wants to point out that it could also inevitably block the question of truth, because as soon as we raise questions concerning the truth of assertions, for example, we must then also raise the question concerning the truth not only of beings but also of the horizon. This first verification of Heidegger's philosophy is important not only historically but also philosophically because it shows that the connections he drew between truth and disclosedness mark a decisive turn in the history of the reflection on truth.[56] Heidegger incorporated previously unnoticed issues and also opened a space for future ones.

Tugendhat concludes his investigation of Heidegger's concept of truth by noticing how, with the equation of truth and disclosedness, Heidegger was able not only to dissolve static phenomenological points of departure but also phenomenology's metaphysical foundations. By declaring that truth "coincides entirely with disclosedness"[57] and with the "horizon of understanding inside which one understands statements," Heidegger takes philosophy beyond the problem of truth understood as the classical agreement between knowing and its object in order to question this same theoretical platform or horizon.[58] This expansion of the problem of truth requires "giving up the idea of a critical demonstration"[59] in favor of interpretations of horizons.

TRUTH VERSUS METHOD

Tugendhat, in a review of *Truth and Method*, notes that precisely because Gadamer had fundamentally accepted Heidegger's concept of truth, his great attempt at a hermeneutical theory could not orient itself to the (traditional) concept of truth, because

> his hermeneutical conversation in which history is always at work remained without a regulative principle. And renewing the orientation of hermeneutics to truth in a more specific sense would not once again orient itself primarily to that which stands over against one (that is, the truth of the historical object)—an orientation which Gadamer had overcome—but it also could not see truth in the dialectic of historical conversation. Rather, his hermeneutical quest for truth had to take the appearing of truth within one's own horizon as its starting point.[60]

Gadamer's philosophical hermeneutics have always been a point of contrast for Tugendhat, not only because they were both Heidegger's disciples but because they interpret Heidegger's concept of truth in precisely opposite directions. Gadamer distinguishes himself from Heidegger, according to Tugendhat, by his different conception of hermeneutical philosophy. Since hermeneutics, for Gadamer, is not a method for philosophy but rather an encounter with the other, it is only productive when it simultaneously reflects upon oneself. It is just this reflection upon "oneself" and the "other" understanding (which is the initial situation and retrogression into the historical dimension of Dasein) that characterizes hermeneutics in Gadamer's sense of the word.[61] Although Tugendhat mentions Gadamer in his book on Husserl and Heidegger and reviewed[62] two of his books in 1978, two years later he felt he had "come to a point where the limits of my previous non-historical method are becoming evident and I recognize my need for dialogue with the hermeneutical philosopher, which in turn refers me to dialogue with history."[63]

One of Gadamer's main concerns has been to extricate the historical sciences from what he considers to be their obsession with "method," in order to acknowledge how truth does not always have to be identified or achieved by a method. This is why Tugendhat has proposed, creating a certain curiosity in many readers, that the title of Gadamer's most original work, *Truth and Method*,[64] should not be understood as the connection of the two terms but rather of their contraposition, as "truth *versus* method."[65] Tugendhat notes that if one should start "with Heidegger's conception of truth, but disregard his ontology and then replace both the existentialism of his earlier philosophy and the mysticism of his later writings by a profound sense of humanist tradition, you get what Gadamer calls 'philosophical hermeneutics.'"[66] Gadamer understands the truth of hermeneutics according to the model of encountering works of art, without bringing back truth to the realm of *Aussagenwahrheit*, propositional truths. The problem with the truth of different works of art, according to Tugendhat's analysis of Gadamer's philosophy, is that they do not relativize one another. In contrast to this, it belongs to the very sense of propositional truth that different philosophical conceptions of something do relativize one another, and Tugendhat thinks that "one can only properly conceive a theory of philosophical hermeneutics when one succeeds in making this mutual relativization compatible with propositional truth, and that means, in giving it a sense which is not relativistic."[67] As soon as we become aware that our previous understanding of some object is dependent upon certain historical conditions, one cannot rest content but must create new understandings in order to free it from this relativity. It is only from the perspective of an absolute claim to truth, says Tugendhat, that "the insight into the relativity of a particular view or understanding lead[s] not to relativism, but to a de-relativization."[68] It is the so-called hermeneutical experience that is always encountered after the original view, which Tugendhat claims to be at the origin of Gadamer's relativism.

Initially, according to Tugendhat, the point of departure toward an object is always naïve and prehermeneutical, hence with an absolute claim to truth. Within this original perspective, whatever is asserted is called into question as soon as one becomes aware of the relativity of one's view and also whenever another different object is encountered. But a synthesis can arise out of the unified understanding of the object, into which both views (the original and the one encountered in the hermeneutical experience) can be integrated. This hermeneutical process proceeds one step at a time, but no hermeneutical experience can be preliminarily anticipated, because the point of departure always remains within one's own contingency. Tugendhat specifies, against Gadamer's hermeneutical approach, that a productive "hermeneutical experience must start out from pre-hermeneutical, naïve experience. Only insofar as the absolute claim of the naïve experience to truth is maintained can, I believe, relativism be avoided."[69]

> By abandoning the clarification of our present understanding as the point of departure, Gadamer thus surrendered even the remainder of methodology that was still left in Heidegger. But Heidegger had prepared the way even for this further development. That Gadamer could oppose "truth" and "method" presupposes Heidegger's notion of truth as "disclosedness" or "unhiddenness." Heidegger's search for a concept of truth wider than the truth of propositions could have been a fruitful enterprise. But if this concept is deprived of its essential contrast to what is false, apparent, etc., it is not being extended but destroyed. For instance, it may be correct that art has something to do with truth, but this can hardly be demonstrated merely by pointing out that a work of art has the function of showing something. And if Gadamer claims that Heidegger has overcome the problem of historical relativism, we have to ask ourselves whether it is not rather a way of avoiding than of overcoming a problem if somebody so changes the meaning of the word "true" that the problem can no longer be meaningfully posed.[70]

Tugendhat's interpretation of Gadamer's hermeneutics is, like his analysis of Heidegger's ontology, a confirmation rather than a correction, because by exposing his position he is indirectly confirming how it is not only a development of Heidegger's idea of truth but also a different approach. According to Gadamer, the proper way to study the philosophers of the past is to listen to what they have to say within the horizons of our own understanding. We must learn to listen to their truth together with the conditions and limitations of our own understanding, our "prejudices." For this reason, truth is not achieved through the methods of scientific investigation but rather through dialogue and conversation, which become the best way to deal with what we encounter in history. Gadamer's contraposition between truth and method presupposes Heidegger's notion of truth as disclosedness, which inevitably flows in the so-called fusion of horizons, thus in something that for Tugendhat is nothing more than a way to avoid a critical analysis of truth. If truth is something you confront yourself with, not something you question through the ideal of historical receptivity against the critical-methodological approach, then a serious investigation of truth must also question its validity. But since Gadamer's hermeneutics does not presuppose any criteria of validity, then the "idea of 'fusion of horizons' is then all that remains."[71]

Tugendhat's criticism of Gadamer's "fusion of horizons" goes so far as to notice how it plays absolutely no role in solving the problem of historical relativism regarding social norms. Even if this has been a latent problem of the romanticist tradition from Schelling and Hegel to the hermeneutical approaches of Heidegger and Gadamer, it is their broad concept of truth that blocked, through an ontologically "inflated" conception of art, the concrete question of the justification of norms. Both Heidegger and Gadamer interpret the Enlightenment and modern rationalistic objectivism, says Tugendhat, "as expressions of a trend toward domination and control. This is contrasted with an attitude of control of receptivity which in Heidegger surrenders itself to Being, in Gadamer to the voices of tradition."[72]

Through his criticism of Gadamer's urbanization of Heidegger's ontology, Tugendhat asks himself what the basic differences between Heidegger's and Gadamer's understanding of hermeneutics are. It is quite clear that for Heidegger hermeneutics was only the method that philosophy had to use in order to describe our own understanding, which needed to be traced back to its historical presuppositions. Within these parameters, the task of hermeneutics is to retrace both the "escape-route of human understanding and to unearth what is being repressed" and "the philosophical tradition in order to recover the original meanings of its concepts."[73] For Gadamer, the meaning of hermeneutics is quite different, because it is simply a phenomenon of philosophical significance whose object is the understanding of others. But in order to make this enterprise meaningful, it must be connected with our present understanding, where the study of history does not become a necessary condition for arriving at something else, as it does for Heidegger, "but is presupposed as a fact, as something going on anyway, whereupon the question is raised of how it can become meaningful."[74] Tugendhat explains that through Gadamer, hermeneutics acquired significance in contemporary philosophy because of Heidegger's influence within German universities in the 1930s. Heidegger made everyone believe that "philosophy as a going concern disappeared."[75] In this way, Gadamer's hermeneutical goal, to "interpret" the great philosophers of the past instead of "doing" philosophy, can be understood as a justification of the climate created by Heidegger.

What guides not only hermeneutics but also analytical philosophy is language understood as the universal element of our understanding. Not only is language not waterproof, it is also not structured in a way to create a closed horizon around us. Language is an open horizon capable of allowing us the comprehension of different worlds and cultures.[76] Tugendhat has probably felt the need to begin a dialogue with Gadamer, as I quote him earlier, because the treatment of language in hermeneutics was closer to analytic philosophy than to Heidegger's.[77] It is Gadamer's "Semantics and Hermeneutics" (1972)[78] that becomes for Tugendhat the perfect bridge to hermeneutics for the English analytic philosopher, because it shows how they both deal with the same problems of linguistic meanings. In semantics, the primary unit of meaning is the sentence, not only because it remains on the level of mere understanding but because everything that is said is drawn of a broader dimension that cannot be expressed explicitly. Gadamer in this essay explains that this dimension is "interpretation," where no isolated propositions are possible because "a sentence can be understood only if the question is understood to which it is an answer."[79] Tugendhat sees Gadamer's explanations in this essay as a "reformation" of hermeneutics that seems to call for a new concept of rationality both wide enough and critical enough to challenge analytical philosophy. More than a challenge, it is a "possibility" for analytical philosophy, since both semantics and hermeneutics originate in the linguistic form of our thought and possess a point of reference of authentic universality.[80] Finally, I should point out again how Tugendhat's criticism of Gadamer's philosophy, like his criticism of Heidegger's, will seem destructive if it is read without taking into account the real intentions of these authors. His criticism in this case is very constructive because, on the one hand, it has guarded hermeneutics from considering the truth of works of art as a unique paradigm and, on the other, it confirms that Heidegger was just looking for a different conceptual platform for the concept of truth.[81] The "right path for modern philosophy between romanticism and positivism is yet to be found,"[82] and hermeneutics will certainly contribute to finding it. Tugendhat gives a good example in this clear passage, which also warns against the metaphysical-positivist intentions that is one of the subjects of chapter 3:

> Hermeneutics is more comprehensive in subject matter than linguistic analysis and phenomenology. In its method, however, hermeneutics is closer to linguistic analysis, despite its origins in phenomenology. Linguistic analysis can be regarded as a reduced hermeneutics, as a first-floor hermeneutics. What linguistic analysis still lacks is a historical dimension and a comprehensive concept of understanding. Hermeneutics, in turn, lives dangerously in the upper story without especially troubling itself about the supportive capacity and the renovation of the floor below, which it has taken over from phenomenology or from an older tradition. The hermeneutical critique, and Heidegger's above all, of metaphysics in general and therefore of phenomenology too, bears only on their limitations; the inherited ground floor is protected like a monument and then either

built upon or dug out underneath by representatives of hermeneutics. Linguistic analysis has never pressed so far. Yet it does not want just to tear the building down, as positivism did. Rather, linguistic analysis believes it has new means and methods for a reconstruction that would be better able to bear the load.[83]

THREE

SEMANTIZING ONTOLOGY

AFTER THE METAPHYSICS OF LOGICAL POSITIVISM

TUGENDHAT, TO HIS CONTINENTAL READER, WANTS TO DEMONSTRATE THAT ANA-
LYTICAL PHILOSOPHY DOES NOT OCCUPY A POSITION IN ORDER TO DENOUNCE
THE CLASSICAL PROBLEMS OF PHILOSOPHY AS FALSE OR IN ORDER TO TURN TO-
WARD NEW QUESTIONS (HENCE, THE QUESTION OF LANGUAGE), BUT RATHER TO
FURNISH NEW MEANS OF APPROACHING MORE RIGOROUSLY THE SAME PROBLEMS
PUT FORWARD BY TRADITIONAL PHILOSOPHY.

— VINCENT DESCOMBES —

Tugendhat begins his famous essay "Phenomenology and Linguistic Analysis" by explaining that, ever since it was noticed in the European Union that "linguistic analysis is not reducible to logical positivism, parallels between analytic philosophy on the one hand and phenomenology and hermeneutics on the other have been noted."[1] These parallels allow Tugendhat not only to push even further his criticism of Heidegger's and Gadamer's too "broad" use of language but also to capture some metaphysical aspects of logical positivism. The logical-positivist criticism of ontology, such as Rudolf Carnap's critique of Heidegger, is not a real linguistic analysis, according to Tugendhat, because it has its foundations within a "dogmatic metaphysical assumption concerning the meaning of the meaning."[2] In this chapter, I study the analytical interpretation that Tugendhat applies to the question concerning the meaning of "Being," hence its semantization and nominalization through language. The logical positivism of Bertrand Russell, Carnap, and Willard Quine, according to Tugendhat, characterized metaphysical statements as "meaning-less" because it considered them empirically unverifiable and analytically nonexplicable. Tugendhat believes that their criticism was not complete because it is also necessary to consider seriously the questions that stand behind the words of metaphysics. The characteristic that determines the word "Being," from a metaphysical point of view, is that it is capable of capturing a first substantive meaning of what the word "everything" sig-nifies. Tugendhat explains that it is understandable that the word "Being" became the guide of universal thought, making metaphysics take the form of an ontology: we can say that "everything" "is, is being" because other-wise it would be "nothing."[3]

In Carnap's most famous essay, "Überwindung der Metaphysik durch Logische Analyse der Sprache" (1932; "The Elimination of Metaphysics Through Logical Analysis of Language"),[4] although ontology is treated as simply meaningless, the word Being has a very important role. It is always used in logically formalized statements, but because of its various disparate meanings—existence, predication, identity, and so on—he uses it with caution since it could create ambiguity. Tugendhat agrees with Carnap that metaphysics, by not taking this ambiguity seriously, became surrounded by meaningless questions that logical positivism avoided by "symbolizing the different meanings differently."[5] But Tugendhat notes that this cannot be the only possible solution, because ontology could still be understood as confined "exclusively to one of the meanings of the word Being, for instance, to that of existence. Carnap is therefore forced to declare that the word Being makes sense if one merely uses it, but that any questions that somehow make it thematic would be meaningless."[6] Quine, in his "On What There Is" (1948),[7] on the other hand, finds the term "ontology" admissible again and also fashionable to the point that he decides to introduce the terms "to-be" and "entity" as indices of the universal. To the fundamental question "What is there?" Quine responds with "everything"; in other words, any language that we decide to use will involve definite determinations of Being, specifically in its subject expressions or in the variables of its existential and universal statements. Although Quine thought to achieve a linguistic criterion for deciding when and whether we can consider an attempt at phenomenological reductions, Tugendhat observes not only that Quine's concept of ontology was grounded upon Carnap's meaning of Being as existence but also that ontology for Quine cannot stand for a philosophical discipline, but only for ontological "assumptions" or "commitments" of a person.[8] Tugendhat observes that

> Quine does not recognize any such thing as a question about the meaning of existence of different types of entities; indeed, he expressly rejects the idea that the existence of different types could have different meanings. But he also does not recognize anything like a question about the meaning of existence in general, or what would be the same thing, about what makes an entity an entity. This second limitation indicates how much Quine remains oriented toward Carnap's logical positivism. That this limitation does not belong to the essence of language-analytical philosophy is shown by more recent English philosophy, especially by Strawson. . . . With Strawson, a position has been reached in which, to certain extent, everything ideological in the rejection of traditional ontology has been dropped—a position in terms of which, therefore, the genuinely substantive analytic critique of traditional ontology can be recognized and made intelligible in its relevance to ontology.[9]

Although Strawson is one of the first analytical philosophers to put aside this ideological prejudice,[10] it is in Russell that concrete affinities can be found with continental philosophy. Tugendhat believes that through Russell's "On Denoting" (1905)[11] we can still understand by "Being" what we mean in natural language when we use the verb "to be." But at the same time, we must remember that by "is" we cannot assume content, because it is not a "real predicate." Since we cannot understand the universality of the verb "to be" as a way to bring out a wider universal determination, the universality of the "is" can only be of a formal universality, not a material one. Tugendhat believes that after Carnap, Quine, and Russell's logical criticism of ontology, the traditional concept of *essentia*[12] vanished because its objectivist nature became more latent. In other words, their criticisms help us understand ontology's nature even better. "Is" and "is not" were so exclusively oriented toward content that metaphysics was simply transferring "Being into the content, and could think of non-being only as null content—as 'nothing.' That '*essentia*' should form a possible meaning of Being would have to be shown anew, in any case, in terms of the verbal sense of 'is,' and cannot simply be assumed as self-evident."[13] Tugendhat observes that it should not be surprising that this critique corresponds to Heidegger's thesis that traditional metaphysics transferred Being (*das Sein*) into entities (*das Seiende*), because both Russell and Heidegger started "out from what Being means in language."[14] It was the ideological antagonism between continental and analytical philosophy that concealed their interrelations and similarities, but with this division at its last strokes, Tugendhat can show how both interpretations can help the other overcome the metaphysical vocabulary that conditions them.

BEING IS NOT A REAL PREDICATE

Tugendhat learned from Heidegger and Gadamer's hermeneutic attitude that a critique is functional not only if it tries to gain from what it criticizes recognition at least of its own relevance, but mostly by its ability to criticize that other position in the belief that it could be right. For this, of course, the critique must have a positive, open-minded attitude from the beginning. This is what was missing in the language-analytical criticism of ontology, because it characterized its metaphysical statements only negatively. Logical positivism ended up by considering metaphysical statements meaningless because they could never be verified either empirically or analytically. This attitude stifled and prevented ontology from making any reply. Having said this, Tugendhat clarifies how the thesis of meaninglessness was not reached by a genuine language analysis (hence, Russell's version of logical positivism), because it had at its foundation a concealed and dogmatic metaphysical presupposition.

> On the other hand, the more radical, hermeneutic turn toward language in recent analytic philosophy was bound to lead to the rediscovery of metaphysical perspectives in language itself. . . . This rediscovery of metaphysical questions provides a new chance for metaphysics itself, because the traditional terminology has not been simply taken over, but from the very outset was subjected to language-analytic criticism. And yet, from

the point of view of metaphysics, this way of doing philosophy has the handicap of still being oriented on the very array of questions from which it is emancipating itself; that is, on the scientistico-epistemological questions of the older analytic philosophy and the traditional spectrum of disciplines. This partiality in the selection of problems is itself a traditionalism; it is not a consequence of the hermeneutic intentions of the philosophy of ordinary language.[15]

Although I have already discussed the hermeneutic nature of analytic philosophy above in chapter 2, it is interesting to note how it is confirmed here once again. It is this same "nature" (or "intentions," as it is here called), according to Tugendhat, that pushed analytic philosophers to retort and attempt anew to answer the question of the meaning of Being. Since the history of our philosophy began with the idea of *hen-pan* (everything-one), Tugendhat is certain that the classical metaphysical distinctions of Being really consisted in this thought, and thus in the fact that it seemed to the classical metaphysical philosophers (Plato, Aristotle, Descartes, Duns Scotus, Thomas Aquinas, Hegel, Heidegger) suitable for capturing a first substantive and formal meaning of what the word "everything" signifies. This concept had so much success because the tradition thought its meaning could be used as a universal thematic guide for philosophy. Tugendhat came to want to investigate the role and meaning that Being had for this guiding principle within language, as Russell and Heidegger had tried to do, because language is the new and most appropriate realm for avoiding the ambiguities into which metaphysics has always fallen.[16]

The distinctions among the three classical meanings of Being (existence, predication, and identity) were already acknowledged by Plato in the *Sophist*, but analytical philosophy claimed, until Quine, that these meanings had nothing in common and that there was no principle that could hold them together. Although Quine's ontology included the concept "everything," though only in the sense of "all objects" and "all entities," Tugendhat points out that it is not only "objects" and "entities" that belong to the universe of our understanding but also their properties, relations, and activities, because of the universality of the ontological problem. It is the nature of this problem that showed Tugendhat that the universe of our understanding is not only a universe of objects, and that it cannot be limited to existence, to the Being of objects. Although analytical philosophy has gone back to investigate the verbal meaning of the word "Being," Tugendhat believes that its analyses have only served to confirm what Heidegger already showed in *Being and Time*, that philosophy since its origins remained so traditionally oriented toward objects that it ended up only considering the word "is" acceptable when it referred to entities. Tugendhat believes that not only for traditional but also for analytic ontology, the word " 'everything' by no means suffices as a genuinely universal thematic guide, because it has the same reifying effects as the word 'beings' or 'entities,' since it likewise refers only, or primarily to objects."[17]

In order to overcome this objectifying attitude, Tugendhat thinks we must begin to consider Being not as content but as a word, that is, formally. Only in this way will its universality not be reduced to an object.[18] But a new problem arises that Tugendhat immediately spots: can the word Being, adequate to this formal universality, become broader than the universality of entities? In order to answer this question, it is necessary to begin (as Tugendhat did with the concept of truth) from the genuine understanding that Being, not only in the sense of "existence" but also in the sense of "predication," is a word, not a real predicate. It is with the Aristotelian dictum of *pollachos legesthai* (according to which basic, philosophically relevant words often have several meanings) that the classical tradition has tried to explain how Being is not subsumed under the unity of a genus. But they did not apply *pollachos legesthai* to the idea of existence and predication and therefore spelled out the postulated unified interrelationship. According to Tugendhat, only Kant, in "The One Possible Basis for a Demonstration of the Existence of God" (1763),[19] tried for a unified clarification of Being as existence and predication.

> Existence is there defined as "absolute position," and "Being" in the sense of predication as "relative position." Common to the two would thus be the concept of "position," and this concept is, as Kant says, "identical with that of Being in general." But what does "position" mean? To make certain

that a unified point of view is designated by "position," an identifying feature must be provided that would be common to absolute and to relative position. Now, what is more obvious than to characterize position by its antithesis to negation? Therewith exactly the point of view would also be denoted which, from the first, was decisive for establishing the word "Being" as the guide for reflection with regard to universality. The universality of "is" indeed resulted from its antithetical relation to "is not."[20]

Tugendhat is trying to explain how this antithesis to the negation is characteristic and unifies Being in its predicative, existential, and identity meanings. This new criterion of universality, which Tugendhat goes on to formulate in order to form a positive conception, is negatability. "Negatability" is the desired uniform characteristic and the new criterion of universality that the tradition of metaphysics was looking for but could not bring forward because it was oriented to objectivist content instead of verbal language. Although the word "Being" owed its eminence to the circumstance that, through its antithesis to "not" it seemed to possess universality, Tugendhat notices how it now turns out that the antithesis to "not" has a wider scope than "Being." One would immediately think that ontology would just have to renounce Being and substitute for it a positive correlate of "not" in order finally to obtain a genuine guide to universal reflection, but this is not possible, because Being is not the universal positive correlate of "not." Tugendhat explains that although language uses a special word for negation ("not"), "it has no special word for affirmation, because it makes an affirmation in every sentence," which implies that "the real theme of universal reflection is accessible to us in language only in the mirror image of negation."[21]

Tugendhat's analysis not only shows (1) how the word "not" has a uniform meaning, (2) how it did not share the fate of the word "Being" (of being differently distributed in empirical languages), (3) how there is no language in which sentences are not subject to negation, but most of all (4) how every sentence is constituted as a sentence by its possibility of negation, which is affirmation. The fact that an affirmation is made in every sentence, regardless of what it says, demonstrates that language has no special word for affirmation; therefore, Being is not a real predicate because the "universal phenomenon of affirmation is wordless."[22]

Tugendhat reaches this conclusion by questioning what "Being means in language" and not what "language means in Being," because he always thought, following Heidegger's and Gadamer's emphasis on language, that the "universal dimension in which we live with understanding is not primarily a world of objects, entities, or facts, but a world of sentences."[23] Where Heidegger used the concept of "openness" and Gadamer that of "language" to discuss the realm of Being, Tugendhat uses the practical concept of the "sentence." But if our understanding constantly transcends its articulation in sentences, what is the dimension through which we pass from sentence to sentence? According to Tugendhat, it is not possible to answer this question, because every naming of entities, objects, or sentences itself remains within language, which is always imbedded in sentences. In other words, Tugendhat believes that argumentation has to be propositional; that is, argumentation can only be about the meaning of propositions and therefore philosophical discourse must be propositional if it is properly to be called argumentative.[24] Tugendhat is certain that the universality of the question of Being does not arise from any assumption regarding the unified sense of the verb "to be," but instead from the universal phenomenon of "affirmation," because affirmation is implicit in all expressions. Yet, as I have demonstrated, affirmations and negations apply universally to expressions of all kinds (not only assertions and sentences containing the verb "to be"). Although the word "is" can be used for a variety of distinct linguistic functions, all of them contain affirmations and negations.[25] I will carefully analyze in chapter 4 the claim that "every sentence makes an affirmation and therefore a truth claim," but it is interesting to note now how Tugendhat goes beyond the metaphysics of the logical positivism of Carnap and Quine, who did not even question their own criteria in criticizing ontology. The most significant way in which Tugendhat overcomes the "metaphysics" of neopositivism is by recognizing that although the affirmation available in the "not" would have to provide guidance both for the universal theme as a whole and for its subdivisions, this is not possible. It is not possible because the universal dimension in which we understand the "not" is not, in the end, a dimension of Being but "a dimension of praxis." This dimension in its totality cannot be cleared up by a simple reflection; one would have to "investigate the entire complex of linguistic features that are irreducible vehicles of affirmation in their interconnections." The important thing is to recognize that we cannot question the universal dimension of our experience with "linguistic means that are already within language demonstrably limited."[26]

SEMANTIZING BEING

One of Tugendhat's last attempts to see if Heidegger's question of Being can really be justified as a philosophical question takes place in *Self-Consciousness and Self-Determination*, in which, according to Habermas, Tugendhat "attempts a semantic reconstruction of the content of the second part of *Being and Time*."[27] More than a "reconstruction," it is, as was Tugendhat's work on the problem of truth, a search for a confirmation. Tugendhat recalls that "whenever we used overly grandiose expressions in his seminars, Heidegger time and again demanded, 'Let's have the small change'":

> It seems that we only find the being of entities, their "is," in language. Thus, the question of the meaning of being appears to be the question of the sense of the word *is* in its different meanings. . . . By insisting upon the question of the *meaning* of being did he want to return to the question of what we mean by the expression *Being* and *is* in opposition to the established terminological use of *Being* in traditional ontology? It might seem this way, since Heidegger begins his book with the following quote from Plato: "For manifestly you have long been aware of what you mean when you use the expression 'being.' We, however, used to think we understood it, have now become perplexed." Heidegger continues: "Do we in our time have an answer to the question of what we really mean by the word 'being'? Not at all. So it is fitting that we should raise anew *the question of the meaning of being*." I have written the last two sentences on the blackboard so that you can immediately recognize the ambiguity: In the first sentence the talk is explicitly of the word *being*, and for that reason *being*

stands in quotation marks; but in the second sentence it remains open as to whether the word is still meant, and that it is not the word that is meant is indicated by the fact that *being* no longer stands in quotation marks.[28]

Tugendhat is certain that if Heidegger intended the question of the meaning of Being to be a questioning of the meaning of the word, then the first step would have been to ask whether this word has a unitary meaning and if a unitary link exists between the word and the meaning. An analysis of the intersubjective clarification (that is, when the meaning of an expression is explained through the form in which the expression is used, as demonstrated in chapter 1) of the different meanings of "Being" is missing in Heidegger. Tugendhat believes not only that Heidegger radically questioned traditional concepts and structures through his phenomenological descriptive method but that in doing so he also "went much farther than analytic philosophy." But since his descriptive method lacked a criterion of verifiability, his ideas "remained intuitive and unproven theses."[29] A verification of Heidegger's philosophy can only take place through a language-analytical intersubjective and semantic examination because Heidegger himself emphasizes the "linguisticality of the understanding of Being." According to Tugendhat's investigations,[30] Heidegger shrinks back from the necessary conclusion that the understanding of Being, and particularly one's relation to one's own to-be, should be "expressed in sentences."[31] Heidegger did in fact consider the subject of philosophy to be "understanding," the "phenomenological description" to be interpretation, and his method to be "hermeneutic," but he did not try to work out any criteria for this "hermeneutic method" in order to proceed beyond Husserl. It is the lack of criteria that renders the communicative character of his philosophy "evocative." But it is just this flaw in Heidegger's philosophy that Tugendhat wants to fill through analytical philosophy.[32]

The problem for Tugendhat is to find out to what extent the insights that Heidegger only evokes can be transferred into controllable statements and intersubjectively checked through an accurate analysis of the structures of language. He is convinced that the question of the meaning of Being is still ambiguous after Heidegger's work because it was not studied as a question of the meaning of the word. The fact that only in language do we find the Being of beings, its "is," is not enough to conclude that its meaning, hence the sense of Being, resides in language. Tugendhat finds two places in Heidegger's thought from which to extrapolate his real intentions in raising the question of the meaning of Being, which will start to bring about the semantization of his philosophy. The first is in section 2 of *Being and Time*, where Heidegger explains that Being can only be clarified by recourse to the understanding of the *Seinsverständnis*, of being. But isn't this only the specifically transcendental turn by means of which he overcomes traditional objectivistic ontology? Heidegger's particular thesis, according to Tugendhat, lies in the fact that he talks in such a way as if all human understanding is based upon an understanding of Being: the essence of human understanding depends on the meaning of Being. Tugendhat, following Heidegger's own demand of his seminar students to use "the small change," transforms this thesis into the smaller question of understanding just the word "Being," which can only be found in sentences. This transformation implies that in relation to the problem of understanding, it is only the understanding of sentences that is really at issue here, since the word Being only occurs in sentences. But a serious problem arises for Tugendhat here because Being does not occur in all sentences. However, he finds that in Heidegger's lecture *What Is Metaphysics?* (1929), a thesis was advanced that would solve the problem in his favor. Heidegger, in this famous lecture, says that there is only an understanding of Being in conjunction with an understanding of nothing, and Tugendhat concludes from this that

> if we dispense with the tendency to speak only in substantives (which Heidegger shares with the tradition) and replace the talk of the "nothing" with the word *not*, it follows that Heidegger wants to grasp the extension of the word *is* in strict correlation with the use of the word *not*. Thus, according to his conception it is the connection between affirmation and negation—the yes/no—that underlies the understanding of sentences; and if understanding extends even further, it underlies this as well.[33]

If in the metaphysical tradition, in which ontology based itself exclusively in assertoric sentences, Being meant something like "presence-at-hand" (an existence that is to be stated), then now, after the end of this tradition, Tugendhat believes we must ask ourselves if there is an alternative to this orientation toward assertoric sentences. There seem to be two theses in Heidegger's thought that could provide an alternative to this orientation toward assertoric sentences. The first one Tugendhat calls the "weak thesis," where the meaning of Being differs in accordance with whether it is taken theoretically (as something that is asserted) or practically (as something to be carried out). But the "stronger thesis is that Being in the sense of presence-at-hand is not the only sense of Being, but also a sense of Being that is derivative in contrast to that of the to-be."[34] Although Heidegger advanced the stronger thesis in *Being and Time*, he originally proceeded from the weaker one. The distinction in this weaker thesis involves a type of Being that would have to belong to every assertoric sentence. The veridical Being "is" expresses the assertive aspect of assertoric sentences because "that *p*" says the same thing as "*p*." Tugendhat, through this semantization, is certain that what Heidegger meant by Being must be extended as far as the use of the words "yes" and "no." He explains that if the "yes/no" by which we answer assertoric sentences has a descriptive meaning and expresses Being in the sense of presence-at-hand, and if there is still another sense of Being, "then there has to be another mode of use of yes/no for which the content of what is affirmed or denied is not that of an assertoric sentence." This other mode, concludes Tugendhat, does exist "related to imperatives and sentences of intention."[35]

Tugendhat shows that these *Absichtsätze*, sentences of intention, are always indicative sentences formulated in the first-person future, because they are employed in those cases that involve one's own actions: "the yes/no of sentences of intention has the meaning of choosing to act (to be) in such and such a way, and generally we only speak of actions in those cases in which this latitude of freedom obtains."[36] This distinction concerns two different meanings of veridical Being, in other words, two fundamentally different ways to assume a position toward sentences: on the one hand, the assertoric yes/no (with which something is stated or asserted), and, on the other, the practical yes/no (in which a decision is expressed to carry out or not to carry out something). These two different modes of assuming a position are explicit or implicit answers to different types of questions: the theoretical and the practical. Heidegger, as I show in chapter 2, tried to avoid separating these different types of questions, and Tugendhat understands this because he shows how for Heidegger the main problem was to explicate a dimension of understanding and inter-pretation when we encounter things beyond their differences (truth and falsity). But in doing so, Heidegger also emphasizes that Being is sup-posed to be a universal thematic guide for philosophy. Tugendhat fol-lowed Heidegger's indications and concludes from his investigations that (1) truth must differentiate true from false in order to be called "truth," (2) nothingness cannot be opposed to Being if we overcome the idea of Being as presence, and (3) "the question of Being has definitively lost its sense as an orientation for serious research . . . because we have no word—neither 'is' nor 'not'—in which that which determines our understanding in a uni-fied manner can be expressed."[37]

NOMINALIZING BEING

Tugendhat did not give up trying to develop and answer Heidegger's question about Being through its foundation in language until the early 1980s. Although his efforts to find a new conception of this fundamental question of philosophy have gone unfulfilled, this does not mean he has not contributed to its understanding and development, as demonstrated in his analysis of the concept of truth in chapter 2. Tugendhat explains that this fundamental question was rejected throughout the history of phi-losophy not only because (1) it was held to be inappropriate in content (ideologically conditioned), (2) it was the wrong theme for philosophy (when problems such as knowledge, history, or man were considered pri-mary), but also because (3) the word "Being" had no unitary meaning, as I have just demonstrated. But Heidegger's concern for the question of Being (*Seinsfrage*), explains Tugendhat, does not stand in continu-ity with the tradition but rather results from a reaction to those newer themes that have taken its place. Questions about knowledge, history, or man that claimed to be more fundamental "than those about Being, would (according to Heidegger) for their part remain without foundation if the Being of knowledge, the Being of history, and so forth, were not to be questioned."[38]

Although Tugendhat admits that his whole generation of German philosophers was swept along by Heidegger's magical insights into philosophy, he is one of the only disciples and admirers of Heidegger to notice, as we have seen, that right after his citation from Plato in *Being and Time*, Heidegger concludes by saying that "it is fitting that we should raise anew *the question of the meaning of Being*."[39] Tugendhat found this quite strange, because he would have expected Heidegger, in order to ask the question about Being in opposition to the metaphysical tradition, not only to return to language for the understanding of the *expression* Being but also to find out whether the word Being has a unitary meaning at all.

> It is extremely remarkable that Heidegger has passed over this problem and has immediately gone on to the question about *the* meaning of Being [*den Sinn des Seins*], as though it were obvious that there is such a thing at all and that such a question had an identifiable meaning. Thus his question that was supposed to provide a foundation for everything else remained itself without foundation.[40]

Since Heidegger, according to Tugendhat, never brought forward a clarification of the linguistic doubts about the question of Being, it is now the moment to do it through its nominalization. Tugendhat's contribution to Heidegger's Festschrift in 1969[41] was entitled "Das Sein und das Nichts," and in that, along with other essays of this period,[42] he explains how Being in our language has always being nominalized. The German for "nothing" is *nichts*, but *nichts* has been nominalized as "*(das) Nichts*," not only "since the sixteenth century, especially to say that God created the world out of '*das Nichts*,'"[43] but much earlier, with Parmenides. According to Tugendhat's investigations, Parmenides, Hegel, and Heidegger always expressed nonbeing as "Nothing," because they understood the nature of Being as a contentless intuition.

> Heidegger applies this Hegelian formulation in *What Is Metaphysics?* and also in his later writings as if it was natural to do so. In Sartre's *L'être et*

le néant, Being and Nothingness [but more accurately it might have been translated as *Being and the Nothing*], it appears even as the title of a book. In this case the combination is very surprising indeed. Two expressions are being connected that do not seem compatible at first: the infinitive of a verb and an indefinite pronoun. One would have imagined instead "*Das Sein und das Nichtsein,*" *Being and Non-Being* or "*Etwas und Nichts,*" *Something and Nothing.* What sense does it have that in the place of "*Nicht seins*" "non-Being," (". . . ist nicht . . ."), ("is not"), the expression "das Nichts," "the nothing" takes its place, and also what meaning does this expression have anyway? What is implied for the understanding of Being if this term in connection with "das Nichts," "the nothing," takes the place of "something"?[44]

According to Heidegger, Western philosophy has misunderstood the nature of Being because the "question of Being" (*Seinsfrage*) was displaced by the "question of what is" (*frage nach dem Seienden*). Tugendhat argues that this is not the only reason it has been misunderstood. He emphasizes the fact that ontology, by treating Being only in positive terms (as "what there is"), has pre-formed the answer into an "objective theory" of beings that are "present." Tugendhat is convinced that whatever is objective for Western philosophy, whatever "is," must also "be thinkable," because thinking itself is understood as holding an object before the mind. But what happens with thought that refers to nonexisting beings? Parmenides' model of thought consisted in differentiating "thinking about Being" and "thinking about nonbeing." Thinking for Parmenides functioned just like perception. But then "nothingness" is also an object; therefore we would have to assume that a nonexisting state of affairs is construed as one that presents itself to the mind as "nothingness." If there is a noise, for example, one either hears something or nothing, in such a way that there is either Being or nothingness, which seem to be opposite. But if this becomes a model of thinking, as it has, about existence and nonexistence in general, the result is that thinking, for example, "the castle does not exist" is equated with "thinking nothing," with the consequence that any particular predicate we attach to Being can be affirmed or negated, but Being is never altered by this.

A nonexisting state of affairs for Western philosophy was constructed as one that presents itself to the mind as "nothingness." Tugendhat's conclusion is that Heidegger can oppose and equate Being and Nothing only because, and only as long as, he continues to share with the whole tradition the appeal to the nature of Being as a contentless intuition. It is this metaphysical model of thought, based on perception, that allows Parmenides, Hegel, and Heidegger to talk about "Nothingness" and fall into the contradiction, first noticed by Carnap,[45] of talking about something (a being) that does not exist.[46]

According to Tugendhat's investigations, this Parmenidean problem of nonbeing, with which Western metaphysics begins, arises because "the complex structure of 'something as something' is compressed into a simple 'something' . . . [and] it can no longer be said of the 'something' that it 'is not' because the 'is' has, so to speak, become one with the 'something' ('Being' is 'mistaken for,' as Heidegger says, 'entities')."[47] Tugendhat shows us that until analytical philosophy[48] started to go back to the origins of Greek ontology, the concepts of Being and Nothingness could only be understood as a polar opposition (as Hegel and Heidegger did), because we were only referring to them in analogy to perceptions. But now that this tradition has been overcome through the linguistic turn,[49] we are able to notice not only how the metaphor of seeing dominates all traditional thought but also why and how it is "the fundamental metaphor to which one can appeal in using any other metaphor."[50]

Tugendhat, instead of worrying about the "meaning of Being," wants to return to language in order to comprehend the meaning of the expression and to find out whether it has a unitary meaning at all. The problem now becomes one of finding out if the universality of the question of Being arises from any assumption about the unified sense of the verb "to be" or instead from the universal phenomenon of affirmation that is implicit in both affirmative and negative statements, as I have shown. But in order to retain the word Being, to guide universal reflection, Tugendhat believes we must first emphasize the claim that every verb can be negated only because there is Being contained in it implicitly.

In fact, it has been usual in ontology since Aristotle to preserve the universality of Being by translating verbal sentences into corresponding nominal
sentences with "to be" and a participle. We say "He swims" means the
same as "He is swimming." Linguistics rightly objects that this translation
actually implies a modification of sense. What gets expressed in the verbal
sentence as activity of the object is, in the nominal sentence, set off by itself
as a real content and is, as it were from outside, established as a state or
condition.[51]

It is from Aristotle that Tugendhat understands the nature of nominalized forms. Aristotle does not only speak of "to be" but also of "being";
in other words, he makes a nominalization, a grammatical transformation
of "p" into "that p" in order to preserve its universality. Although the
expression "that p" seems to have the same content as the assertoric sentence "p," "that p" is not a sentence but a "singular term."[52] According to
Tugendhat's analysis, we can tell this from the fact that "that p" "requires
supplementation by a (higher-level) predicate in order to become once
more a whole sentence,"[53] because nominalized forms are semantically
secondary relative to the predicative forms. But why is this relevant for
the question of Being? It is relevant because, as Tugendhat says, ontology
translated verbal sentences into nominal ones in order to "preserve the
universality of Being"; therefore, what gets expressed in verbal sentences
as the activity of the object is, in nominal sentences, set off by itself as a
real content and is, as it were from outside, established as a condition. In
the next chapter, I will go further and analyze why the predicates in sentences like "the sky is blue" should not also stand for something, in this
case the blueness of the sky. Blueness is indeed an object (something) and
thus could also be designated as a Being. Our criterion of objects leads us
to understand that the expression "the blueness" is a singular term. But in
moving from "the sky is blue" to "the blueness of the sky," we are always
also changing the form of the expression: the predicate "is blue" has been
changed by a so-called nominalization into the singular term "the blueness." In other words, Being becomes the ineliminable basis upon which
we can revise our ideas of what there is: the structure of our thinking about

what we consider to be Being is therefore a "propositional structure" of "something as something" ("that p"), not just "something" ("p").[54]

Tugendhat explains that since the conceptual systems that philosophy wants to explain are not always suggested in the constellations of meanings of a language's words, one "cannot determine whether such a conceptual system exists on the basis of an orientation toward a word."[55] Heidegger and Gadamer would, of course, object to Tugendhat by appealing to the fact that a word already exists, is already suggesting a system, and probably also is suggesting some prejudices that determine it, but Tugendhat believes that even if this same prejudice proves to be correct in the end, it is always more difficult for the conceptual labor to elucidate a state of affairs if there are already some systems behind it. Although Tugendhat believes that the effect of verbal ambiguity on thinking is negative, never positive, this "does not mean that the philosophical labor of conceptual explanation takes place in some dimension transcending language,"[56] because concepts are usages of words and words can have different meanings. This is also why Tugendhat ends his criticism of ontology by denying that the global orientation toward Being can be of any use for philosophy, which is always going "upstream" against the tendencies of words and against the tendencies of other prejudices. Although it would not follow that the orientation toward Being, according to Tugendhat, is of "permanent importance," he thinks "we will still be able to learn from the philosophers who have proceeded from the system of meaning that the word 'be' has in Greek, not because of, but in spite of, the fact that they have oriented themselves toward it."[57]

FOUR

PHILOSOPHIZING ANALYTICALLY

THE SEMANTIC FOUNDATION
OF PHILOSOPHY

ON THIS PATH FOCUSING ON LANGUAGE OF COURSE ONE CAN PROCEED IN VARI-
OUS WAYS. THE ANGLO-SAXON TRADITION SOUGHT TO WORK OUT THE IMMANENT
LOGIC OF ACTUALLY SPOKEN LANGUAGE AND IN THIS WAY TO CHALLENGE THE
ARTIFICIAL WORD-IDOLS OF TRADITIONAL PHILOSOPHICAL CONCEPT FORMA-
TION WITH A NEW ANALYTIC CONSCIENCE. HERE THE WORK OF QUINE WAS VERY
INFLUENTIAL—AND ON THE GERMAN SCENE THE ESPECIALLY USEFUL BOOK BY
ERNST TUGENDHAT, *TRADITIONAL AND ANALYTICAL PHILOSOPHY: LECTURES ON
THE PHILOSOPHY OF LANGUAGE.*
— HANS-GEORG GADAMER —

In so-called analytic philosophy, as Tugendhat explains in the foreword
to his famous lectures on analytical philosophy, there is little reflection on
its own grounds. For the most part, the problems treated by philosophers
are inherited problems that are not questioned. This is partially due to a
lack of historical consciousness: a way of philosophizing can only become
a fundamental philosophical position when it is confronted with earlier
conceptions of philosophy. "This reflection on foundations is not just an
additional act of self-clarification. It is a condition of a philosophy's ability to perceive the task that has always been the genuinely philosophical
task: the examination of existing questions, methods and basic concepts,
and the development of new ones."[1] With these words, Tugendhat accuses analytical philosophy of a "lack of historical consciousness" and
an "insufficient confrontation" with the history of philosophy. Contrary

to Michael Dummett, who in the same period tried to reaffirm the original analytical program,[2] Tugendhat establishes the basis for a conception that designates philosophy, under the name of a formal semantics, as the fundamental discipline. This systematic conception recognizes a methodological principle that consists in the idea that concepts may be clarified only by examining the rules of use of the corresponding words. To understand the meaning of a word does not mean to see something:

> There is nothing there to be seen, and even if there were something, it would be of no service to you in attaining intersubjective understanding—rather, I show you how the word is used. This insistence upon the mode of use is certainly not the end of all philosophical wisdom, but it is surely its beginning ... what is at issue here is the elimination[3] of a metaphorical mode of speaking in philosophy, and above all the removal of the metaphor of seeing that dominates all traditional thinking, since this is the fundamental metaphor to which one can appeal in using any other metaphor.[4]

Formal semantics becomes the inheritor of ontology and transcendental philosophy: its objects of analysis are not conscience, intentionality, and representation, as they were for traditional philosophy, but language.[5] Tugendhat explains that it is not possible to find a new, complete, and adequate conceptuality for the new semantic thematic he has in mind, because it is not possible to "overcome metaphysics": "for the main the categorical means available to us still stem from an object-orientated tradition; and it seems to me doubtful whether it is possible to develop a new conceptuality other than by debating with the inadequacies of previous ones."[6]

Tugendhat is indicating here the need to eliminate the centrality of any theory of knowledge and avoid the metaphysical trap of objectivity (*Gegenständlichkeit*), turning, on the one hand, to the semantic theory of Frege, according to which "only in the context of a sentence do words have meaning," and, on the other hand, to analytical philosophy, which considers understanding as a linguistic factor.[7] The philosophical analysis of language not only demonstrates that truth occurs exclusively in propositions and not in facts, but also that our understanding of truth is a linguistic one. From Plato and Aristotle to Husserl and Heidegger, the focus on the object has prevented an adequate understanding of "predicative sentences," since the relation between a singular term and its object was considered a *Zuordnung*, a synthesis of two different planes. This synthesis of two different elements does not occur in language because, in order to be understood, language can never be abandoned.[8] Tugendhat is certain that although the linguistic term stands for an object, this same object "is not accessible nonlinguistically." The idea of an attribution presupposes that the object is also accessible nonlinguistically, while instead "the reference to an object is comprehensible only through an indication of which of all the objects is the one in question. But this is only possible on the basis of a complex system of links composed of demonstrative expressions that are located in space and time because, in general, one may refer to a single object explicitly only by referring to all objects."[9] Tugendhat is trying to explain that, contrary to what the metaphysical tradition taught us, the use of singular terms is much more complicated than the use of general terms. Thought is a linguistic factor, the essence of language is all in its use, and for this reason, formal semantics must introduce everyone to the correct use of language.[10]

Since Kant, psychology has been the discipline that modern philosophy most had to confront, but this place is now held by linguistics. Modern philosophy's collision with a determined empirical science, Tugendhat believes, derives

> from what is called its *reflective* character. It conceives of its enquiries as consisting not in the direct thematization of such and such objects but in simultaneous reflection on how these objects can be given to us, how they become accessible to us. In classical modern philosophy the field of givenness reflected upon was conceived as consciousness, a dimension of representations or ideas; whereas in the new conception of philosophy it is conceived as the sphere of the understanding of our linguistic expressions.[11]

The problem of philosophy consists in the solution of philosophical questions by means of linguistic analysis of the terms in which these same questions are expressed. But then what is the goal of philosophy? What does philosophy aspire to? Philosophy differentiates itself from other sciences, and from linguistics in particular, because it aspires to a universal knowledge. It is a reflection on our a priori knowledge, and Tugendhat calls it "linguistic-analytical." While science researches the unknown inside a specific field of objects, philosophy instead investigates reflectively on what we already know. "What we are here striving for is not the explanation of something that is not yet understood, but the clarification of what is already understood. And this clarification can only be achieved by reflection on our understanding itself, not by experience."[12] In this way, language becomes the new field of the a priori, a field that philosophy must investigate methodologically through an analysis of our linguistic understanding, in other words, through an interpretation of knowledge reduced to the "meanings of linguistic expressions." Success in articulating linguistic understanding in linguistic statements becomes the goal of philosophy—but if these analytic statements base their truth or falsity on the meaning of the linguistic expressions in them, on what do the synthetic a priori statements base their truth?

> It seems that one must conceive, in the sphere of the *a priori*, an analogue of sense-experience. In this way there arises the idea of a non-empirical experience, a spiritual seeing, an intellectual intuition. Plato and Aristotle called this intellectual intuition *nous*; and in Latin this was translated as *intuitus*. More or less explicitly this idea of an intellectual intuition plays an important role in large parts of the philosophical tradition. In our time it has been taken up and theoretically developed by phenomenology. The language-analytical thesis that there is only an analytic, only a linguistic a priori can therefore be seen as a counter-thesis to the idea of an intellectual intuition. . . . For philosophy the demand that we should turn our attention to the things can only mean: that we should conceive of the a priori subject-matter in connection with experience. The danger of losing contact with the things (and that means: with experience) arises precisely when a philosophy constructs in the *a priori* sphere its own fictitious world of things with its own non-empirical mode of access. Precisely if experience is the only subject-matter for philosophy then what is specifically philosophical can only be linguistic analysis.[13]

The Aristotelian conception of philosophy as the science of being as being establishes the primacy of philosophy toward all the other sciences:

philosophy no longer embraces the particular sciences as regards to their "content" (as the generalization of their material), but "formally" (beyond any reference to objects). Philosophy does not thematize language as sciences do, with their specific spheres of objects. Language does not appear to philosophy as the generalization of the sphere of objects but, on the contrary, as the "formalization" in which linguistic terms do not substitute for objects by abstraction. "Formalization" is determined by reflection.

> One could provisionally describe it by saying that it presupposes a move of reflection. Whereas the particular sciences are concerned with the objects of a domain and their proprieties, the subject-matter of ontology is not to be sought in a transcendent domain (for where should this be?). But then the only alternative is that one arrives at this subject-matter by reflecting on the manner of our reference to objects. . . . From the linguistic perspective we can at any rate give a definite meaning to the distinction between generalization and formalization.[14]

Concepts are not only principles of classification, to which correspond, in language, the so-called general terms or predicates, which may be also called "classification-expressions"; they may also be subsumed to a "progressive abstraction." This progressive abstraction consists in subordinating particular concepts to larger and larger ones. From the passage of the predicate "Ernst" to more abstract predicates such as "German," "human," "living thing," and "spatiotemporal object," each predicate is more general than the preceding one because it is applicable to all objects to which the preceding one is applicable, but the converse is not valid. Tugendhat explains that

> it is the concepts or predicates themselves and not the objects which fall under the concepts, or to which the predicates are applicable, which fall under the description "classification-principle." . . . Now the specifically language-analytical position would be that one can only explain what is meant by "concepts" by references to the use of predicates, and that one can only explain what is meant by "objects" by reference to the use of singular terms.[15]

Aristotle, according to Tugendhat, was on the right path when he rejected the reduction of predicative determinations to abstract objects but not when he called "predicative determinations" both *onta* (beings) and *legomena* (something said). This undecidedness became the starting point, in the Middle Ages, of the nominalism controversy.[16] One must now ask why Aristotle objectified the meaning of predicates after having refused to follow Plato in treating the meanings of predicates as independent objects. Inaugurating ontology, Aristotle oriented himself, on the one side, toward the "objectual" formula "being as being" and, on the other hand, toward the verbal form "is," but in this way he

> lets himself be guided by this verbal form even where it does not connote being in the sense of existence, i.e. where the "is" is not the "is" of a being; and since the formula "being as being" nonetheless remains the guiding principle, formalizing the approach, which in itself would have led away from the restriction to the problem of objects, is again being cast into an objectual terminology.[17]

Although it is true that the Aristotelian ontology overcomes the formal theory of objects in the direction of a formal semantics, it does so in such a way that what emerges is misinterpreted in terms of a metaphysical object-oriented perspective caused by the lack of awareness of its semantic foundation. We must now ask: why should not the predicate of a sentence like "the sky is blue" also stand for something, in this case the blueness of the sky? According to Tugendhat, this conception

> would be comparatively harmless because something like *blueness* is indeed an object (something) and thus could also be designated as a being. Our criterion of objects fits: the expression "the blueness" is a singular term. But in moving from "The sky is blue" to "the blueness of the sky" we have to change the form of the expression; the predicate "is blue" has been changed by a so-called nominalization into the singular term "the blueness." And since singular terms and predicates are semantic classes, we must also understand this grammatical change as one of semantic form. . . . [Although] the nominalized form is semantically secondary relative to the predicative form I cannot assume this here. But then I do not need

to, for Aristotle himself, in his debate with Plato, does not merely regard objects like blueness, hence abstract objects, as secondary; he rejects them altogether.[18]

Aristotle had already captured the connection between the concept of object and the notions of "being," "unity," and "something" (*ti*). The connection with these notions was also retained in Scholasticism under the titles *ens*, *unum*, and *aliquid*, hence the transcendentals. The Being of objects can only be reached by reflecting on the mode in which we refer to them, that is, the correctness of the use of the linguistic expressions with which we nominate them. How can something like "reality" be given to us, if not by means of linguistic usage? What is the meaning of linguistic analysis for philosophy? What has prevented traditional ontology from flowing into a formal semantic?

As I show in chapter 3, the meaning of a linguistic expression was conceived in traditional ontology as the relation between the singular term with a nonlinguistic object. In other words, all the decisive steps resulted from an objectifying reinterpretation that concealed the linguistic dimension of the reflection. The problem of Being (*Sein*) and not-Being (*Nichtsein*) was interpreted by Parmenides as the problem of what is and what is not (*von Seiendem und Nichtseiendem*). In consequence, according to Tugendhat's investigation, "there is just a single unmoved Being ('*Seiendes*'), because with what is not ('*dem Nichtseienden*') not-Being ('*das Nichtsein*') was also excluded."[19] It was Plato who discovered for the first time, analyzing definitions, the meanings of predicates, but he immediately objectified them in his doctrine of ideas as supersensible entities. Although Aristotle started out from the form of the singular predicative sentence, he nonetheless developed on this basis an objectual metaphysical ontology.[20] The expression "something" indicates everything that is an object, while, conversely, by "object" is meant everything that is "something." But this formulation is linguistically faulty because the word "something" is not a predicate "but an indefinite pronoun."[21] Aristotle, explains Tugendhat, coined the expression "a this" (*tode ti*) for "object," but we must try to "avoid such ungrammatical expressions, and to this end there is no alternative but to go back even further to the linguistic background."[22] There is a class of linguistic expressions that are used to stand for an object, and here we can also say: "to stand for something. These are the expressions which can function as the sentence-subject in so-called singular predicative statements and which in logic have also been called *singular terms*."[23] The Aristotelian idea of a fundamental philosophical discipline turns out to be unsatisfactory because the perspective on objects corresponds to "just one semantic form among others." In order to bring to an end the philosophical goal that Aristotle set himself, to thematize what all sciences formally presuppose, one must take traditional ontology beyond itself to a new formal science, which, in the shape of a "formal semantics," grounds all the other sciences. This "formal semantics" is not only "language-analytical" because it analyzes the meaning of linguistic expressions, but is also "formal," says Tugendhat, "in the same sense that ontology was formal; and because it removes weaknesses of ontology, which are incapable of immanent resolution, it can lay claim to being ontology's legitimate successor."[24]

If we follow Aristotle's path and try to construe philosophy as the highest science, we must then understand that the formal element common to all sciences cannot be "objectivity," because we only refer to objects through predicative statements about them; the theory of objects is a part of formal semantics. Also, Aristotle did not only direct himself toward being but also toward the verbal form "is." Now, since ontology has a larger extension than a mere theory of the substance, formal thematization does not include only objects but also predicative determinations: these are determinations of objects. Language is not a simple medium between us and the reality of objects, because in its semantical dimension there are some determinations that do not depend from mere objectivity but do contribute to their understanding. It is wrong, according to Tugendhat, to think that the distinction between objects and meanings is leveled by the semantic turn. In this passage he explains why the opposite is the case:

> It was the old ontology in which this distinction was leveled out; for want of other categories the meaning of a linguistic expression was interpreted as an object. By contrast, there is no reason, from the semantic perspective, for neglecting the object for which an expression stands in favor of its

meaning. All linguistic expressions which we understand have, in so far as we understand them, a meaning. Some of these expressions, singular terms, stand for objects. An expression can presumably only have this function of standing for an object in virtue of how we understand it, thus in virtue of its meaning. If this is correct . . . then the objecthood of objects cannot be thematized independently of the meaning of singular terms. . . . Here then the dimension of objects does indeed fall away; and the impression therefore arises that we are dealing with the "merely linguistic." But the linguistic is not the mere sign; it is that which one understands and which many can understand in the same way. It is, therefore, nothing subjective.[25]

THE HISTORY OF OPTICAL PHILOSOPHY

Frege's semantic theory sought to help philosophy free itself from the traditional attachment to objects and therefore to pass from questions such as "what object or quasi-object does this word (e.g., 'Being' or 'consciousness') stand for?" to "how do we put words together?" If we continue questioning to which object of representation words refer, we will never, according to Tugendhat, be capable to grasp language as the appropriate sphere of philosophy. The objectivistic metaphysical questions presuppose that our knowledge of language is preceded by the understanding of the relation between language and something else (world or reality). This orientation toward objects has obliged traditional ontology to formulate its most difficult question as "what is Being as being?" Tugendhat is certain that this question must now be reformulated if we want to avoid talking about meaning in an objectual way. We must now not only ask "how can one refer to objects with linguistic expressions?" but also "in what does the meaning of a singular term consist?" To determine in this way the subject matter of philosophy means linking all these specific philosophical concepts to linguistic structures that we can analyze. In this form, the sphere of the a priori, the clarification of the meaning, is reduced to the narrower structure of understanding presupposed in each understanding of particular linguistic expressions. I have already shown that traditional ontology tended toward a formal semantics, therefore a perspective on the form of sentences, and even Aristotle himself was oriented toward the concept of *logos*, and more precisely, the *logos apophantikos*, the assertoric sentence. The ontological question must then be to find an adequate formulation in formal semantics, a question that concerns the form of all sentences or the connections of sentence forms, a question such as: "what is it to understand a sentence?" In this way, the traditional ontological question as to the Being of being will be reformulated in semantical terms. But it could appear strange that this question does not need the formulation "what is it to understand a sentence as a sentence?" Tugendhat explains that

> Aristotle however only had to introduce the "as"-formulation because he formulated the question objectually. That made it necessary to exclude the misunderstanding that ontology studies beings in the sense of individual being, individual objects. As soon as one formulates the ontological question semantically (what does it mean to speak of Being?) a corresponding misunderstanding can no longer arise and the "as"-formulation drops out.[26]

The problem of Being in traditional ontology from Parmenides to Hegel did not really question "truth," but the not-Being that is hidden in each being. If Aristotle or the tradition that followed him had taken the veritative Being as the guiding thread of analysis, then a semantic of the assertoric sentences would have developed within the framework of our ontology.

> Instead of this, however, the problematic, which Aristotle had at least touched upon, became unrecognizable in the shape of the inadequate doctrine of the *verum* as another "transcendental" determination of *ens*, together with *unum* and *aliquid*, a doctrine in which the veritative meaning of "is" was assimilated to the others and thereby finally objectified. Moreover for medieval ontology the starting-point for the demonstration of the universality of Being was no longer the usage of "is" but the thesis that the determination *ens* is the first determination that is given to the mind. How this proposition, which, to the impartial observer, must appear far from evident, indeed unintelligible, could be regarded as supremely evident by

an entire tradition, can be explained only by reference to the concept of representation ("*Vorstellen*").[27]

Trying to understand the relationship of Being to objects without considering language implies the hypothesis that our consciousness can represent (*Vorsichhaben*) these objects. Transcendental philosophy has conceived the consciousness of objects in too simple a fashion because, as Tugendhat explains, "it fails to take account of the fact that we refer linguistically to objects by means of expressions which—as singular terms—belong to a certain logical (formal-semantic) sentence-structure."[28] Representing objects, until now, meant making them present to oneself in the sense of an inner picture in order to bring it before one sensuously: inner representations as representatives of outer objects. But this is impossible, according to Tugendhat, because in this way something that belongs to a sensuous relationship (*Anschauungsbeziehung*) is *transferred* to a "relationship that is logical." The consciousness of an object, according to this tradition, was like "the sensuous of having before oneself a picture, only this having before oneself is not sensuous. From the beginnings of Greek philosophy, explains Tugendhat, up to Husserl philosophers, through the neglect of language-analytical reflection, have operated with a sensuous and even optical model."[29] For this reason, in medieval thought, Being was the primary object of the intellect (*ens primum objectum intellectus nostri*).[30] At the time it was thought that from this content, which the intellect has "before it," one removes all determinateness, and what is left is the concept of Being. This same concept of Being afterward did not have anything to do with the actual use of "is," which Hegel took as his point of departure in *Logic* (1812), as I discuss in chapter 3.

The orientation toward consciousness, characteristic of modern philosophy, was interpreted as a critical extension of ontology, because Aristotle had neglected in his ontological interpretation the aspect of grounding and justification. Ontology's turn toward consciousness concerns the problem of assertions insofar as they make a claim of knowledge. But this knowledge not only is always knowledge of an individual; it also concerns something that must find its legitimation outside the interior certainty from which it arises. Descartes, explains Tugendhat, showed that this state of certainty itself cannot be doubted by the person in the condition I am analyzing now: his certainty or state of doubt are indubitable because they are an indubitable knowledge in which he is in. This same sphere of consciousness is something inner that is immediately given to the individual. With Husserl's so-called transcendental-philosophical turn, the mode of givenness of objects is not a matter of certainty, but only "constitutive for the object-hood of objects."[31] In regional ontologies, the fundamental concepts that characterize the sphere of objects as such ("material things," "state of consciousness," or "number") not only possess a gradually higher generality than the concepts that belong to the object-sphere but are also completely different from them. This is a metaphysical perspective that, since it does not reflect from and through language, is only one possible interpretation of its state of affairs or reality: it is "only concerned," notes Tugendhat, with "the mode of givenness of objects. For Husserl the form of objecthood is constituted in the form of mode of givenness of these objects. Correspondingly one can also, according to Husserl, only clarify the sense of objecthood as such in a transcendental study of givenness."[32]

This process is different in Kant, where the reflection on consciousness invades ontology because the determination of objects depends upon the conditions of the possibility of experience. His transcendental turn only showed how objecthood, which was already the problem, could now be analyzed in a new way, extending the thematic field. Tugendhat notes that although Kant, unlike Husserl, understood the necessity of a transcendental enquiry through the recognition that our experience of objects is essentially always spatial and temporal, in a "world-relation" (*Weltbezug*) he does not explain how the "subjective turn was made necessary by something which does not become accessible in an objectual approach." Kant only thematized the nonobjectual consciousness that belongs to the context of objectual experience. By "object" (*Gegenstand*), Kant only meant what we now call "objectivity" (*Objektivität*), which is "a mode of veritative being." But Kant, says Tugendhat, "could not explicitly conduct his enquiry in this way, for despite the fact that he started out from the forms of judgment he was not oriented towards sentences."[33]

As much as Heidegger tried to separate the understanding of consciousness from the orientation toward objects, he also, like Kant, overlooked the veritative being to which they were oriented.[34] It is true that he abandoned the term consciousness (*Bewusstsein*) because this term, in Husserl as in Kant, was tied to the concept of an object in that "consciousness means *eo ipso* consciousness of objects."[35] Heidegger uses the term "disclosedness" (*Erschlossenheit*) instead of "consciousness," as I discuss in chapter 2, in order to show that the disclosedness (traditionally understood as our "self-consciousness") that each person has of himself or herself is not to be understood metaphysically, in other words, with reference to *Gegenstände*, objects.[36] The problem, according to Tugendhat, is that this Heideggerian extension of the philosophical enquiry beyond the sphere of objects failed completely to take account of linguistic sentences and therefore of the whole dimension of nonobjectual consciousness. Tugendhat sees Heidegger's situation as particularly "confused," because he was not only concerned with an extension (overcoming) of the disclosedness thematic "beyond objects"[37] but also wanted to show that the real, basic disclosedness is one that does not relate to objects at all. In *Being and Time*, by "objecthood" or "presence-at-hand" (*Vorhandenheit*) Heidegger meant not only that for which singular terms stand but the whole ontological perspective that results from the orientation toward the statement. Rather than the disclosedness that is expressed in sentences, he sought to exhibit a prelogical and prelinguistic (and, I should add, prephilosophical) disclosedness as more authentic.

> This exclusion of sentences from the core-area of the analysis which results from the rejection of the logical contradicts the central importance which Heidegger attributed to language ("Language is the house of Being"). In his statements about language Heidegger therefore reverted to the level of the most primitive theories of language, in that he emphasized the significance of the *word* for the disclosedness of beings. Because Heidegger restricted the notions of objecthood and objectification to the level of statements, objects could once more gain access through the backdoor of another terminology (that of "beings" and "things") and take up a dominant and analytical uncontrollable position. Heidegger's conception of "world" is correspondingly ambiguous: on the one hand it appears as a

whole of significance, on the other hand—and increasingly so in the later works—as the sphere of disclosedness of *things*.[38]

AFTER THE FICTITIOUS WORLD OF INTUITION

In Kant and Heidegger, the problem of the world is put aside because the dimension of consciousness absorbs not only the understanding of sentences but also the reference to objects. Tugendhat is convinced that "if all that is given to us of something is of speaking about it then we can only elucidate it by examining how we can speak about it."[39] This means that we can clarify any thematic that extends beyond the understanding of sentences only by means of linguistic analysis—therefore an analytical philosophy in the broad sense of an analysis of meaning, not merely in the narrow sense of an analysis of the sentence form. According to Tugendhat's program, this linguistic analysis, understood in such a broad sense, actually "takes the place of descriptive phenomenology, if one rejects as fictions the peculiar forms of intuition—inner intuition and intuition of essences—presupposed in phenomenology."[40] The consciousness of an object is not a representation of an object, but "means it" (*Meinen*), which by means of a singular term indicates it. If we recognize that this singular term that "means" the object is a constitutive component in the understanding of predicative sentences, then to mean an object rests on what Tugendhat calls "propositional consciousness," which consists in holding to "be true an existential sentence."[41] The intentional relation between a concrete object and a state of affairs as it was intended by phenomenology is actually grounded in the understanding of a sentence, because there is no consciousness of something that is not founded in a holding-to-be-true of an existential sentence, hence an *Existenzsatz*. That particular quality of consciousness that Husserl called "intentionality," which in supposedly intuitive descriptions he characterized as directedness to an object, turns out to be, according to Tugendhat, sentence-understanding (*Satzverständnis*). Tugendhat is certain that the transcendental philosophy schema of consciousness as a subject-object relation is impossible because, when a subject has such a relation, it is actually founded in the understanding of a sentence. The inevitable consequence of this transcendental interpretation of consciousness was the German idealists' attempt to interpret self-consciousness in accordance with this schema. This consciousness was interpreted as a subject-object relation in which subject and object were "identical": a relation of something with itself. If the meaning of a sentence is not the representation of a state of affairs, then the explanation of that same state of affairs will depend exclusively on the sentence and its meaning, hence from the understanding of a non-nominalized sentence.

The new fundamental question of philosophy—"What does it mean to understand a sentence?"—helps us avoid the idea that the predicate and subject of the proposition refer to objects they could represent. For this reason, Tugendhat believes "we can summarize the result by saying that there is no such thing as a sign-free reference to an object (an individual)."[42] If to understand a sentence does not mean to represent the object for which it stands, the only possibility left is to understand the rules that determine its correct engagement. "The sentence thus seems to be the primary unit of meaning."[43] The sentence (*Satz*) has always been considered a synthesis of two elements: subject and predicate. Although meaning should emerge from this synthesis, this meaning, according to Tugendhat, should now be conceived as the understanding of linguistic rules, because the predicate no longer stands for any object. If the reference to objects, after the linguistic turn, only occurs through the singular term, and this same singular term is an internal part of the sentence, then the singular term should always be placed side by side with the predicate. The function of the predicate is not to stand for something but to characterize something, hence the object of the singular term: understanding the predicate is to understand its characterization function. Tugendhat explains, through the example of a red castle (which is situated in Heidelberg, where he gave these lectures), that a sentence such as "the castle is red" is "no longer to be explained by saying that the predicate stands for a characteristic (redness) which is synthesized with the object, but rather by saying that the object—the castle—is characterized in a specific manner by the predicate 'is red.'"[44] The predicate (is red) does not link the indicated object by the singular term (the castle of Heidelberg) to an objective characterization (the redness), but rather determines the object according to a nature that belongs to the same object. The truth of the entire sentence will not depend on the object but from the meaning of the parts that constitute the sentence.[45] Tugendhat's insistence upon the predicative form (is red) against its nominalization (the redness) is directly related to his antiplatonic (hence, antimetaphysical) attitude. This attitude falls into the so-called nominalist tradition, according to which there are no general essences for which predicates stand. The "only objects given to us in understanding these signs are the signs themselves, the *nomina*."[46] The nominalist, Tugendhat firmly believes, will deny that we represent something when we significantly employ a predicate.

> Take, e.g., the sentence "Heidelberg Castle is red." If we make this state-
> ment in the perceptual situation, thus in a situation in which we perceive
> the castle and perceive that it is red, then clearly we do so on the basis of a
> particular color-representation. But suppose we utter such a sentence here
> in the lecture-room, for example, where we cannot see the castle; we can
> have a corresponding color-representation in our imagination, but clearly
> we can also understand the sentence without having any such representa-
> tion corresponding to the word "red."[47]

Thanks to the fundamental principle of analytic philosophy, nominalism not only is part of a skeptical position but also contains the possibility of explaining predicates positively without making them objects.[48] According to Tugendhat, this fundamental principle consists in Wittgenstein's formula that "the meaning of a word is what is explained by the explanation of the meaning."[49] If one wants to clarify the meaning with which the predicate "red" is used, even if the "redness" could be represented in general, it would be useless to appeal to it. We may only explain a predicate appealing to the use made in the judgment according to a personal understanding. The understanding of names such as "red" or "redness" is based on the understanding of the predicate "red" and not the inverse, because singular terms such as "the red" or "the redness" are nothing more than the nominalization of the predicate "is red." When Tugendhat says that the castle is red, he does not affirm thinking that the object must be placed under the perception of the red. The truth of a predicative sentence will depend on the predicate's correct characterization of the object denoted by the singular term. And this same object must be completely entrusted to the name that therefore designates it, but the object never appears in flesh and blood. "The function of the singular term is to indicate which of all objects that could come into question is meant. Thus it is the function of the singular term to pick out one thing from a plurality as what is meant—and this means: as that to which the predicate is supposed to apply."[50] Tugendhat calls this function of picking out one thing from the presupposed plurality "specification." In a predicative assertion, it is by means of the predicate (which is specified) that the singular term will be characterized. Analytic philosophy, understood as formal semantics, does not seek objects that linguistic expressions refer to in the use we make of them. It does not try to construct metaphysics, but only to return to the prephilosophic consciousness to which meanings belong. Just as ontology, Tugendhat explains, did not only mean a metaphysical foundation by "Being" but was asking what the beings with which we have to do prephilosophically are *as* beings, so for analytical philosophy what is meant by "meanings" is not a metaphysical foundation. When we ask how to use linguistic expressions, we are trying to ask with a prephilosophical sensibility how an individual expression is used, emphasizing its mode of employment as such through a formal generality.[51]

Tugendhat has insightfully noted that this question concerning the semantics of predicative sentences could also be understood as the question concerning simple "predicative form," hence the question of how the meaning of the whole sentence comes from the meaning of its two components (predicate and subject). Although the metaphysical, object-oriented position understood the question in this way, Tugendhat is certain that its attempts to produce the manner in which the meaning of the sentence arises out of the two parts as composition failed because it was conditioned by the objectual interpretation of predicates.

> It thereby became clear that the meaning of the predicate can only be understood by reference to the meaning of the sentence-whole. And since in the meantime it has emerged that to understand an assertoric sentence (if we disregard deictic expressions) is to know its truth-conditions we are now in a position to understand the alternative to the object-oriented

conception of the predicative sentence in terms of the sentence-whole. If we attempt a formulation of this alternative analogous to the one for truth-functional sentences . . . we can again say: the error of the object-oriented conception is not that it speaks of objects that can be true or false—states of affairs, or assertions—but that it thinks of a predicative state of affairs, that a is F, as composed of a and that for which the expression "F" stands; and further we can now again say: the dependence of the assertion is to be construed not as composition but as a dependence of truth-value.[52]

The declarative sentence is true when the predicate is inherent in the object denoted by the singular term, without allowing this inherence to descend from some synthesis of two elements of the sentence. Tugendhat gives a clear definition for the predicative assertions: *"the assertion that* a *is* F *is true if and only if the predicate* 'F' *applies* [zutrifft] *to the object for which the singular term* 'a' *stands."*[53] What is meant by the word "applies"? The predicate (red) is inherent to the object (the castle of Heidelberg) only if the castle of Heidelberg is red. The proposition is so structured (*gegliedert*) that the two components (singular term and predicate) have different and mutually supplementing functions. It is through the proposition that the state of affairs is understood because its truth will depend on whether the predicate applies to an object for which the subject-expression stands. Plato, in the *Sophist*, was the first to show that the possibility of sentences being true or false will depend upon their predicative structure. Although Plato was concerned with the problem of explaining the possibility of falsity (how is it possible to assert and believe something that is not), he solved this problem by explaining the complex structure of the predicative statement because, in regard to this question, the fact that the two components have different functions (as we have just seen) could be ignored. And it was ignored because the metaphysical tradition could not see this fact and took for granted that both sentence components had the function of standing for objects. Tugendhat saw that in this form (the condition of the possibility of being true or false is the synthetic form of the statement), Plato's insight became, through Aristotle's *De Anima*, a permanent item in the philosophical tradition, because statements other than predicative ones were just not considered. "The foil against which Plato and Aristotle posed the problem of falsity was the idea of a representation [*Vorstellen*] of objects that could only be true. Both the truth-relation and the object-relation were thus taken for granted and treated as unproblematic."[54] In this way, explains Tugendhat, the much more radical question of the conditions of the possibility of a relationship to truth lies outside the horizon not only of traditional philosophy but also of today's analytical philosophy for the simple reason "that, through lack of reflection on the relation of their own position to the philosophical tradition, analytical philosophers confined themselves to the traditional problems."[55]

This reference to objects was considered so natural that it was not even considered a problem, yet Tugendhat shows, combining Heidegger's and Frege's intuitions, that if the truth of the predicate "is red" does not connect to "redness" or "red" understood as objects, then its inherence to the singular term (the castle of Heidelberg) is purely of a linguistic nature. The truth of the predicate "is red" will not rely on the perception of the color nor from the image of the color in the imagination: the sentence is true or false on the basis of the meaning of the elements that compose it, not on the properties of the synthesis of the real or imaginative objects. The meaning of a predicate indicates a function that refers always and exclusively to the singular term.

THE TRUTHFUL ASPECT OF LANGUAGE

Toward the end of *Traditional and Analytical Philosophy*, Tugendhat tries to summarize his investigations by acknowledging that there is no such thing as a sign-free reference to an object, because it would be a complete misunderstanding to suppose that the rule-governed use of signs would somehow take the place of objects, as happens with predicates.

> This misunderstanding would correspond to the prejudice that linguistic analysis is concerned with linguistic usage rather than with things [*die Sachen*]. Faced with this objection one must always ask what is meant by "things." Here it can only mean the objects in space and time. But not only do these objects remain intact; it is only the mode of employment of singular terms, as this has been presented, that makes it intelligible both

that and how one can mean an individual spatio-temporal object. The rule-governed use of these signs does not take the place of these *objects*; rather it takes the place of a fictitious sign-free *reference* to these objects. In fact it was this reference, interpreted as representation, which replaced spatio-temporal objects by something else, namely by representations.[56]

According to the metaphysical tradition, objects could also be given to us without the signs that represent them, because objects would represent something that is given to us independently of language. For this fictitious, sign-free reference to objects, our use of the "sign" must be seen as something arbitrary that overlaps onto the object, whose foundation is thought of independently from other signs. But Tugendhat showed that the sign does not represent the object but only individuates it, since we can explain to someone what it is for an expression to stand for an object by demonstrating to him the reference-rules (*Verweisungsregeln*) that govern the expressions that supplement the predicates of this same object-domain. What is meant in general by such a rule is explained by "demonstrating by means of examples how the use of expressions is explained in the particular case in accordance with such a rule."[57] Therefore we can show to someone what the word "red" indicates not because we can refer to the "red" as an object but because we can indicate, using negative and positive examples, the use we make of this word. The word will be understood in its meaning when our interlocutor uses it in the same way. It is not necessary to draw the attention of general representations.[58] Since the relation with objects occurs only through language, the meaning of a sentence may only be verified inside the same language. In the case of a predicate sentence, the path followed for its verification is that of the identification of the object denoted by the singular term. The last stop of this path will be the verification in the perception, but this verification (which once again is expressed in a proposition) does not contain any general reference.

The metaphysical tradition has ignored the communicative nature of language because it has understood the comprehension of sentences as representations of objects. This tradition has interrogated objects, demanding how they are given to us without asking the question of the function of the signs that correspond to the objects, hence without noticing that only an abstraction could separate the sign from its objects. Analytical philosophy instead intends the relation with objects as a reference (*Bezugnahme*) that exists only on the basis of a sign. The understanding of an object fully coincides with the analysis of the sign that corresponds to it. Tugendhat has delineated a nonobjective semantics, in other words, a postmetaphysical philosophy capable of overcoming objectivity toward language.[59] Tugendhat calls this process "a dissolution of the traditional conceptuality"[60] because it helped to transcend and reinterpret the semantic foundation of philosophy. Some distinguished analytical philosophers, such as Strawson, Russell, Saul Kripke, and Keith Donnellan, have all, according to Tugendhat, fallen back into metaphysics because they consider the relation with the object as an immediate relation instead of understanding it as a specification that happens through the proposition. Although Dummett did think that the meaning of a singular term is to be understood as the contribution it makes to the meaning of the assertoric sentence (into which it enters as a constituent), he did not develop, as he should have, a formal semantics of singular terms. Tugendhat believes he remained the only one to have understood the absolute, primary role developed by the meaning of the singular term in the formation of the meaning of the declarative sentence. But the main factor in this problem is understanding that there is no such thing as a reference to an object that can be detached from the context of a sentence, and this is also so in the case of theories of consciousness. The use of signs thus acquires a fundamental significance for the theory of consciousness.

> Linguistic signs are not representatives of other functions which would also be possible without them. Hand in hand with this "up-grading" of signs goes the new conception of their mode of employment. Whereas according to traditional semantics one understands a sign—any sign—if one knows what it stands for, according to the language-analytical conception one understands a sign—including a sign that stands for an object—if one could explain its mode of employment to someone who does not yet understand it. And in the particular case of the components of predicative sentences this means: explain their identification-rule or verification-rule;

and *that* means: explain the contribution they make in establishing the truth of sentences into which they can enter as components.[61]

Habermas, following Tugendhat's formula, according to which there are no facts but only true propositions, has recently observed that we can only explain "what a fact is only with the help of the truth of a statement of fact, and we can explain what is real only in terms of what is true. Being, as Tugendhat says, is veritative being. Since the truth of beliefs or sentences can in turn be justified only with the help of other beliefs and sentences, we cannot break free from the magic circle of our language."[62] The essential thing is not to be able to "break free from the magic circle of our language," as Habermas says, but to stay in the "circle" in the right way. Aristotle, in *De Interpretatione*, was able to stay inside this circle even while finding a truth criterion. This criterion consisted in distinguishing assertoric sentences or statements from other sentences (such as imperative sentences, optative sentences, or interrogative sentences) by asking "whether one can call what is said with the sentence true or false."[63] Tugendhat has noted that Aristotle in his discussions of the various meanings of the word "is" distinguished this prefixed "is" by whether it is said that something is true and with the corresponding "is not" that something is false. Aristotle justified this thesis by referring to the equivalence of "it is the case that *p*" and called "this meaning of Being *einai hos to alethes*. We can accordingly speak of *veritative Being*."[64] Since Aristotle does not only speak of *Sein* (to be), but also of *Seiendes* (beings), Tugendhat thinks we must ask if the veritative "is" is the "is" of an object. Each grammatical transformation in our metaphysical tradition from "*p*" into "that *p*" must be conceived as a "nominalization." Expressions such as "that it is raining" still seem to have the same content as the assertoric sentence "it is raining," but actually, "that it is raining" is not a sentence but a singular term, because "that *p*" requires a "supplementation by a (higher-level) predicate in order to become once more a whole sentence."[65] That yesterday it snowed is a fact only if it is true that yesterday it snowed; therefore Tugendhat's analysis shows that we use the predicate "is a fact" as equivalent in meaning to the predicate "is true." We are obliged to ask at this point: what are these objects that are designated by an expression of the form "that *p*" and which are only facts if they are true for themselves? The answer is "that which can be true or false and which, if it is true, is a fact, is what is asserted when we utter an assertoric sentence. So it seems that we can characterize the objects in question as what is said or asserted. This also seems to correspond to our ordinary use of language. We ask, e.g., 'Is what he asserted (said) true? Is it a fact?' "[66]

Tugendhat's analytical philosophy pushes us to finally understand that assertion moments—since they can be expressed with the predicate "is true"—always contain truth claims. Anyone that utters an assertoric sentence asserts something ("the castle is red" or "it is raining") and at the same time also thereby asserts that what he asserts (that the castle is red or that it is raining) is true. At this point I must admit with Tugendhat not only that the veritative "is" is used as equivalent to the predicate "is true," but also that this "is" expresses the assertion moment of the statement. This assertion moment is to be understood as a truth claim, but we must not fall into the wrong assumption that there is an affirmative and a negative sentence form, or that affirmation and negation are on the same level. Tugendhat explains that it is not possible to divide sentences into affirmative and negative blocks, although it is true that "for every assertoric sentence there is an opposite sentence. But there is no general criterion by which we could tell which of the two is the negative one; for the criterion that the sentence is negative in which a generation-sign occurs is of only limited application."[67] For example, the predicate "is immortal" is as positive as the apparently opposite predicate "is mortal." It only seems negative because it is equivalent to "is not mortal," and the predicate "is mortal" equally seems negative because it is equivalent to "does not live forever." Although Tugendhat tries at the end of his lectures to give an answer to the question of the "criterion," he acknowledges that "its applicability is, however, restricted,"[68] giving further credence to the end of metaphysics. Instead, feeling obliged to follow the linguistic turn, he recognizes how any consciousness of objects must rest on a propositional consciousness, which "consists in holding to be true an existential sentence."[69]

LANGUAGE IS THE CONSCIOUSNESS OF MAN

Tugendhat, continuing his semantization of Heidegger's ontology, explained in *Self-Consciousness and Self-Determination* (1979) that although Heidegger "emphasizes the linguisticality of the understanding of Being," he does not reach the "necessary conclusion that the understanding of Being, and particularly the relation of oneself to one's own to-be, is expressed in sentences."[70] Traditional thought was not able, according to Tugendhat, to take from the different functions that words have inside language any indication that could serve the pure philosophical investigation. The consequence of this missed linguistic reflection in the history of philosophy produced the so-called objectification of determinations that actually belong to language. The metaphysical tradition believed that names were signs by means of which we could refer directly to objects, but, as we have seen, they are only singular terms, verbal means through which the speaker can specify which object among all objects he is referring to. The singular term indicates the object to "apply" to the predicative expression, which, joining to the singular term, forms a complete sentence. If we say "Tugendhat is German," with the singular term "Tugendhat" we are indicating which object we want to indicate as German. The linguistic turn in philosophy has shown to what extent ontology had conceived philosophical problems through metaphors modeled primarily on "seen," especially including the metaphor of objects put outside the consciousness and indicated by names. Tugendhat has individuated three main models upon which the traditional theory of self-consciousness has been based:

> The first is the ontological model of a substance and its states, a model that has characterized the tradition since Aristotle and, moreover, is deeply rooted in the fundamental structure of our speech, that is, in the subject-predicate structure. The second model is the so-called subject-object relation. It is presupposed as self-evident that consciousness involves having something before oneself, the "representation" of an object. Hence, it is presumed that it consists in a peculiar relationship between the subject and an object: One has something before oneself. This has led to the concep-

tion of self-consciousness and the relation of oneself to oneself in general as a relationship between the subject and himself qua object: One has oneself before oneself. The third model is based on the epistemological presupposition that all immediate empirical knowledge must rest upon perception. This presupposition has led to understanding even knowledge of oneself and the relation of oneself to oneself as a kind of inner perception.[71]

According to these models, consciousness was envisioned in analogy to a brain in which images are to be found that were then grasped as representatives for the object by the subject. The subject in this way was conceived through the analogy of the rear wall of a camera obscura. Tugendhat remembers that, since Kant, conscious beings do not relate to the objects of their consciousness through proxies or substitutes, but directly. In German idealism after Fichte, the subject-object relation presupposes self-consciousness in the sense of knowledge of an isolated self, or, as the idealists put it, of an isolated ego.[72] And even the Heidelberg school, represented by Dieter Henrich, Konrad Cramer, Ulrich Pothast, and Manfred Frank, proceeded from this tradition, considering self-consciousness primarily founded on intuition: to believe that the "I" can be conscious of itself only through reflection means to consider self-consciousness as consciousness of an object. Self-consciousness, self-reflection, and absolute reflection are considered as an identity of the knower and what is known. Tugendhat is certain that the only way to deconstruct this immediate access to the phenomenon of self-consciousness is to reconsider the whole problem from a semantic point of view, that is, from the point of view of language.[73]

Self-consciousness was comprehended until now as a relation in which the subject considers himself as an object: the subject is characterized by expressions that do not belong to ordinary language but instead derive from a substantivization of linguistic determinations such as "consciousness," "I," "oneself." Tugendhat, in *Self-Consciousness and Self-Determination*, begins by saying that in order to talk about self-consciousness, one must abandon the idea of taking the idea of inner perception as a starting point. Even when Husserl talked about "intentional experiences" he was actually talking about the way we speak about these phenomena in language. The peculiar feature of the verbs to which metaphysics brought our attention is most of all a semantic feature, since "consciousness," "self-consciousness," and "consciousness of something" are given to us only through language. Tugendhat explains the "triviality that the words consciousness, self-consciousness, and so on are just words, and a clarification can begin in no way other than as an inquiry into their meaning. . . . The paths first begin to diverge at the point at which we think we can discern the meaning of words by intuiting something with a spiritual eye."[74]

Tugendhat's argument consists of three points: (1) that an object exists is a proposition, (2) believing that an object exists is a propositional consciousness, and (3) all intentional consciousness is either directly propositional or implies a propositional consciousness. The fact that our access to objects happens in linguistic propositions does not allow us to imagine any existence outside our language. As consciousness is not related to objects in the ordinary sense, neither is self-consciousness related to ourselves as objects. Self-consciousness is not the consciousness through which I know myself but a conceptual knowledge that implies the structure "consciousness that *p*." If self-consciousness has the form "I know: I φ," where φ is a predicate that designates a state of consciousness, then "knowledge does not merely imply, but possesses the structure *knowledge that p*."[75] Contrary to the traditional models, the subject does not have any direct access either to himself or to his mental states because he can only articulate his experiences by saying: I *know, feel,* or *notice that* I *P.* The subject cannot have a knowledge either of his "I" or of his states independently; he may only know that he finds himself in this or that state. Consciousness and self-consciousness are not phenomena of an objective nature; they are linguistic because self-consciousness is a knowledge that is expressed by means of sentences. On the one hand, the subject, in Tugendhat's analysis, ends up by being completely absorbed in language, sentences, and propositions: *language is the consciousness of man.* Understanding, on the other hand, is unavoidably intersubjective, as I show in chapter 1. "All knowledge and all objective cognition, specifies Tugendhat, presupposes understanding. Thus, even if one wanted to set the topic of theoretical philosophy as narrowly as Descartes or Kant did, it is not obvious that one could ground this conception by appealing one-sidedly to a putative pre-intersubjective self-consciousness."[76]

Tugendhat, remaining faithful to his motto (*philosophy not as the explanation of something that is not yet understood, but the clarification of what is already understood*), recognized that if the ontological and epistemological model employed by traditional theories of self-consciousness are now proven to be untenable thanks to the linguistic turn, we obviously must turn to those modern philosophers who have tried to break through this traditional categorical apparatus. This is what, in different ways, Heidegger and Wittgenstein have done. German idealism understood the relation of oneself to oneself as the structure of a relation of something to itself and thus as a sort of "self-mirroring," but Heidegger, explains Tugendhat, proposed an alternative model:

> The Human being relates to *himself* in relating himself to his existence—to his life as it is impending at any given time. . . . The late Wittgenstein . . . initiates a new line of reflection upon the nature of the meaning of our linguistic expressions, and hence upon what it means to understand a linguistic expression. . . . Apart from names and pronouns, linguistic expressions do not stand for objects. Therefore, the form of disclosure (*Erschlossenheit*), in Heidegger's terms, that is involved in understanding linguistic expressions is not consciousness of an object, that is, not intentional consciousness: thus, the subject-object model is again rejected in a radical manner. Above all, Wittgenstein is unremitting in opposing the view that conceives of the meaning of linguistic expressions as mental pictures, which we somehow have before us in a mental seeing.[77]

This is a critical rupture in the traditional model of understanding linguistic expressions, because it makes it possible for Wittgenstein to regard a person's knowledge of his own inner sphere in such a way that it is not construed as inner seeing. Tugendhat believes that this traditional model of self-consciousness guided by the metaphor of inner seeing is inadequate because propositions that express "intentional acts" and "experiences" have a tripartite structure. They do not indicate a relation with an object, but rather the constitution of a "state of affairs." A state of affairs cannot be referred to through nominal expressions: this state requires that something is predicated on something. Propositions in which we express the state of affairs constitute the minimum semantical unit of any understanding, because when I reflect on my inner states, I do not regard my "feeling" or my "thinking" as something that could be seen as an object. Instead, I capture my inner states in *propositional attitudes.* Tugendhat explains that this is because "one can identify an object through perception only if one discerns the object at the same time as a bearer of specific predicates of perception."[78]

What we designate as "objectivity" or "states of affairs" cannot be determined without the help of propositions, and a state of affairs can have a meaning only within language, since meaning is nothing other than a constitutive and dependent part of the use of signs. Just as the truth value of the predicate "is red," referring to the castle of Heidelberg, does not refer to the real sensory intuition of the red, in the same way, conscious relations such as "believing," "fearing," and "wishing" are never expressions that designate ordinary objects, that is, spatiotemporal objects, but rather they are always referred to a nominalized sentence. It is impossible to wish or know spatiotemporal objects because one only wishes that something is or would be the case: the expression *I know*, explains Tugendhat,

> is not to be completed by expressions such as *the chair*, *Mr. X*, and so on, but rather we find "I know that it is raining today," or "that this chair is brown," or "that a chair stands here." If we take any assertoric sentence "*p*" such as "it is raining today," we can always objectify what is expressed by reformulating it through nominalization as "that *p*," for example, "that it is raining today."[79]

The object of the expression "the sheet" is certainly a spatiotemporal object; in other words, it is a fact that the sheet in this moment is here, but this fact or state of affairs does not possess a precise place in space and time. After the linguistic turn, the ontological status of objects rests upon a "propositional consciousness," a relation that consciousness establishes not with objects but with propositions, and the ontological question of Being turns out to be a question about the understanding of sentences. Thus, says Tugendhat, the "demonstration that all intentional consciousness is propositional gives an additional historical significance to the language-analytical programme of a theory of sentences."[80] The pronoun of the first-person singular replaces the absolute "I." This pronoun refers to the spatiotemporal empirical person characterized by the consciousness it has of itself. Having said this, does it imply that all intentional consciousness is necessarily linguistic? Tugendhat obviously suggests this, because a proposition for him is an object that cannot be identified spatiotemporally. "If we ask *what* it is that he is afraid of or that he aims at or that he believes, we identify the proposition at issue by means of the linguistic expression 'that *p*' ('he fears, believes, that it will rain'); and 'that *p*' refers back to the simple expression '*p*,' that is, to a declarative sentence."[81]

These semantic reformulations of metaphysical theories of self-consciousness through the linguistic turn have allowed Tugendhat to highlight the communicative and truthful aspects of the subject. These were neglected by object-oriented positions because the linguistic access to our states of consciousness only takes place in secondary propositions that are subordinated to the general structure of declarative propositions. The identification rule fixes the grammatical subject of propositions while the rule of verification supplies the criteria thanks to which we can understand and use the predicate. The only possible access to phenomena is the one that passes through the rules of use of the correspondent predicative expressions.[82]

If the repetition of the problem of Being by Heidegger has led to an interpretation of the sense of the truth of Being as disclosure, and this same disclosure must include language, then (1) consciousness is a propositional consciousness that does not refer to objects but to propositions, (2) self-consciousness is a relation of a person to propositions, and (3) language is the consciousness of man. But why are so many philosophers still inclined to find this semantic condition so paradoxical? Tugendhat believes the answer to this question lies in the fact that "we are so strongly oriented by the model of perception that we assume that there cannot be any non-inductive empirical knowledge that is not based upon perception."[83] His semantization of Heidegger's ontology has pushed contemporary philosophers to understand how the linguistic turn is the best internal emancipation from metaphysics.

THE LINGUISTIC TURN AS THE END OF METAPHYSICS

INDEED, THE NONFORMALIZABILITY OF THE NONPROPOSITIONAL ELEMENTS OF MEANING IS PRECISELY WHAT THOSE WHO STRESS THIS DIMENSION (HEIDEGGER, GADAMER) WANT TO INSIST ON, EVEN WHILE THEY ARGUE THAT THIS ABSENCE OF "METHOD" OR "SYSTEM" DOES NOT ENTAIL THE IMPOSSIBILITY OF COHERENT "INTERPRETATION." AND, FINALLY, TO REPEAT, THE POX LAID ON THEIR HOUSE BY TUGENDHAT SEEMS JUST AS RELEVANT TO HIS OWN VERY UNSYSTEMATIC (NONFORMALIZABLE) USE OF EPISTEMOLOGICAL CONSIDERATIONS.
— ROBERT B. PIPPIN —

Tugendhat, by his own honest admission, shows himself to be a post-metaphysical philosopher who never tried to correct his master. After working on Heidegger for twenty years, he acknowledged that his own interpretation of Heidegger's philosophy "does not correspond exactly to Heidegger's self-understanding, but . . . is the best I could make of Heidegger's question of Being."[1] Even at the end of his four-hundred-page magnum opus, *Traditional and Analytical Philosophy*, he admits that the "question of what it is to understand a linguistic expression seems, if we do not deceive ourselves, as unclear as ever."[2] He must then be considered a philosopher who did not set himself up to solve philosophical problems but rather placed himself in a dialogue in order to dissolve unanswerable problems. These honest affirmations by Tugendhat confirm (1) how he pursued the attitude of his master, Heidegger, not as part of a power-laden relation, an *Überwindung*, but rather as a distortion (*Verwindung*) that establishes a relationship of conformity; (2) how philosophy is becoming "a matter of therapy rather than discovery";[3] and (3) how well he fits in the "Gadamerian culture of dialogue," where philosophical success is measured by "horizons fused rather than problems solved, or even by problems dissolved," as I suggest earlier.[4]

I conclude this book by asserting that Tugendhat's philosophical position did not really consist in a turn from phenomenology to analytical philosophy but rather in an interpretation of the end of metaphysics as a linguistic determination.[5] Tugendhat recalls that after having spent a semester in 1965 as a guest at the University of Michigan, attending courses by William Alston and Alvin Goldman, he finally understood the importance that analytical philosophy held for him. His philosophical origins in Husserl and Heidegger suddenly obtained a sense of purpose that gave a direction to his work that he never abandoned. "Analytical philosophy," he recalls, "showed how this new way to proceed allowed me also new possibilities to approach to the philosophy of the past."[6] The passage from phenomenology to analytical philosophy is nothing else than the linguistic clarification of the transcendental conditions of any experience: metaphysics concludes its journey with the linguistic turn because the clarification of things is replaced by the clarification of words and their dispositions in the human discourses. The fact that "Being that can be understood is language" does not mean (1) that from now on Being is identified with language, (2) nor that the experience of the world only happens in language, and most of all, (3) it does not allude to a metaphysical discovery of the linguistic nature of reality. It is only the awareness that experience occurs through language. Tugendhat, Putnam, Kuhn, Pareyson, Davidson, Derrida, Apel, Rorty, Vattimo, Sellars, Badiou, and Brandom: the work of all of these represent the philosophical consequences of the twentieth century's linguistic turn. This turn is the end of metaphysics, hence of objectivity, of any metalanguage and of any privileged description of Being. If there is no way to surround language to reach the object in itself, not only is Being that can be understood language, but the ground of language itself needs to be interpreted, since in it there are no facts but only true propositions.

That truth does not occur in the sphere of facts but only in the sphere of propositions is the cultural *koiné* that characterizes the end of traditional metaphysics and the beginning of the Gadamerian culture of dialogue, in which analytical and continental philosophers may find a common linguistic ground of exchange. Tugendhat is the paradigmatic example of this culture, since he has shown how, in the traditional ontological terminology, Being has primarily been captured in an objective or Platonic perspective. It must now be reconsidered as a linguistic problem. Tugendhat himself specifies that

> meanings do not exist in a Platonic heaven; they are meanings of signs. And they are meanings of signs only in virtue of the fact that certain sensible forms are used ("interpreted") as signs. If this is so, then it is fundamental to a satisfactory theory of meaning that one correctly characterize the mode of behaviour, or consciousness, in which an expression is interpreted as meaningful.[7]

There is no doubt that the two most original disciples of Heidegger were Gadamer and Tugendhat. Both centered their philosophy on two sections from *Being and Time*, paragraphs 33 ("Statement as a Derivate Mode of Interpretation") and 44 ("Da-sein, Disclosedness, and Truth"). These paragraphs are extremely important because they are where Heidegger formulates his ontological understanding of the concept of truth, which he never abandoned. Tugendhat and Gadamer interpret these paragraphs in different ways, the former favoring the idea of truth as linguistic propositions and the latter of truth as a unique ontological event. Both Tugendhat and Gadamer emphasize the two main linguistic particularities of Heidegger's philosophy: the *propositional* and *dialogical* nature of language. Although Heidegger did not take either of these very seriously (considering hermeneutical philosophy "Gadamer's business"[8] and not even mentioning Tugendhat's work on his concept of truth as *aletheia*, as discussed in chapter 2 of this work), it is through them that the linguistic turn has become the guiding concept for the overcoming of metaphysics. As we have seen, Tugendhat believes that the principal false presupposition of modern philosophy was conceiving the field of givenness as consciousness, a representation in ideas, whereas it should be conceived as the understanding of our linguistic propositions. Gadamer, on the other hand, constructing a "hermeneutization" of onto-theology, rejects Tugendhat's construction of logic on the basis of propositions because he considers a reliance on logic among "the most fateful decisions of Western culture"; instead, he suggests understanding language on the basis of "dialogue": "Therefore language is realized not in statements but as conversation, as the unity of a meaning, that develops out of the word and answer. Language attains its completeness therein"[9] because propositions can never be excluded from the historical context of motivation (tradition) in which they are embedded and which is the only place they have any meaning. But, as we have seen, Tugendhat is probably one of the only philosophers to have given a historical justification to his semantical and propositional theory: analytical philosophy.[10]

If, as Habermas phrases it, Gadamer has "urbanized" Heidegger's ontological province,[11] we should say that Tugendhat has "semanticized" it. Of what does this semantization consist? According to Heidegger, the problem of "understanding" must be approached as the problem of "understanding of Being," and an understanding of Being is always also an understanding of the *Nichts*, nothingness. Tugendhat shows that Heidegger shares with the tradition the tendency toward nominalization: the *Nichts* used by Heidegger itself comes from the linguistic expression *nicht*, "nothing," which ought to be understood first of all as a predicative function. The ontological problem posed in *Being and Time* must be kept rigorously in the house of Being, and hence of language.

In the foreword to *Philosophische Aufsätze*, Tugendhat explains that he is the cause, with his essay "Heidegger's Idea of Truth"—which Heidegger read in manuscript—of a correction that Heidegger was forced to make to his theory of truth. But as I pointed out in chapter 2, Tugendhat did not really want to "correct" Heidegger's concept of truth, indicating in the equalization of "truth" and "disclosure" the loss of any criteria to distinguish true from false, but only to show that deep in Heidegger's reformulating of the concept of truth a whole new idea of understanding was rising.[12]

If "what is ahead of philosophy as its goal, after deconstructionism, is a labor of stitching things back together, of reassembly,"[13] as Vattimo emphasizes, then analytical philosophy, as it is meant by Tugendhat, is not really a protest against any sort of return to metaphysics but rather a critique of the philosophical terminology that attaches to objects perceived by the senses. This critique primarily helps Tugendhat to dissolve those philosophical problems that still maintain the illusion that philosophy has its own sphere of objects beyond language. Focusing on analysis or on synthesis, analytical philosophers try to solve the delineated problems by "reducing them to their . . . parts and to the relations in which these parts stand" instead of "parts [of] larger unities," as Matson Wallace writes.[14] And Rorty is certainly right when he says that "the distinction between 'analytic' and 'continental' philosophy is very crude"[15] because it is only a methodological opposition.

In other words, analytical philosophy after Tugendhat is not characterized by adherence to particular philosophical theses but by a style. Tugendhat has said that "if after 1975 I dedicated myself to practical philosophy, [it] is not only due to my own new concerns, but also because I lost any interest in theoretical philosophy. . . . I think that the question of Being has definitively lost its sense as an orientation for serious research."[16] Hence, my dialogue with Tugendhat on Heidegger and ontology was very difficult not only because of these matters of style and the personal concerns that pushed Tugendhat toward a practical and mystical philosophy,[17] but also because he has been one of the least subservient disciples of his master, Heidegger.[18] Without implying that I understand Tugendhat's philosophy better than he (Friedrich Schleiermacher would say that one always understands a work "at first just as well and then better than its author"),[19] in the following dialogue he considers my interpretation of his philosophy too Heideggerian but recognizes, at the same time, that the two were very close when he wrote the works I concentrate upon in this book. This dialogue took place on February 11, 2002, in Tubingen.

THE DISSOLUTION OF ONTOLOGY INTO FORMAL SEMANTICS:
A DIALOGUE WITH ERNST TUGENDHAT

SANTIAGO ZABALA: What is the function of language in Aristotle's ontology?

ERNST TUGENDHAT: The problem of the function of language in Aristotle is something difficult. In the fifth book of his *Metaphysics*, he talks about the different meanings of the fundamental words for metaphysics, and although he does not explicitly talk about language, he actually does. It's all about the different meanings of words. But what significance does this have for metaphysics? If one questions what Being means, one should start by acknowledging that it is a word of language. From this acknowledgment one can understand what Aristotle and Heidegger wanted to do with ontology. This is what I wanted to do with my book on analytical philosophy: ontology dissolves into semantics.

sz: What does this dissolution consist of?

ET: What are beings? They are those objects of which we talk in predicative statements. "Dissolution" means that reflecting on objects gives birth to reflection on what is more than a pure object, and these are statements, or also the meaning of statements.

sz: Then there are no facts, but only propositions?

ET: No. I do not want to say this because it would imply that the world dissolves. I do not intend this. The way in which we relate to the world is such that we always understand that objects have certain characteristics, and we reach this conclusion only through reflecting on the mode of talking about objects.

sz: How would you characterize the significance Heidegger gave to language?

ET: His thoughts about language are quite vague. I've said in one of my last articles that Heidegger talks a lot about language but does not say anything productive, while Aristotle does not talk about language but worked in a way that is actually a linguistic reflection.

sz: You criticized a lot the metaphysical tendency toward "nominalization."

ET: In our languages we have a tendency, for example, to talk about "the death" when we want to say that life ends. But it is easier to reflect on the underlying verb instead of the nominalization. Although this happens a lot in Plato, in Aristotle it is different. When Aristotle talks about a predicate, he uses the form of a predicate as a predicate; in other words, he talks about "white" and not "whiteness."

SZ: Why shouldn't we consider this "turn" a change, your passage from phenomenology to analytical philosophy a turning point?

ET: It was not a turn, because in the reflection on the meaning of words I've only tried to rescue traditional problems and this, in a certain way, I keep on doing.

SZ: Habermas has said that Gadamer "urbanized" Heidegger's ontology. May we say that Tugendhat has "semanticized" it?

ET: Yes, we can say it. But I do not see either the "metaphysics" or "the philosophy of Heidegger" as things with which we can do something. I do not see it in this way. I'm now concerned with human problems and how one should understand them. I cannot give too much significance to this Heideggerian idea of overcoming metaphysics because I do not see this entity. You are making me depend a lot from Heidegger if you say that I've done something with Heidegger. My book *Traditional and Analytical Philosophy* [1976] was only in part an elaboration of some problems of Heidegger, but I could not characterize myself in this way. I believe that there is very little left of Heidegger's philosophy. I would not be able to say what Heidegger's contribution to philosophy is. This has been for me a very long development that started with *Der Wahrheitsbegriff bei Husserl und Heidegger* [1967]. In the past twenty years more and more of Heidegger's concepts have given way. You are right in saying that many philosophers have done this or that with Heidegger, but I just cannot include myself under this group. And I cannot understand how anyone can talk about philosophers as figures: "Heidegger," "Gadamer." I think that in this way philosophical thoughts get lost.

SZ: I would like to talk about your *Der Wahrheitsbegriff bei Husserl und Heidegger*. How do you evaluate this important book today?

ET: In this book I tried to save a lot in Heidegger because at the time I thought that his philosophy was something very important, with the exception that he was completely mistaken about the concept of truth, but now I think there were many more errors.

sz: Is it still possible to talk about Being today?

et: Yes, but we have to distinguish the different meanings of this word. Being is not useful anymore as a central concept.

sz: Of what do real philosophical problems consist?

et: I do not know which are the philosophical problems, I only know which are mine. An important problem is to understand morality, and another one is that of the relation of a person to oneself. Also the question: How does a human being live?

sz: But doesn't this become a practical philosophy?

et: Yes, of course, because we are practical beings. I'm not interested in problems of the theory of science or of mind-body relation. I'm partly interested in theory of action because it enters into the form of how people relate with themselves or with others, but most of what goes on in analytical philosophy are problematizations of certain aspects, of certain concepts, without any relation to the life of each one of us. These are theoretical problems.

sz: What significance does the history of philosophy have for philosophy?

et: Little. I see the history of philosophy as a *Steinbruch* [quarry], a place from which one can extract stones. The idea that we philosophers are inside a history that begins with the pre-Socratics and that our task is to reflect on this history seems to me wrong. If in Aristotle I find many things that he says that help me understand problems, I take these things and leave the others. I do the same things with other philosophers. This is why I do not find interesting either the history of philosophy or the history of the West. Right now I'm working on matters that are in Chinese, Buddhist, and Hindu thought. They are as valuable as the thought of philosophers of the West. What seems to me important is "who brings something." I've given conferences on mysticism in several countries, and people always ask me why I have so little investigated Western mystics or philosophers who were also, in some way, mystics, such as Heidegger, Spinoza. The answer lies in the fact that what I'm interested in can be found in a more simple, pure state, in other cultures, while in the history of our philosophy, mystic thought was already introduced in conceptualizations that I find strange. In a recent article, I write on how a person relates to his own life. At first I wanted to write it as an interpretation of Heidegger, since it is something central in his philosophy, but then I realized that in this way I was only complicating things. I see no sense in reflecting on history in itself or on the history of philosophy because I consider it a historical prejudice that everything should be explained historically. This has much to do with Christianity, Heidegger, and Marx: as if we were in front of a history, as if this would be our main theme. This does not seem to me true.

SZ: Does this have anything to do with postmodernity?

ET: No, although it has become a custom to think in this way today. But I do not see it in this way. For example, the political and moral modern thought is not something of this culture. It is something of modernity. And for me there is no postmodernity. This is accepted also in other countries of the world when some religious thoughts are left aside. Other cultures are also for me pure *Steinbruch*. I can extract thoughts from there, but I'm not interested in reflecting either on this culture or on the others. I think that our main problem is to understand one another as human beings. For this we can extract thoughts from anywhere if we believe them to be interesting since we are not just interpreting a culture nor the relation of this culture with others.

SZ: We all have our history.

ET: Using thoughts from various cultures I hope to convince people that certain problems can be interesting. I want to elaborate them in such a way that all human beings may find them interesting.

SZ: Thirty years ago you used to do philosophy in a very different way.

ET: In my *Traditional and Analytical Philosophy* I had a very specific goal, which was to lead people with presuppositions of the continental side toward analytical philosophy. I wanted to construct a bridge. But today I would not say that this is the goal of philosophy. It was rather a step toward a philosophy inside modernity, but modernity for me does not mean a specific culture. I would say that the specific culture of Europe is Christianity. Once what I call modernity developed, something developed that had universal implications. Let's take the example of human rights: if we examine the volumes published on human rights, many talk about "the human rights inside the Chinese, Hindu, etcetera traditions." This seems to me absurd, because there are no human rights, in a specific sense, in a premodern culture. In the specific sense, it has more to do with the conception of a legitimate state inside modernity, and this should, according to me, be the same for all. As far as in China a conception of a modern legitimate state develops, the Chinese will have to include human rights. This has nothing to do with the West except for the fact that the West began with these universalistic thoughts. They are universals; in other words, I do not see anything parochial in the idea of human rights. In South America there are many intellectuals who believe that the idea of human rights is an invention of Europe and that it is not valid for them: I think this is an error.

sz: Do you think that philosophy has been replaced by democracy?

et: Philosophy cannot be replaced with a political order. Philosophers must continue to think on fundamental concepts of our thought and life. A democratic politics is certainly part of our life, but philosophy can not be replaced by politics.

sz: What does the work of the philosopher consist in?

et: First of all, it does not consist in interpreting philosophers. It is not about interpreting a philosophical tradition. Instead, it's all about clarifying problems of our life, in its individual character as much as in its intersubjective one.

sz: What place does ontology have in all this?

et: Ontology had a sense in Aristotle, but not anymore today. A legitimate question today would be why *it was* important. Aristotle started from something very thoughtful when he said that philosophy has to do with everything, the totality. For Aristotle the totality meant the totality of beings, and for this reason philosophy had to be ontology. This arose from a certain interpretation of what everything is, from our comprehension. Once this is taken into account, ontology may have a certain place inside something much larger. One should ask why Heidegger has revitalized this question of Being. If I ask myself what he meant by Being, I would answer that although he thematized the word Being, he did it because all human understanding is grounded on an understanding of Being, and this seems to me true.

sz: Do you feel close to any contemporary philosopher?

et: When I worked on morality, I felt near to Habermas, but now I do not feel close to anyone, even if this sounds exaggerated. Now I'm concentrating on the problem of the relation to oneself and the problem of self-relativization, which concerns religion and mysticism. But I do not think there are any other philosophers working on these matters.

sz: How do you see your philosophical path today?

et: I started in Heidegger's environment, but the decisive experience was when at the age of thirty-five I stayed for four months at the University of Michigan. When I got back, I was appointed to my first chair at Heidelberg University, and I started to do analytical philosophy. At the beginning I was not sure how it would work out, but it took a concrete form in my *Traditional and Analytical Philosophy*. I knew I was doing something German because I was a German trying to show other Germans the reasons for philosophy in an analytical way. Afterward, when I started to work on morality, I found myself close to Habermas. But after having worked on morality for over twenty years, it is enough.

sz: In your *Der Wahrheitsbegriff bei Husserl und Heidegger*, you strongly criticized Heidegger for having lost the concept of truth. Did you ever talk to Heidegger about this?

et: Yes, Heidegger loses the specific concept of truth, and I talked with him about this. Just today Heidegger's son told me that he will allow me to see some papers with notes by Heidegger on my book. Apel believes that Heidegger made a correction because of my book. With Heidegger I discussed the essay "Heidegger's Idea of Truth" [1969], where I said he shouldn't have called what he meant by *Unverbogenheit* truth. He more or less accepted this remark but continued to think that *Unverbogenheit* was a profound idea. I tried to show that it was a catastrophe if one left behind the normal concept of truth because it is a basic concept of philosophy.

sz: In your essay *Phenomenology and Linguistic Analysis* [1970], you make a very interesting comparison between hermeneutics and analytical philosophy.

ET: This is a problem that I did not pursue. Analytical philosophy thematizes individual statements, while hermeneutics believes it thinks about the horizon of understanding inside which one understands statements. This is a path I've indicated but not pursued.

SZ: Don't you think that the distinction between analytical and continental philosophy is ridiculous? At the end you contributed to its dissolution.

ET: No. I do not find it ridiculous. I still think this distinction is very real. Today I would say that the nature of continental philosophy is that it considers itself a reflection upon a historical situation. Instead, the questions posed in analytical philosophy are rather unhistorical, and if we see the difference in this way, I belong to the analytical side and you to the continental one.

SZ: Could you please explain once again what you mean when you say that ontology dissolves?

ET: My path on the problem of Being ends with the review I did of C. Kahn's book in 1977. Perhaps I would pick up again certain themes that Heidegger expressed in terms of Being, but I do not think that Being is an adequate term. Wittgenstein said in his conference on ethics, "how remarkable that the world exists." Although this continues to be a fundamental problem for me, it isn't simply the question of Being, but a phrase in which a word such as "Being" or "existence" has a place. This seems to me a fundamental question, as it was for Heidegger. But one can not say that this is ontology. The reason why the idea of ontology explodes is that the word "Being" does not have one single meaning. This does not mean that the questions posed with this word are not serious. What's more, it's possible that some of them might only be used with a certain meaning of the word Being.

SZ: So the question of Being does not make sense anymore?

ET: Wittgenstein said: "I wonder [*staunen*] that anything exists." I believe this continues to be an important question, but one cannot say that this is the question of Being. What does it mean that there are beings, or that something exists? In the word "existence," the word "Being" is used in a very specific way. This never was the question of ontology. The ontological question was formulated by Aristotle concerning objects. This ontological question is not well formulated, but this does not mean it is not important. Many things were said by Heidegger and by many Western philosophers that just have no meaning. I think that we philosophers continue to have a task in the history of philosophy, but only that of clarifying things that are not clear in the form in which many people have formulated them.

SZ: You have said many times that philosophy is not the explanation of something that is not yet understood but the clarification of what has already been understood.

ET: Both things. Naturally it is the philosopher's goal to clarify things that have been said and that we do not understand clearly. But the idea of philosophizing with philosophers, with the figures of philosophers, seems to me to lack any interest. No philosopher, even Heidegger, has ever philosophized like this. It seems we are in front of a sky where many stars can be seen. Stars might be interesting, they might even shed light on certain problems, but this does not mean that we are in front of stars, but of certain problems.

SZ: Gadamer said that "Being that can be understood is language." What do you think of this?

ET: When Gadamer says such things, they are confused. One cannot say that Being is language. He should not talk about Being if he thinks it is language. I just do not understand him. Language does not mean anything; we have "many" words and "many" linguistic structures that we should understand. There is nothing that we may call "language" or that we may call "Being" and of which we may say it's the same thing. Regarding Heidegger, I think there is an important distinction that we cannot leave hanging: the difference between appearance and truth. This is something that dissolves in Heidegger. This is a very specific theme that has nothing to do with what I've just said about Gadamer. Don't you feel anything wrong when you read Gadamer's assertion? "The language": What is this? We have something very important, which is propositional language and which I distinguish from other animals' languages and where one must question what is structurally characteristic of it. This already means that "the" language does not exist. We may say "the human language" or "structures of human languages," on which we ought to reflect and find out the importance they have for human life.

sz: In the last paragraph of *Being and Time* Heidegger says: "the distinction between the Being of existing *Da-sein* and the beings of beings unlike *Da-sein* (for example, reality) may seem to be illuminating, but it is only the *point of departure* for the ontological problematic; it is not something with which philosophy can rest and be satisfied." What does this difference mean for thought?

et: Heidegger has substantized something like Being and set against it beings. I consider this an *Irrweg*, an absurd path, even if it would be interesting to investigate this. There was something magical about Heidegger: I would say that he got confused in his own rhetoric.

INTRODUCTION

1. Rorty alluded to the "future Gadamerian culture" for the first time at the conference he gave to celebrate Gadamer's hundredth birthday on February 12, 2000, at the University of Heidelberg. This conference can now be found in a marvelous book edited by Bruce Krajewski, *Gadamer's Repercussions: Reconsidering Philosophical Hermeneutics*, 21–29.

2. Bubner goes on to specify that Tugendhat "has taken seriously Heidegger's emphasis on the *concept of truth*, and for that very reason has found fault with the obscurity of Heidegger's analysis of truth as the locus of an original 'disclosure' of Being. That has brought him back, in opposition to the common opinion of the school, to the position prior to Heidegger's advance beyond Husserl. The transformation of the exact method of phenomenological analysis of conscious experiences into a comprehensive hermeneutic of Da-sein in the historical context is not simply reaffirmed, but painstakingly scrutinized to see what has been gained and what lost." Bubner, *Modern German Philosophy*, 91.

3. D'Agostini, *Analitici e continentali*, 273. Hans-Johann Glock reminds us that some German philosophers after the war "approached analytical philosophy from their own indigenous perspective (many of them taught for some time at Heidelberg, the University of Gadamer). One important example of this approach is the critical hermeneutics of Apel and Habermas. But their use of analytical philosophy is eclectic: they invoke certain points in support of their own position, without altering their preconceptions or style of thought.... Ernst Tugendhat is a German Jew who, in 1949, returned from exile to study with Heidegger, and later immersed himself in analytical philosophy.

Throughout he has used analytical tools to pursue his own questions, derived mainly from Aristotle and Heidegger. Moreover, he has done so in a way which transforms both the traditional questions and the analytic methods. His discussion of analytical and traditional philosophy is not based on pointing out interesting but ultimately inconsequential analogies, e.g. between Frege and Husserl, or Heidegger and the later Wittgenstein." Glock, "The Object of Philosophy," 234. Barry Smith and Kevin Mulligan have critically noticed how "Tugendhat turns out to resemble Martin Heidegger: Heidegger, too, was happy to emphasize the importance of something called 'ontological analytic' without ever saying what the 'analytic' means." Smith and Mulligan, "Traditional Versus Analytical Philosophy," 202.

4. Tugendhat has accepted the term "semantization" to characterize his own position toward Heidegger. See the epilogue to this volume. Barthes also talks about an "universal semantization" to characterize the linguistic turn. See Barthes, *Elements of Semiology*, 42.

5. Rorty, "Being That Can Be Understood Is Language," 28.

6. This fusion is well explained by Jean Grondin when he states that "with Continental hermeneutic philosophy, analytic philosophy remains dominant, especially in Anglo-Saxon countries, though it has endured fundamental changes affecting its self-understanding. Following the steps of the late Wittgenstein and under the auspices of the older pragmatic tradition (Peirce, James, Dewey), Quine, Goodman, Rorty, and Davidson have gradually detached analytic philosophy from its early program of logical critique of language. In doing so, they reoriented it toward general questions such as the possibility—given perspectivism and cultural relativity—of binding truth, as well as of responsible behaviour and knowledge, a task that had been entrusted to Continental philosophy since the advent of historicism. Today, quite unlike formerly, it seems that analytical philosophy stands for no precisely formulated program. In the very pursuit of its own tradition, analytical philosophy came to the recognition that it is faced with the same challenges as is transcendental hermeneutics on the Continent. Both are impelled toward a pragmatic philosophy of finitude that must take its chances and weigh its risks. That is one way of describing the dissolution of philosophical analysis, or at least its convergences with hermeneutic philosophy." Grondin, *Introduction to Philosophical Hermeneutics*, 9–10. D'Agostini also observes that the "dichotomy 'analytical and continental' . . . does not have an effective empirical collateral reality. More so, for some time, tight connections between the inheritors of neo-positivism (analytical) and those of the phenomenological-

existential (continentals) can be found and young researchers study without any discrimination authors of one or the other side." D'Agostini, *Breve storia della filosofia nel Novecento*, 193. For a historical reconstruction of contemporary philosophy, see Prado, ed., *A House Divided*; Niznik and Sanders, eds. *Debating the State of Philosophy*; Brogan and Risser, eds., *American Continental Philosophy*; Cavell, *Philosophical Passages*; Rorty, *The Linguistic Turn*; D'Amico, *Contemporary Continental Philosophy*; and Grondin, "Continental or Hermeneutical Philosophy."

7. In the German term *Überwindung* we should think of the "overcoming" of metaphysics; *Verwindung*, instead, is the "turning to new purposes," as Rorty says, or even "surpassing" or "twisting" metaphysics. R. P. Pippin has explained, commenting on Vattimo's investigations, that "etymologically, the term suggests a convalescence from an illness, a twisting, or even distorting, as well as a resignation (one can be *verwunden* to a loss). It suggests both an acceptance of Western humanism and a taking leave from it at the same time, much in the manner of the later Heidegger's remarks about the always intertwined nature of revealing and concealing truth. Metaphysics is not 'responsible' for the obscuring of Being as presencing; Being always *must* be obscured as presencing." Pippin, *Hegel's Idealism*, 138.

8. Vattimo, "Pensiamo in compagnia," 193.

9. Rorty, review of *Traditional and Analytical Philosophy*, 727.

10. Bubner, *Modern German Philosophy*, 97.

11. Rorty, "Being That Can Be Understood Is Language," 26.

12. Ibid., 23.

13. Jürgen Habermas, "After Historicism, Is Metaphysics Still Possible?" 18. Andrew Bowie, commenting on Habermas's philosophy, noted how in his taking up key ideas from the analytical tradition, "he was influenced by Heidegger's pupil, Ernst Tugendhat, who had, in turn, come to reject many of his teacher's ideas in favour of arguments from analytical philosophy." Bowie, *Introduction to German Philosophy*, 182.

14. R. Brandom believes that when "we talk of the 'end of metaphysics,' whether that be in Nietzsche's sense, or in that of Dewey and Rorty, the point ought to be that we give up the idea of a vocabulary that is final in the sense of unrevisable and irreplaceable, a set of concepts and categories that can be counted on as fully adequate as we develop and our circumstances change." Brandom, "Hegelian Pragmatism and Social Emancipation," 561. Habermas, discussing Rorty, has also noted how Tugendhat fits in this list of postmetaphysical philosophers: "like, for example, Apel and Tugendhat, Rorty regards the history

of philosophy as a succession of three paradigms. He speaks of metaphysics, epistemology, and the philosophy of language." Habermas, "Richard Rorty's Pragmatic Turn," 37.

15. "So the result seems to be: thoughts are neither things in the external world nor ideas. A third realm must be recognized." Frege, English translation of *Der Gedanke*, in Beaney, ed., *The Frege Reader*, 336–337.

16. D'Agostini observes that "reconnecting analytical thought to its Austrian and Bretanian origins helps one to understand the affinities (explained by Tugendhat) with continental ontology. Not only did Husserl start with Bretanian introductions, but even Heidegger's interest in ontology is due to his early reading of Brentano's dissertation." D'Agostini, *Analitici e continentali*, 228.

17. Tugendhat, *Traditional and Analytical Philosophy*, x.

18. "Tugendhat is the author of penetrating books on Aristotle and on the concept of truth in Husserl and Heidegger, and the present work deservedly drew attention to itself on its first appearance, not least because in it we find a philosopher steeped in traditional philosophy giving an account of the results of his confrontation with the thought of Frege, Wittgenstein, Searle, Strawson, '*et frères.*'" Smith and Mulligan, "Traditional Versus Analytical Philosophy," 194. John. R. Williams has rightly observed that Tugendhat's main aim is this book was to "demonstrate that linguistic philosophy does indeed answer the questions of traditional philosophy, such as the question of the meaning of 'Being,' and does so better than any form of traditional philosophy has been able to do." Williams, "Traditional and Analytical Philosophy," 346–347.

19. Tugendhat, preface to the Italian edition of *Traditional and Analytical Philosophy: Lectures on the Philosophy of Language* (Genova: Marietti, 1989), 4.

20. Tugendhat, *Traditional and Analytical Philosophy*, 8.

21. Tugendhat, *Self-Consciousness and Self-Determination*, 30.

22. Bubner, "Zur Wirkung der analytischen Philosophie in Deutschland," 448.

23. Although Dummett has also reconstructed the origins of analytical philosophy in his *Origins of Analytical Philosophy*, I agree with H.-J. Glock when he says that "Tugendhat traces the origin of a cultural theme of analytical philosophy in a way which is more conscientious and less myopic than comparable attempts by Anglophone writers like Dummet. He shows that philosophy's concern with the concept of an object and the role of singular terms has deeper (and in many respects more important) roots than Frege's distinction between objects and concepts or the logical atomism of Russel and the *Tractatus*, notably in Aristotle's ontology and Kant's transcendental philosophy. . . . He shows how analytical philosophy can profit not only from 'classi-

cal' traditional philosophy, but also from contemporary Continental philosophy. For example, he intimates that the understanding of sentences in turn presupposes a larger context, namely membership of an intellectual tradition, an idea which could be developed by reference both to the historical dimensions of understanding discussed by hermeneutics and to Wittgenstein's claim that speaking a language is part of a 'form of life.' For all those who are interested in a serious debate between analytical and Continental philosophy, Tugendhat's works the best place to start." Glock, "The Object of Philosophy," 240.

24. On this matter, see Pothast, "In assertorischen Sätzen wahrnehmen und in praktischen Sätzen überlegen, wie zu reagieren ist, Ernst Tugendhat, *Selbstbewusstsein und Selbstbestimmung*," 26–43.

25. Rorty, review of *Traditional and Analytical Philosophy*, 726–727.

26. For an ethical-political profile of Tugendhat's later works, see Wolf, *Das Problem des moralischen Sollens*; Constantineau, "L'éthique par-delà la sémantique et la pragmatique"; Willaschek, ed., *Ernst Tugendhat. Moralbegründung und Gerechtigkeit*; Zambelli, "Tugendhat, filosofia e impegno antinucleare"; F. Brezina, *Die Achtung*; Guess, "Equality and Equilibrium in the Ethics of E. Tugendhat," in Guess, ed., *Morality, Culture, and History*, 51–77; Raulet, "L'éthique à la hauter de l'exigence de fondation scientifique: Ernst Tugendhat," in Raulet, *La philosophie allemande depuis 1945*, 186–190. Tugendhat's ethics was celebrated in 2006 in Germany with a book edited by Scarano and Suárez with contributions from Nida-Rümelin, Wolf, Rössler, and other important German philosophers and entitled *Ernst Tugendhats Ethik. Einwände und Erwiderungen*.

27. Henrich, "Noch einmal in Zirkeln"; Soldati, "Selbstbewusstsein und unmittelbares Wissen bei Tugendhat."

28. R. B. Pippin supports Tugendhat by recalling how "philosophers traditionally took themselves to be discovering the 'real' nature of 'objects' in the world (or at least their real, formal characteristic; that required to be an object, and so not accessible empirically), and the real nature of our relation to them. But actually, there is no way to talk about objects ('in themselves') independently of reference and predication in language. Thus the true philosophical domain should be to discover how anything can be said or understood at all, and it should abandon any notion of special 'objects' of inquiry: Being, forms, universals, or even 'meanings.'" Pippin, "Traditional and Analytical Philosophy: E. Tugendhat," 166.

29. Richardson, *Heidegger: Through Phenomenology to Thought*.

30. Heidegger, preface to Richardson, *Heidegger: Through Phenomenology to Thought*, xxii.

31. The only review of this book available in English was written by Andrew Bowie, where he lucidly considers that "Tugendhat himself is an exemplary figure for contemporary philosophers concerned with the relationship between the traditions of 'analytical' and 'continental' philosophy: rather than accept the received wisdom of the dominant philosophical tradition in his own country, he has sought to renew it by confronting it with other traditions. Having returned to Germany after the Second World War from enforced exile in Venezuela, in order initially to study with Heidegger, Tugendhat gradually moved away from the hermeneutic tradition, and, after a stay in the USA in 1965, began, with others like Karl-Otto Apel, to introduce important aspects of the analytical tradition into German philosophy." Bowie, "Review Essay: 'Ernst Tugendhat, Philosophische Aufsätze,'" 345.

32. Recently, Charles Parsons, commenting on chapter 4 of Donald Davidson's *Truth and Predication*, noted how "something of the overview of Davidson asks for was given by Ernst Tugendhat in *Vorlesungen in del Sprachanalytische Philosophie*. Although that work has been translated into English . . . it hasn't gotten the attention it deserves in the English-speaking world." Parsons, in Davidson, *Truth and Predication*, 94. These are the published studies so far: Lütterfelds, *Bin ich nur öffentliche Person? E. Tugendhats Idealismuskritik (Fiche)—ein Anstoss zur transzendentalen Sprachanalyse (Wittgenstein)*; Tomasello, "La svolta linguistica nell'ermeneutica tedesca contemporanea"; Peschl, *Transzendentalphilosophie—Sprachanalyse—Neoontologie. Zum Problem ihrer Vermittlung in exemplarischer Auseinandersetzung mit H. Rickert, E. Tugendhat und K.-O. Apel*; Meuter, *Das Problem der personalen Identität im Anschluss an Ernst Tugendhat, Niklas Luhmann und Paul Ricoeur*; Mauersberg, *Der lange Abschied von der Bewusstseinphilosophie. Theorie der Subjektivität bei Habermas und Tugendhat nach dem Paradigmenwechsel zur Sprache*; Zabala, "Che cosa significa pensare dopo la svolta linguistica? La filosofia di Ernst Tugendhat." The bibliography of this work contains references to all the reviews of Tugendhat's books by Rorty, Marconi, Taylor, Bouveresse, Descombes, Pöggeler, Larmore, Brenner, Crowell, Smith, Mulligan, Pippin, Tomasello, Williams, Steinvorth, Rochlitz, Pothast, and others.

33. It is interesting to note that the only recent history of contemporary philosophy that discusses Tugendhat is Bubner, *Modern German Philosophy*. In Italy, Pagnini, "Tugendhat: Dall'ontologia alla semantica formale"; and

D'Agostini, *Analitici e continentali*, 273–276, have also discussed his position. In English, he is mentioned in Bowie, *Introduction to German Philosophy*, but not in Wheeler, *Deconstruction as Analytic Philosophy*, which is probably one of the best works of analytic-continental bridge building available today. In France, he is discussed in Raulet, *La philosophie allemande depuis 1945*. The most recent account of Tugendhat's biography can be found in Reemtsma, "Laudatio en la concesión del Premio 'Meister Eckhart' a Ernst Tugendhat"; and an essay on his life by Crothers, "La odisea del filósofo Ernst Tugendhat."

34. Prado confirms this in his introduction to the important book *A House Divided*, when he states that "the past three or so decades have seen a widening of the gap by the weighing in of postmodernist thought on the Continental side. But more recently there has been growing interest on the part of some philosophers on both sides of the divide in narrowing the gap." Prado, *A House Divided*, 9. J. Grondin gives probably the most remarkable expositions of the analytical-continental divide in two essays: "Hermeneutical Truth and its Historical Presuppositions" and "Continental and Hermeneutic Philosophy: The Tragedies of Understanding in the Analytic and Continental Perspectives."

35. Rorty, review of Tugendhat's *Traditional and Analytical Philosophy*, 729. Bubner thinks that Tugendhat's *Traditional and Analytical Philosophy* "creates a bridge, perhaps for the first time, between the state of problems, as handed down the tradition, which is the major preoccupation of continental philosophy, and the methods of linguistic analysis, which have developed in the Anglo-Saxon school in a way which has been more or less unencumbered by traditional modes of posing the questions." Bubner, *Modern German Philosophy*, 95.

36. On Tugendhat's linguistic turn, see Bubner, *Modern German Philosophy*, 92–103; Frank, *What Is Neostructuralism?*; O. Höffe, "Ist die Transzentale Vernunftkritik in der Sprachphilosophie aufgehoben. Eine programmatische Auseinandersetzung mit Ernst Tugendhat und Karl-Otto Apel"; A. Pagnini, "Tugendhat: Dall'ontologia alla semantica formale"; Wyller, "Wahrheit und Bedeutung bei Tugendhat und Davidson"; Tomasello, *La svolta linguistica*, 52–81; Hrachovec, "Unterwegs zur Sprachanalyse. Uber Jacques Derrida zu Ernst Tugendhat"; Peschl, *Transzendentalphilosophie—Sprachanalyse—Neoontologie*, 199–292; Enskat, "Von der Semantik zur Seinsfrage E. Tugendhat"; Glock, "The Object of Philosophy"; Mauersberg, *Der lange Abschied von der Bewusstseinsphilosophie*; Zabala, "Che cosa significa pensare."

1. OVERCOMING HUSSERL

1. Tugendhat, "Phenomenology and Linguistic Analysis," 336. It is interesting to note that this book includes a foreword by Paul Ricouer in which, without mentioning Tugendhat, he refers negatively to Tugendhat's analytical interpretation of Husserl by saying: "Another merit, and not the least, of this collection of essays is to bring phenomenology out of its relative isolation and to open a discussion with other schools of thought, in particular with the dominant philosophy in the Anglo-Saxon world, analytic philosophy. . . . I would like to say how much today it seems to me necessary to undertake an intersecting reading of phenomenology and analytical philosophy. It may look at first as though these two schools of thought take their points of departure in two different regions, that of the speech act for analytical philosophy and that of lived experience for phenomenology. Upon reflection, however, this opposition is revealed as superficial. . . . Phenomenology and linguistic analysis, I would say, operate on two different strategic levels: that of the conditions of possibility of meaning and that of the articulation of this meaning in speech acts where it is brought to language." Ricouer, foreword to *Husserl*, x–xi. Dermot Moran, in the introduction to the English translation of Husserl's *Logical Investigations*, noticed how Husserl "has been a major influence on both Ernst Tugendhat and Karl-Otto Apel's philosophy of language." Moran, introduction to *Logical Investigations*, 1:lxiii.

2. Tugendhat, "Phenomenology and Linguistic Analysis," 325.

3. Tugendhat, *Der Wahrheitsbegriff bei Husserl und Heidegger*.

4. This is one of Heidegger's characteristic themes in *Being and Time*, §31: "the tradition of philosophy has been primarily oriented from the very beginning towards 'seeing' as the mode of access to beings *and to being*" (138).

5. R. Gasché explained that Husserl's goal was to achieve a retrogression to the most self-evidence of experience, to a stratum of experience that has not yet been thematized: "To achieve this goal, Husserl proposes a double retrogression: one that leads from the pregiven and 'objective' world to the original life-world, and another that reaches through the life-world toward the transcendental subjectivity constitutive of both life-world and 'objective' world. The objective world 'is there as that on which contemporary science has already done its work of exact determination.' In fact, it is the 'theoretical world,' a world inseparable from the natural sciences, whose tradition determines its mode of givenness and informs the way one experiences it." Gasché, *The Tain of the Mirror*, 110. On the end of subjectivity in the linguistic

turn, see the precise investigation of Mauersberg, *Der lange Abschied von der Bewusstseinsphilosophie*. Hrachovec said that "whereas Jacques Derrida, in a Heideggerian move, shows the metaphysical assumptions hidden in unmediated presence, Ernst Tugendhat exchanges Husserl's emphasis on phenomenological explorations of the human mind for the tools of analytical philosophy of language." Hrachovec, "Deletion or Deployment," 51. Hrachovec has also analyzed the similarities between Derrida's and Tugendhat's treatment of Husserl in "Unterwegs zur Sprachanalyse."

6. Tugendhat explains clearly that if "you want to know what a word means, says Wittgenstein, I do not refer you to something that you see—there is nothing there to be seen, and even if there were something, it would be of no service to you in attaining intersubjective understanding—rather, I show you how the word is used. This insistence upon the mode of use is certainly not the end of all philosophical wisdom, but it is surely its beginning. I do not see how anyone can deny this, assuming that he wants to do philosophy in such a way that others understand him and he understands others. Hence, what is at issue is the elimination of a metaphorical mode of speaking in philosophy, and above all the removal of the metaphor of seeing that dominates all traditional thinking, since this is the fundamental metaphor to which one can appeal in using any other metaphor." Tugendhat, *Self-Consciousness and Self-Determination*, 30.

7. Tugendhat, "Description as the Method of Philosophy," 415.

8. Tugendhat, "Phenomenology and Linguistic Analysis," 328.

9. The best study so far on the phenomenological movement is Spiegelberg, *The Phenomenological Movement*.

10. Tugendhat, "Description as the Method of Philosophy," 420.

11. Tugendhat, "Topic and Method of Philosophy in Wittgenstein," 10.

12. Tugendhat, "Reflections on Philosophical Method from an Analytic Point of View," 117. Jacques Bouveresse explains that "as Tugendhat emphasizes the negation of Wittgenstein's principle, which reduces the question of meanings to that of the explanation of meanings, in the way we just explained, has as consequences the fact 'that a philosophical semantics would directly lose its meaning because philosophy only wants to make explicit what we already understand in a philosophical form'" Bouveresse, *Herméneutique et linguistique*, 60.

13. Tugendhat, "Reflections on Philosophical Method from an Analytic Point of View," 117.

14. Tugendhat, "Description as the Method of Philosophy," 418.

15. In an interview, Robert Brandom, author of *Making It Explicit*, *Articulating Reasons*, and *Tales of the Mighty Dead*, explained the concept of "making something explicit" in his work; his explanation has many analogies with Tugendhat's philosophy. He says that "making something explicit is putting it in a form in which it can serve as a *reason* for another claim, and for which in turn reasons can be demanded. Second, the function of vocabulary of most interest to philosophers (starting with logical expressions) is to make explicit those *inferential* connections that articulate the contents of all concepts, and the *normative* aspects of our social practice in virtue of which we can keep track of how our *commitments* and *entitlements* are changed by performing speech acts (giving and asking for reasons). I see mastering discursive practice as a matter of knowing what one is committing oneself to by performing certain speech acts, and what would entitle one to them. My project in the book is to make explicit the fine structure of such discursive practice. It puts forward an expressive, normative, pragmatic rationalism." Brandom, "Interview with R. Brandom by Carlo Penco," 149.

16. Tugendhat, "Description as the Method of Philosophy," 421.

17. In the dialogue included as the appendix to this volume I ask Tugendhat about this point, and he replies positively.

18. "It is the origin (specific of a philosophy as an activity marked by a certain history in the traditional European culture) which calls philosophy to argumentation. It only offers it a repertory of arguments, the only to which it has recourse to." Vattimo, "Diritto all'argomentazione," 70.

19. Tugendhat used the phrase "*hermeneutischen Charackter der analytischen Philosophie*" for the first time in the essay "Philosophical Method from an Analytic Point of View" (1989), translated by W. Rehg. Although the English translator of this essay translated the German term "*Charackter*" as "character," I prefer to translate it as "nature," not only because this better expresses the meaning it refers to in the context of Tugendhat's philosophy but also because in an earlier essay ("Language Analysis and the Critique of Ontology," 1967) he uses a similar expression: "the hermeneutic intentions of the philosophy of ordinary language." Tugendhat, "Language Analysis and the Critique of Ontology," 101.

20. Bubner also explains that since "analytical philosophy and hermeneutics have recognized more clearly the connection between speaking and acting, a great deal has been said about how they work together. The heterogeneity of the elements has tended rather to fade into oblivion behind the dominant idea of a similarity of structure. Speaking and acting—so it may seem to the ad-

vocates of a harmonistic program—are ultimately one or at least to be explained as springing from the same roots." Bubner, *Essays in Hermeneutics and Critical Theory*, 147. On the relation between semantics, phenomenology, and hermeneutics, see Gadamer, "Semantics and Hermeneutics," in his *Philosophical Hermeneutics*, 82–94; Ricouer, "The Problem of Double Meaning as Hermeneutic Problem and Semantic Problem," in his *The Conflict of Interpretations*, 61–76; Bouveresse, *Herméneutique et linguistique*; and the first part of Brandom, *Tales of the Mighty Dead*.

21. Tugendhat, "Reflections on Philosophical Method from an Analytic Point of View," 118.

22. Ibid., 122.

23. On the convergence between the linguistic and continental turns, the study by Tietz, *Sprache und Verstehen in analytischer und hermeneutischer Sicht*, gives very clear examples of Tugendhat's position.

24. Tugendhat, "Philosophical Method from an Analytic Point of View," 118.

25. On the contribution of phenomenology to analytical philosophy, see Grondin, "La contribution silencieuse de Husserl à l'hermeneutique," 383–393; and Benoist, *Représentations sans objet*.

26. Tugendhat, "Reflections on Philosophical Method from an Analytic Point of View," 119.

27. Ibid., 120.

28. Ibid., 121.

29. Ibid., 121–122.

30. Ibid., 122.

31. Ibid., 123.

32. For a historical and conceptual account of the end of metaphysics and the start of postmodernity, see Welsch, *Unsere postmoderne Moderne*; and Vattimo, *The End of Modernity*.

33. Tugendhat, "Reflections on Philosophical Method from an Analytic Point of View," 124.

34. Ibid.

35. Tugendhat, "Phenomenology and Linguistic Analysis," 326. Dahlstrom has lucidly explained that the point here is not only that there is a way of imagining something without the medium of an image, but also "that this is a way for it to be 'given itself' (*Selbstgebung*). The latter thesis, in particular, is controversial. Tugendhat, for example, regards this thesis as false (from Husserl's standpoint) and even as rightly contradicted by Husserl himself. 'Husserl allowed himself to be misled in the Ideas into understanding the "self" on the

basis of the contrast with the image. .... In this sense [namely the contrast to the image] the "self" comes to be directly represented even in the empty intention of meaning.' ... In the simple or straightforward re-presentation (*Vergegenwärtigung*) of which Husserl and Heidegger are speaking, what is meant is 'intuited or observed as "itself,"' not by means of an image but 'immediately,' though in 'the modified character of "something vaguely hovering before us (*Vorschwebendes*)."' Since the same does not hold for the empty meaning-intention, there is reason for Heidegger, following Husserl, to speak of a stage of self-givenness in regard to simple re-presentation. Moreover, even if Tugendhat rightly maintains that the 'self' remains 'without further qualification even in the latest writings [of Husserl] the characteristic of the genuine presence of what is meant, to be attained only in the evidence of perception,' he also recognizes the fact that 'from now on when Husserl wants to be exact in his terminology, he names the self-givenness of perception "given in person" or "originally givenness" in order to distinguish it from the self-givenness of the imagination.' ... However the talk of self-givenness (by Husserl and Heidegger) refers not to the source of the givenness but simply to what is given in contrast to what is meant. Husserl speaks of the self-givenness in the imagination, as Tugendhat rightly notes, in order to distinguish the re-presentation from the consciousness of an image or copy. In the 're-presentative' imagination, what is meant itself is given, albeit not 'in the flesh,' and not merely meant." Dahlstrom, *Heidegger's Concept of Truth*, 61–62.

36. Tugendhat, "Phenomenology and Linguistic Analysis," 335.

37. On the problem of the existence of objects, see Benoist, "La question des objets inexistants et les 'origines communes' de la phénoménologie et de la philosophie analytique," in Benoist, *Représentations sans objet*, 5–16; and Harman, *Tool-Being*.

38. This matter is well developed in Soldati, *Bedeutung und psychischer Gehalt*, and in his essay "Bedeutungen und Gegenständlichkeiten."

39. Against this interpretation of Tugendhat, Smith and Mulligan have said that "Tugendhat wants to foist onto Husserl the thesis that the state of affairs is an objectified meaning, i.e., that it is both a meaning and an object, because this will strengthen his case that, except for brief periods of clarity, Husserl failed to appreciate the crucial differences between sentences and names. But the thesis that Husserlian *Sachverhalte* are *meanings* breaks down in the face of the fact that *Sachverhalte* quite clearly have certain properties possessed by no meanings: they have pieceable and perceptible parts. And the thesis that

Husserlian *Sachverhalte* are objects breaks down because it ignores the fact that Husserl has at his disposal the resources of a subtle syntactic theory of modifications or transformations. These resources enable him to distinguish a hierarchy of levels or forms of discourse about the structures in the world and thereby precisely to avoid any identification of *Sachverhalte* as objects. Thus according to Husserl our simple or unmodified, non-philosophical talk about objects is transformed in a systematic way when we talk about *Sachverhalte*. Hence, it is not as if the world is made up of objects and *Sachverhalte* somehow alongside each other. Nor, a fortiori, are *Sachverhalte* simply another kind of object: if they were, then clearly no modification of our ordinary forms of speech would be necessary in order to refer to them." Smith and Mulligan, "Traditional Versus Analytic Philosophy," 196. Instead, Pippin believes that "Tugendhat criticizes Husserlian phenomenology . . . to show that [the] entire problematic (the consciousness-object model of intentionality) is misconceived. Not surprisingly, Tugendhat adopts a strict 'propositional attitude' approach to the issues Husserl takes up, and tries to show that what consciousness can be said to be conscious of is never an intentional object, and always a proposition (that *p*). Hence if we are really interested in how it is that consciousness intends an object, we should investigate what it is for a speaker or a hearer to understand a sentence." Pippin, "Traditional and Analytical Philosophy," 166.

40. Taylor Carman rightly objects that Tugendhat in this way is telling only part of Husserl's version of phenomenology. "For transcendental reduction does not merely bracket the objects of theoretical, objectifying acts; it is also meant to direct our attention exclusively to consciousness and its supposedly immanent intentional contents. It is precisely this privileging of consciousness that is the target of Heidegger's critique, over and beyond his rejection of Husserl's impoverished conception of the character of everyday experience. Tugendhat thus misrepresents the aim of the reduction and so fails to appreciate how radically Heidegger departs from it." Carman, *Heidegger's Analytic*, 84. On Tugendhat's general interpretation of Husserl's epoché and its relation with Heidegger's notion of being-in-the-world, see the analysis in Carman, *Heidegger's Analytic*, 82–85.

41. Tugendhat, "Phenomenology and Linguistic Analysis," 329.

42. Ibid., 333.

43. Frank observes that "Derrida—much like Tugendhat—approaches the phenomenon of 'self-consciousness' or 'subjectivity' from the angle of the so-called experiences of consciousness or *states* of consciousness. Derrida tries to

demonstrate that Husserl believed it was possible to distinguish a 'pre-expres-sive' stratum from an expressive stratum in these 'states of consciousness.' The consciousness experience, according to this, would thus be cognizant of its meaning or its signification even before it is consigned to the expressive substance (*Ausdruckskörper*). . . . As in Tugendhat's critique of Husserl, it is the idea of a pre-semiotic internal perception against which Derrida lashes out. In his opinion, meaning can be formed only in a language, and language generates its signification by means of the differentiations of expressions. We are already acquainted with this sort of critique of the paradigm of a lan-guage-independent transcendental consciousness from the works of Herder, Schleiermacher, Humboldt, and, of course, Saussure." Frank, *What Is Neo-structuralism?*, 223. This comparison of Tugendhat and Derrida is also ana-lyzed in Hrachovec, "Unterwegs zur Sprachanalyse," 284–295.

44. Tugendhat, "Phenomenology and Linguistic Analysis," 337.
45. Ibid., 331.
46. Ibid., 337.
47. Ibid., 332.
48. Ibid. According to this interpretation, explains Cobb-Stevens, "Husserl was committed to the following problematic theses: (a) that the assertoric force of a statement is included within its nominalized propositional content; (b) that the sense of a predicate ('white') is the object for which its nominalized modification ('whiteness') stands; (c) that the predication is a synthesis of two objects. This criticism seriously misinterprets what Husserl has to say about the relationship between propositions and facts. In the first place, he nowhere holds that meanings function as intermediaries between words and facts. To suggest, as Tugendhat does, that reflection on what has just been said converts not-yet-objectified meanings into objects is to miss the point of Husserl's thesis that propositions *are* facts taken as supposed. The reflective turn that establishes propositions as such converts *facts* into propositions; it does not convert ethereal, un-thematic, non-objective intermediaries into objectified propositions. Moreover, Husserl insists that there is an essential difference between naming and making a statement: 'An assertion can never function as a name, nor a name as an assertion, without changing its essential nature. . . .' Hence, he would never claim that propositions are nominalized facts. Tu-gendhat unfortunately confuses nominalization of a fact with the taking of a fact as a supposition. Nominalization of an articulated fact modifies that fact's structure. It names what had heretofore been asserted, thus compressing the articulated interplay of object and feature into an object that is set up as a sub-

ject of predication." Cobb-Stevens, *Husserl and Analytic Philosophy*, 175–176. On the relation of this problem and the "ontological reference," see the very clear essay by Smith, "Frege and Husserl."

49. Tugendhat, "Phenomenology and Linguistic Analysis," 333.

50. Vattimo and Brandom, both being postmetaphysical philosophers like Tugendhat, have also declared the same idea. Vattimo believes that "for a long time, philosophers and linguistics have dismissed the idea that first we see things and then attribute them their names. On the contrary, we encounter the world already possessing forms, words, grammatical structures through which we give it order, otherwise to us the world would appear to be an indistinct mess." Vattimo, *After Christianity*, 7. And Brandom argues, "facts are just true claims (not in the sense of claim*ings*, which require us for their existence, but of what is claim*ed*, which does not). For there are facts about what follows from what, and what is evidence for and against what other claims." Brandom, "Hegelian Pragmatism and Social Emancipation," 563. Although Tugendhat does not agree with me in our dialogue about the idea that "there are no facts, but only propositions," I still believe his philosophy has clear indications of this, and I give specific examples (as we will also see in chapter 4) of such a generalization.

51. Tugendhat, *Traditional and Analytical Philosophy*, 63.

52. Tugendhat, "Language Analysis and the Critique of Ontology," 110–111.

53. Tugendhat, *Traditional and Analytical Philosophy*, 253. On this definition of the concept of truth, Bubner commented that it is "not particularly startling, if one remembers the oldest account of truth in Plato or Aristotle, who explicated the truth of assertions in terms of the 'existence' (*hyparchein*) of what is asserted. Tugendhat in general makes no secret of this borrowing. However the problem arises of what is denoted by the word 'applies.' Tugendhat falls back for its elucidation fundamentally on the correct use of the predicate, so that understanding of the predicate and the problem of truth become well-nigh indistinguishable. The rules of verification of a sentence refer to the rules of application of predicates. But is truth to be nothing other than correct use of words? Is the wide domain of the false, of illusion, of delusion, of error to be narrowed down to a series of violations of rules of language?" Bubner, *Modern German Philosophy*, 96. Pippin has commented on this definition, noticing that "Tugendhat denies that there can be *any* direct (or 'unmediated') relation between a singular term and its referent. A singular term picks out or singles out one *among many*, and so a way of explaining both how that reference is held on to and how that distinguishing function continues to work in

several different contexts is needed. Tugendhat sticks to one of his general systematic principles here and argues that his explanation must always realize that such a singular term's function can only be understood if we continue to investigate how that term functions in the whole assertion. This means that the function of demonstrative and locating singular terms 'consists in this, that they specify the perceptual object in such a way that one can establish it *as thus specified* whether the predicate applies to it.'" Pippin, "Traditional and Analytical Philosophy," 167. And Dahlstrom noticed that "Tugendhat understands the 'specific' conception of truth (retaining its properly criterial character) in Husserlian terms. Truth consists in the fact that something merely meant by means of an assertion, that is to say, something entertained in its absence, shows itself in person (and is also experienced and identified) just as it was or is intended. On the basis of the evidence and identification, the assertion is not only meaningful but true." Dahlstrom, *Heidegger's Concept of Truth*, 434.

2. CORRECTING HEIDEGGER

1. Tugendhat, *TI KATA TINOS*.
2. Ackrill, "E. Tugendhat. *TI KATA TINOS*," 775.
3. Pierre Aubenque, review of *TI KATA TINOS*, 300. See the bibliography for the other reviews of this book by Ackrill, Allan, and others.
4. Tugendhat, *TI KATA TINOS*, 23.
5. Ibid., 22. I should note that this assumption is common to Aristotle's *Posteriori Analytics* ii, chap. I; and *Metaph. Z*, chap 17, in that a demand for explanation is normally raised in a *ti kata tinos* form. Tugendhat's thesis seeks to retrace Aristotle's thought using *Anwesenheit* and other modern concepts for which neither Greek nor English have equivalents.
6. The historical justification for this, according to D. J. Allan, is that "Aristotle himself tends to take for granted the ideas which provide the framework for his detailed metaphysical discussion, novel though his concepts and terminology in many respects were. The ancient commentators, who had other virtues, hardly gave the explanation which he omitted to give. It thus came about that substance, ancient, necessary being, contingency, and so forth persisted, though with important shifts in their meaning, as the basis of later metaphysics. After Hegel this active metaphysical tradition was cut short, the energy of the learned took a new direction, and classical scholars, armed by now with their own technique, made the thought of Aristotle a principal subject

of study. They discussed his work at first mainly from a systematic point of view, but since Jaeger from the point of view of development also. However, neither class of scholar at once recognized that after so many centuries the opportunity to analyze the Aristotelian metaphysical concepts had at last come, perhaps because the nineteenth century shrank from any relapse into active philosophizing. Today (in Germany) many philosophers are no longer thus shy of metaphysics, but in formulating its problems they display a new historical awareness. The old metaphysics held up to view a timeless super-sensible being; this was prior to time-conditioned existence, and served as a standard by which the latter fell short. Now, thanks especially to Heidegger, the picture is changed. We now have rather an ontology comprising two parts, and the timeless being of older metaphysics has become the occupant of one compartment." Allan, "E. Tugendhat. *TI KATA TINOS*," 221.

7. Very interesting comments are made by C. P. Long on Tugendhat's analysis of the *tode ti* in Long, *Ethics of Ontology*, 88.

8. Hubert Dreyfus explains the ontological difference by showing that "Heidegger conceptualizes the difference between specific coping (ontic transcendence) and world-disclosing background coping (originary transcendence) as the difference between our relation to beings and our understanding of Being. This is presumably the original version of the famous *ontological difference*, which, according to the later Heidegger, the tradition sought mistakenly to capture in its various accounts of the Being of beings." Dreyfus, *Being-in-the-World*, 107.

9. Heidegger, *Being and Time*.

10. A. Bowie emphasizes this connection with the ontological difference, explaining that "Tugendhat sees a fundamental methodological link, via what Heidegger termed 'ontological difference,' between Heidegger and that side of the analytical tradition which rejects the notion of truth as adequate 'representation.' Ontological difference is Heidegger's way of considering the difference between his contested notion of 'Being' and 'entities/beings' ('*Seiendes*'), which were characterized in traditional ontology by the predicates attached to true Being. Once the model of representation, in which the mind is supposed more or less adequately to mirror or 'intuit' a nature of pre-existing entities, is questioned, the character of non-Being can be differently understood, and this, Tugendhat initially believes, gives a vital clue to the meaning of the question of Being in Heidegger. In the metaphor of the 'mirror of nature' which these days stands for what Heidegger terms 'Western metaphysics,' the 'ready-made' world is seen to consist of objects whose es-

sences are somehow reflected in the mind and in language. Heidegger's point is that understanding the meaning of Being cannot be achieved in this manner, because language is the location of the understanding of something *as* something, which, for Tugendhat, and in many ways for Heidegger, is evident in the structure of propositions, not in a mirroring or intuition of pre-existing objects." Bowie, "Review Essay," 346–347. For studies of Heidegger and Aristotle, see Brogan, *Heidegger and Aristotle*; and McNeill, *The Glance of the Eye*. Volpi, "Dasein as Praxis," is also very useful.

11. Etymologically, *a-letheia* means the undoing of *lethe*. Lethe was the mythological river of sleep or oblivion, across which the dead must pass before entering Hades. In other words, *lethe* should also be understood as a forgetting, an absencing. In our context, the Greek word stands for "disclosure," a term composed of the privative prefix a- (un- or dis-) and the root *lethe* (hiddenness or closure). If the finitude of this dis-closure is inscribed in the word *a-letheia*, then to disclose something is to momentarily rescue it from some prior unavailability (*lethe*) and to try to hold it for a while in presence.

12. Habermas, *Pragmatics of Social Interaction*, 174, defines this book as an "excellent study on the concept of truth in Husserl and Heidegger."

13. "Ernst Tugendhat has advanced what is perhaps the most sophisticated philosophical challenge to Heidegger's ontological interpretation of truth." Carman, *Heidegger's Analytic*, 258.

14. The first review of the book was written by Otto Pöggeler (who is still the one who best understood the book), and he clearly explains Tugendhat's goals: "In his book on Husserl and Heidegger Tugendhat picks up on the idea that today we can establish a relation with Husserl and Heidegger which is not determined by a preference for one or the other. Heidegger must not be interpreted starting from Husserl, nor Husserl from Heidegger. Each one should be listened to independently. . . . Tugendhat bases his thesis on the idea that philosophy amounts to 'the idea of founding on truth the human life in its totality.' The question of the meaning of truth is the fundamental question of philosophy. But today, it seems, that just that sense of truth has become lost. . . . We may doubt together with Nietzsche that all interest must be subordinated to the interest of truth, and Marx and Freud have taught us to consider this in different ways. In this situation Tugendhat interrogates himself critically on the 'meaning of truth,' hence using the 'current' concept of truth, the one which we are 'familiar with' to understand under the name of truth." Pöggeler, "Ernst Tugendhat," 376–378. Although today the amount of work done on this book is vast (a complete list of them can be found in the

bibliography), it is Dahlstrom's investigations (*Heidegger's Concept of Truth* and "The Clearing and Its Truth") that contain the most elaborate and extensive analyses of Tugendhat's interpretations.

15. Tugendhat, *Der Wahrheitsbegriff bei Husserl und Heidegger*, 1. There is no doubt that this book is primarily concerned with the search for a truth for practical and moral issues that Tugendhat does not find in either Husserl or Heidegger. It is interesting to note how these same problems are elaborated in Tugendhat's recent work, as he explains in the epilogue (see below). On the problem of freedom, please see not only Tugendhat, *Der Begriff der Willensfreiheit*; but also Schönrich, "Innere Autonomie oder Zurechnungsfähigkeit?"

16. Heidegger's conception of disclosure takes the place of Husserl's intentionality in *Being and Time*, and understanding becomes the fundamental nature of Dasein. Understanding is not a "particular" type of knowing—distinct from other types such as explaining, comprehending, or even grasping something thematically—because understanding for Heidegger is an ontological factor. Understanding entails awareness of certain relations such as the awareness of this *as* that or of this *as for* that. This "as" articulates the significance of the thing, in other words, prior to predicative knowledge, which is expressed in sentences such as *the castle is red*, "*C* is *R*"; human beings already have a pretheoretical understanding of the Being of things (this as *Being for* that). Heidegger calls human beings *Dasein* because their Being consists in disclosing and understanding Being (whether the Being of itself or that of other entities). Although Tugendhat notes that although Heidegger refers often to Husserl's theory of truth as developed in the sixth of his *Logical Investigations*, he does not explain how he "leaps over Husserl's intentionality in general with the concept of 'disclosure.'" Tugendhat, "Heidegger's Idea of Truth," 88. On the relation between Husserl and Heidegger, see Sheehan, "Husserl and Heidegger"; Marion, *Reduction and Givenness*; and Elliott, *Phenomenology and Imagination in Husserl and Heidegger*.

17. Tugendhat, *Der Wahrheitsbegriff bei Husserl und Heidegger*, 351. Mark Wrathall rightly notes that Heidegger did not "equate" the concept of truth: "Finally, Heidegger's warnings to the contrary, it is perhaps understandable that readers often confuse unconcealment with what we ordinarily think of as truth. In any event, in response to criticisms from Paul Friedländer about his etymology of *aletheia*, and from Tugendhat regarding the "natural conception of truth," Heidegger eventually disavowed the practice of calling unconcealment "truth." But since Heidegger himself had never confused un-

concealment with propositional truth, the disavowal should not be taken to mean that he gave up on the platform or any of the planks of the platform. On the contrary, to the extent that the platform was obscured by the tendency to think of truth only in terms of correspondence, Heidegger hoped to make clearer his commitment to it." Wrathall, "Unconcealment," 341. Taylor Carman, commenting on Wrathall, says, "I think Wrathall is right that Tugendhat and others have misunderstood the point of Heidegger's account, which is neither to offer an analysis of propositional truth nor to contest the traditional conception of propositional truth as correspondence. Instead, as Wrathall says, and as Heidegger himself insists, he is offering an account of the ontological conditions of truth traditionally conceived. The uncovering of entities in our practices and in our understanding, that is, is the condition for the propositional contents of assertions and belief being true in virtue of their relation to the way things are. Truth as Heidegger describes it, an unconcealment, is thus the ontological condition of truth conventionally understood, that is, as correctness or correspondence with entities." Carman, *Heidegger's Analytic*, 259.

18. Tugendhat, *Der Wahrheitsbegriff bei Husserl und Heidegger*, 350.
19. Tugendhat, *Self-Consciousness and Self-Determination*, 214. Actually Heidegger, already in *Being and Time*, anticipates Tugendhat's corrections when he observes that his recourse to the original meaning of *aletheia* as "unconcealment" and "discoveredness" should be preserved from "uninhibited word-mysticism," because "to translate this word as 'truth,' and especially to define this expression conceptually in theoretical ways, is to cover over the meaning of what the Greeks posited at the basis . . . of the terminological use of '*aletheia*'" Heidegger, *Being and Time*, 202. Either way, Tugendhat reaches his conclusion considering that Heidegger has not explained the specific meaning of truth but "obscured," "broadened," and "forfeited" it from philosophical thought. Pierre Keller rightly notes, regarding this issue of justification, that "Heidegger's lack of interest in justification and the determination of criteria for truth encourages him, however, to regard rightness and wrongness as extraneous to the notion of truth. There is clearly a problem here. But Ernst Tugendhat somewhat overstates the problem by arguing that this leads Heidegger 'in making the word truth a basic concept to pass over precisely the problem of truth.' To be plausible, Tugendhat's critique must be understood as taking the problem of truth to be the problem of how to distinguish truth from falsity rather than the problem of what truth means. Unfortunately, like Heidegger, Tugendhat does not clearly distinguish the

problem of what truth means from the problem of what the criteria for truth are." Keller, *Husserl and Heidegger on Human Experience*, 97.

20. Apel, "Regulative Ideas or Truth-Happening?" 73.

21. Apel, *Toward a Transformation of Philosophy*. This English edition is not complete; the passage where Apel discusses Tugendhat's correction was left out of the translation. But since this same point was made by Apel many years later in "Regulative Ideas or Truth-Happening?" this essay can be used to cite Apel's "discovery of 1973." "Apel seems to me right," says Karsten Harries, "when, following Tugendhat, he insists on the difference between disclosure, even authentic disclosure, and the truth of assertions. To claim truth is not to be content with the evidence presented by subjective disclosure. Truth demands objectivity." Harries, "On the Power and Limit of Transcendental Reflection," 147–148.

22. Heidegger, *On Time and Being*, 70. Gadamer in an interview in 1986 said that Heidegger "realized that the Greeks never ... meant *aletheia* in his sense, they never meant anything like a play of concealment and unconcealment." Gadamer, "Interview: Historicism and Romanticism," in his *Hans-Georg Gadamer on Education, Poetry, and History: Applied Hermeneutics*, 129.

23. This essay was presented in 1964 and published for the first time in Pöggeler, ed., *Heidegger: Perspektiven zur Deutung seines Werkes*. For an accurate analysis of this essay see Wolin, *The Heidegger Controversy: A Critical Reader*, 245–248.

24. Although the most detailed and best known presentation of this critique is in his habilitation theses, *Der Wahrheitsbegriff bei Husserl und Heidegger*, published in 1967, this essay is the first record of this same critique.

25. For a whole reconstruction of this debate see Lafont, *Heidegger, Language, and World-Disclosure*, 116n9.

26. Pöggeler, "Heideggers logische Untersuchungen," 80–82.

27. Lafont agrees with this when she writes that "Tugendhat's analysis can be recognized as valuable for its *immanent critique* of Heidegger's argumentation. With this critique, we can see in detail the extent to which Heidegger's argument as a whole contains no explication of the sense of truth as correctness, but rather a displacement of this theme." Lafont, *Heidegger, Language, and World-Disclosure*, 123–124. Dahlstrom goes so far as to specify that "Tugendhat is not simply objecting to the fact that Heidegger turns from the problem of truth toward another theme (disclosedness)." Dahlstrom, *Heidegger's Concept of Truth*, 396. Joanna Hodge goes even further in considering that Tugendhat's analysis "of Heidegger's conception of truth is flawed by its fail-

ure to recognize the linkages between the three parts of Heidegger's account of truth and to see its relation to Heidegger's critique of separating out interdependent areas of philosophical enquiry. Truth, for Heidegger, is first of all an epistemological grounded notion revealing of the matter in the world; but he grounds that notion first in a set of quasi-transcendental conditions of possibility, which he sums up with the term '*Erschlossenheit*,' openness. Tugendhat is unimpressed by Heidegger's attempt to ground the analysis of truth in the fact that the entity for which truth is an issue is concerned with its own identity. He fails to recognize that, for Heidegger, truth is not simply a question of knowledge and meaning, but a question of identity and purpose. His critique also overlooks the connection between the account of truth and the analysis of Dasein as care and as essentially concerned with affirming itself as a self with a future." Hodge, *Heidegger and Ethics*, 194. Taylor Carman also agrees with my analysis when he says that "if Heidegger's account fails to distinguish *false* uncovering from *true* uncovering, he [Tugendhat] points out, it can hardly qualify as an interesting or plausible account of truth. It would appear, then, that Heidegger has not so much offered a new account of truth as simply changed the subject." Carman, *Heidegger's Analytic*, 258.

28. Apel, "Comments on Professor Pöggeler's Paper," 100.

29. Vattimo has explained this well when he states that "the misapprehension we are concerned to put right is that in *Being and Time* Heidegger looks for a more adequate description of the meaning of Being and of the idea of truth—as if the notion of Being as presence handed down to us by metaphysics, and the corresponding notion of truth as the correspondence of proposition to thing, were partial, incomplete, or somehow inadequate and therefore false descriptions of Being as it is *really* given and of the experience of truth as it *really* occurs. That this might not be Heidegger's intention is, from the beginning of the work, less than clear. However, it may be appreciated well enough if one reflects that such an intention could only be contradictory, even solely in light of the features at play within truth as correspondence. But with the evolution of Heidegger's work after *Being and Time*, it becomes clear that his ontology cannot in any way be taken for a kind of existentially phrased neo-Kantianism (where the structure of reason and its a priori have fallen into the thrownness and finitude of Dasein's project) and therefore also that his objection to the conception of truth as correspondence is not based on its inadequacy as a faithful description of the experience of truth. For with the acknowledgment of inadequacy it emerges that one cannot keep to a conception of truth as correspondence, since this implies a conception of Being

as *Grund*, as an insuperable first principle that reduces all questioning to silence. Moreover, it is precisely the meditation on the insufficiency of the idea of truth as the correspondence of judgment to thing that has set us on the path of Being as event." Vattimo, *Beyond Interpretation*, 76. Barry Allen is of this opinion when he states that "it was the destiny of Western thinking, or perhaps the destiny of being 'itself,' to obliterate the difference and deliver us over to an epoch of metaphysics from Plato to Nietzsche (supposedly). Heidegger cannot say that this is a mistake. It is not an error in the sense of a falsification or distortion affecting the accuracy with which a being is represented. Yet if not exactly a mistake, still it is something that might have been otherwise, or might one day be otherwise, and which for a reason Heidegger never adequately clarifies it is the outstanding task of philosophy to try to think otherwise." Allen, *Truth in Philosophy*, 94.

30. I agree with Daniel O. Dahlstrom when he says that "the self-interpretation of a thinker is, of course, important, but hardly the last word to the meaning of his or her work. It is also not obvious that Heidegger's later remarks should be read as an endorsement precisely of the sorts of criticism subsequently elaborated by Tugendhat. More importantly, the fact that Heidegger considers his early use of the term 'truth' misleading in some sense does not by any means settle the issue whether the disclosedness characterized in *Being and Time* as the original truth dispenses with the difference that Tugendhat rightly insists is essential to propositional truth. What matters, in other words, is not Heidegger's choice of terms, but their function in his argument. The issue is not whether Heidegger ought to have characterized disclosedness as truth, but whether that characterization forfeits the specific sense of truth (bivalence), as Tugendhat charges." Dahlstrom, *Heidegger's Concept of Truth*, 404. Regarding the enormous consequences of Heidegger's analysis of truth in hermeneutics and in contemporary philosophy, two books are very useful. On the Heideggerian idea that all human thought involves "interpretation" in relation to truth, see Wachterhauser, ed., *Hermeneutics and Truth*, with essays by Bubner, Dostal, Gadamer, Risser, Grondin, and others. A more detailed historical approach can be found in Allen, *Truth in Philosophy*.

31. W. J. Richardson is very clear regarding this issue: "Since the tradition of philosophy from the very beginning has been orientated toward explaining the approach to beings and to Being as 'to see,' Heidegger will accept the metaphor insofar as its sense is broad enough to signify any approach to the Being of beings whatever. Hence all of the traditional formulae for 'seeing' beings, such as Kant's 'intuition' and Husserl's 'intuition of essences,' are for

Heidegger derivative forms of the promordial seeing which is the existential comprehension of Being." Richardson, *Heidegger*, 63–64. And Bowie correctly notes, as I also discuss in chapter 4, that the difficulty here lies in the relationship between truth as a semantic issue relating to propositions and truth as a world-disclosure that is prior to propositions. He explains that Heidegger, "by making a generalized notion of disclosure prior to propositional truth and falsity therefore has questionable social and ethical implications." Bowie, *Introduction to German Philosophy*, 214.

32. Tugendhat, "Heidegger's Idea of Truth," 84.

33. Ibid. A very clear interpretation of this end of philosophy in Heidegger's philosophy can be found in Sallis, *Delimitations*, and in the works of Tugendhat's contemporaneous philosophers such as Rorty, Derrida, and Vattimo, who have also emphasized this matter in their interpretations of Heidegger.

34. "Being and truth 'are' equiprimordially." Heidegger, *Being and Time*, 211.

35. Heidegger, *Being and Time*, 207–208.

36. Lafont has specified the derivative nature of statements very clearly: "Heidegger intends to show that the statement cannot 'primarily disclose entities on its own.' Rather, it 'always already remains itself on the basis of being-in-the-world.' By underscoring the circular character of every understanding (or the holistic structure of language), Heidegger places into question the traditional limited way of considering the statement 'as the only clue for obtaining *access* to the entities which authentically are.' Here it is not a question of thematizing pre-linguistic phenomena, but of emphasizing the priority of understanding over knowing, and thus the primacy of holism in every analysis of linguistic phenomena—such as understanding." Lafont, *Heidegger, Language, and World-Disclosure*, 54.

37. Heidegger, *Logic: The Question of Truth*.

38. Sheehan expands on this: "In other words, prior to predicative knowledge, which is expressed in sentences of the type '*S* is *P*,' human beings already have a pre-theoretical or 'pre-ontological' understanding of the Being of things (this as *being for* that). Since the 'as' articulates how something is understood, and since the Greek verb '*hermeneuein*' means 'to make something understandable,' Heidegger calls the 'as' that renders things intelligible in practical understanding the 'hermeneutical as.' This 'hermeneutical as' is made possible because a human being is a 'thrown project,' necessarily thrust into possibilities (thrownness) and thereby holding the world open (project). Hermeneutical understanding—that is, pre-predicatively understanding the 'hermeneutical as' by being a thrown project—is the kind of cognition

that most befits being-in-the-world. It is the primary way in which humans know the Being of things. By contrast, the more detached and objective 'apophantic' knowledge that expresses itself in declarative sentences (*'S* is *P'*) is evidence, for Heidegger, of a derivative and flattened-out understanding of Being." Sheehan, "Heidegger," 359.

39. Tugendhat, *Der Wahrheitsbegriff bei Husserl und Heidegger*, 260.

40. Tugendhat, "Heidegger's Idea of Truth," 96.

41. Again, W. J. Richardson is very clear regarding this issue: "The traditional concept of truth gives us no satisfying answers. This, of course, is not to deny its validity, but simply to say that it presupposes a more fundamental truth from which it springs as its source." Richardson, *Heidegger*, 94.

42. Tugendhat, "Heidegger's Idea of Truth," 86.

43. Ibid., 88. The problem that Tugendhat sees in the consequences of this "broadening" of the understanding of truth is well explained by A. Bowie: "In the wake of Husserl, Tugendhat argues that an assertion's being true of something must mean that the thing is brought to light 'as it is in itself.' This is the vital function of assertions in social life, where we need this kind of discrimination for knowledge to progress, by showing when things are brought to light in a way which is not 'as they are in themselves.' Heidegger's blurring of the true and the false—can't things be falsely disclosed?—by making a generalized notion of disclosure prior to propositional truth and falsity therefore has questionable social and ethical implications. . . . Tugendhat also contends that the suggestion that the issue of truth has to do with time mistakes the nature of the meaning of Being in propositions. In Heidegger's example of 'the sky *is* blue' the assertion is evidently only true for as long as the sky is blue on a particular day. However, the truth of the assertions about the sky's being blue at that time is itself timeless. Otherwise one is not using the sense of 'true' which we must rely on in everyday communication, which seems inextricably connected with meaning. We don't mean 'I think the sky is blue, but I may be wrong about this at some point in the future' when we say 'the sky is blue.' " Bowie, *Introduction to German Philosophy*, 214.

44. Tugendhat, "Heidegger's Idea of Truth," 93.

45. Gadamer is the philosopher who, in his *Truth and Method*, mostly developed the idea of disclosing horizons, which Tugendhat criticized, as we will see in the final section of this chapter, "Truth Versus Method."

46. Tugendhat, "Heidegger's Idea of Truth," 96.

47. Ibid. Again, R. Schürmann rightly notes how the last ten pages of Tugendhat's *Der Wahrheitsbegriff bei Husserl und Heidegger* suffer from the absence of

a "historical perspective": "I agree that the conflictual ('*gegenwendig*') essence of '*aletheia*' 'buries the very possibility of the question of truth' understood as the question of the 'regulative idea of a measure.' Truth is indeed rendered inoperative as a standard for 'choice.' But this is not to say the 'question of truth need no longer emerge' in Heidegger's later writings. On the contrary, the concept of truth as 'measure' has changed. 'No formal rule is given.' Not quite: for the era marked by the hypothesis of metaphysical closure, material rules are the epochal principles; for a possible economy after the 'turn,' the formal rule can only be 'presencing,' or '*phuesthai*.' What Tugendhat does not see is that the 'leeway ("*Spielraum*") which is unconcealment' yields an economic measurement because unconcealment has a history whose possible closure transmutes truth from ideal to event-like ('*ereignishaft*')." Schürmann, *Heidegger on Being and Acting*, 357–358.

48. Tugendhat, "Heidegger's Idea of Truth," 89. A. Bowie clearly notes that Tugendhat's exclusive insistence on the propositional level of the argument is very difficult to square with certain aspects of Heidegger's early analyses of the nature of propositions because they "are understood as being dependent on the world's '*Erschlossenheit*,' 'disclosedness.' The world of truth is initially constituted, Heidegger claims, by the hermeneutic 'as-structure of understanding,' which, however implicitly, he relates to a conception of self-consciousness, which need not be linguistic and which *precedes* the 'apophantic "as" of the proposition.' In the Heidegger of before the '*Kehre*' the locus of this disclosure is '*Dasein*,' the term which Heidegger uses, albeit problematically, as a replacement for the metaphysical notion of the subject derived from post-Cartesian transcendental philosophy." Bowie, "Review Essay," 348.

49. Tugendhat, "Heidegger's Idea of Truth," 89.

50. Ibid., 90–91.

51. For an accurate account and analysis of Heidegger's term "being-in-the-World," see Dreyfus, *Being-in-the-World*. For a complete history of the origin of *Being and Time*, see Kisiel, *The Genesis of Heidegger's* Being and Time.

52. Tugendhat, "Heidegger's Idea of Truth," 93–94.

53. Daniel O. Dahlstrom explains why Heidegger does not lose sight of the difference between the ostensive givenness of things and the givenness as it is in itself, as Tugendhat believes he does: "The fact that he [Heidegger] takes into consideration the difference that Tugendhat fails to find is confirmed by the point of departure of the discussion of truth in *Being and Time* as well as in the logic lectures. That point of departure is not simply the truth of an assertion, but the possibility of its falsity as well. In order to be able to as-

sert something true or false about something, it must already be uncovered in some respect. Yet the possibility of an assertion's truth or falsity consists precisely in the fact that what is uncovered can be interpreted either as it is in itself or not. Furthermore, Heidegger grounds the apophantic 'as'-structure of assertions and thus their possibility of being true or false in the existential-hermeneutic 'as'-structure of prepredicative (or at least prethematic) actions that can themselves go awry." Dahlstrom, *Heidegger's Concept of Truth*, 405.

54. Tugendhat, "Heidegger's Idea of Truth," 94.

55. Ibid., 95.

56. For a clear account of the history of the reflection on truth see Allen, *Truth in Philosophy*.

57. Tugendhat, *Der Wahrheitsbegriff bei Husserl und Heidegger*, 117.

58. B. Allen believes it is "worth emphasizing that Heidegger does not think that the 'correspondence theory of truth' is wrong but only superficial. If truth requires correspondence, correspondence requires presencing, and presencing requires ontological difference, which *is not* apart from the *Ek-sistenz* of Dasein." Allen, *Truth in Philosophy*, 89.

59. Tugendhat, *Der Wahrheitsbegriff bei Husserl und Heidegger*, 405.

60. Ibid., 358. Robert J. Dostal gives two clear reasons Gadamer found Heidegger's treatment of truth so persuasive and significant. The examples of these two analyses can also be used, if interpreted negatively, to explain why Tugendhat instead found Heidegger's treatment of truth a mistake: "First, Heidegger shows us how to avoid the impasse between skepticism and Cartesian foundationalism with respect to truth. Put simply, the former denies truth and the latter attempts to refute skepticism and prove that we are capable of truth. Heidegger asserts that the skeptic cannot be refuted and need not be refuted since truth is undeniably an aspect of our experience. We find ourselves inevitably presupposing truth. The philosophical task (considered in *Being and Time* to be phenomenological) is to give an account of our experience of truth and falsity—not to prove that we do experience truth or that there is truth. The second (and closely related) reason that Gadamer follows the Heideggerian account is its thoroughly human perspective. It rejects any implicit divine model of self-certainty, complete clarity, and total transparency, e.g., any god's-eye point of view. It affirms, rather, human finitude. To say that we do not have complete objectivity or certitude does not mean, for Heidegger, that we must assert subjectivity and doubt. Descartes and Hegel yield Nietzsche in just this way. Most important for Gadamer is the way in which the Heideggerian account escapes the dialectical quagmire of subjectivity and

objectivity, doubt and certitude, truth and falsity. Heidegger claims that any revealing of the truth is at the same time a concealing. To bring something into the light is to cast an aspect of it into shadow." Dostal, "The Experience of Truth for Gadamer and Heidegger," 49–50.

61. On the problem of the "other" in Gadamer's philosophy, see the distinguished study by Risser, *Hermeneutics and the Voice of the Other*.

62. Tugendhat reviewed Gadamer's *Truth and Method* and *Philosophical Hermeneutics* for the *Times Literary Supplement* (May 19, 1978).

63. Tugendhat, "Ancient and Modern Ethics," 32.

64. Gadamer, *Truth and Method*. Some very good studies are now available on Gadamer's hermeneutics, such as Grondin, *The Philosophy of Gadamer*; Dostal, ed., *The Cambridge Companion to Gadamer*; Krajewski, ed., *Gadamer's Repercussions*; Lawn, *Wittgenstein and Gadamer*; and Horn, *Gadamer and Wittgenstein on the Unity of Language*.

65. Tugendhat, "The Fusion of Horizons," 426. Gadamer responds indirectly to Tugendhat in an interview with Carsten Dutt by saying: "This interpretation conveys the one-sided impression that I think there are no methods in the humanities and social sciences. Of course there are methods, and certainly one must learn them and apply them. But I would say that the fact that we are able to apply certain methods to certain objects does not establish *why* we are pursuing knowledge in the humanities and social sciences. To me it seems self-evident that in the natural sciences one pursues knowledge ultimately because through them one can stand on one's own feet: one can orient oneself and through measurement, reckoning, and construction eventually gain control of the surrounding world. By doing this we can—at least this is their intention—live better and survive better than if we just confronted a nature that is indifferent to us. But in the humanities and social sciences [*Geisteswissenschaften*] there can be nothing like such ruling over the historical world. The humanities and social sciences bring something different into our lives through their form of participation in what has been handed down to us, something that is not knowledge for the sake of control [*Herrschaftswissen*], yet it is no less important. We customarily call it 'culture.'" Gadamer, *Gadamer in Conversation*, 41.

66. Tugendhat, "The Fusion of Horizons," 426.

67. Tugendhat, "Ancient and Modern Ethics," 33–34.

68. Ibid., 34.

69. Ibid., 35.

70. Tugendhat, "The Fusion of Horizons," 430.

71. Ibid.

72. Ibid., 430–431.

73. Ibid., 427–428.

74. Ibid., 429.

75. Ibid.

76. Gadamer specifies that "our verbal experience of the world is prior to everything that is recognized and addressed as existing. *That language and world are related in a fundamental way does not mean, then, that world becomes the object of language.* Rather, the object of knowledge and statements is always already enclosed within the world horizon of language. That human experience of the world is verbal does not imply that a world-in-itself is being objectified." Gadamer, *Truth and Method*, 447.

77. Although Tugendhat criticizes Gadamer's understanding of language in this volume's epilogue, he reserves his most biting criticism for Heidegger, saying in 1977 that "Heidegger's dictum that language thinks is one of the most gloomy things that has ever been said in philosophy because it is the declaration of the bankruptcy of all philosophy and the deepest expression of anti-enlightenment." Tugendhat, "The Question About Being," 270.

78. Gadamer, "Semantics and Hermeneutics," in his *Philosophical Hermeneutics*, 82–94.

79. Tugendhat, "The Fusion of Horizons," 431.

80. Gadamer himself specifies that "it seems to me to be no coincidence that among the various directions which contemporary philosophical research has taken, semantics and hermeneutics have assumed particular importance. Both have as their starting point the linguistic form of expression in which our thought is formulated. They no longer pass over the primary form in which our intellectual experience is given. Insofar as both of them deal with the realm of language, it is clear that semantics and hermeneutics alike have a truly universal perspective. For of that which is given in language, what is, on the other hand, not a sign and what, on the other, is not a moment in the process of coming to understand?" Gadamer, "Semantics and Hermeneutics," 82. Chapter 4 discusses how Tugendhat, in his *Traditional and Analytical Philosophy*, tries to answer this question.

81. A. Bowie rightly notes how "Tugendhat's work provides an indispensable corrective, especially within the German and French hermeneutic traditions, to many of the more questionable tendencies in European philosophy, that are illustrated in the frequent refusal of Heidegger and his epigones to justify their contentions to a critical public; at the same time his work may, in a dif-

ferent context, be just as questionable for its failure to see the limiting effects
of the positivist tradition upon a philosophical culture which has so far been
largely indifferent to the insights of hermeneutics." Bowie, "Review Essay,"
350–351.
82. Tugendhat, "The Fusion of Horizons," 432.
83. Tugendhat, "Phenomenology and Linguistic Analysis," 325–326.

3. SEMANTIZING ONTOLOGY

1. Tugendhat, "Phenomenology and Linguistic Analysis," 325. A. Bowie explains very well the growth of interest in Heidegger among analytical philosophers and what Tugendhat has achieved by linking Heidegger's notion of
"world" and Gadamer's hermeneutic: "Tugendhat's assumption that import-
ing formal semantics into a traditional philosophical problem will obviate the
problem in its traditional form tends at times to be reminiscent of the now discredited assumption that dominated analytical philosophy in its heroic phase,
namely that it could linguistically redefine most of the Western philosophical
tradition's major metaphysical concerns. Although Tugendhat emphatically
rejects the logical-positivist condemnation of all metaphysics as meaningless, the fact is that the tension between a historico-hermeneutic approach to
philosophical problems and a problem-solving approach is often underplayed
in Tugendhat's work, because the latter almost invariably dominates. This
is perhaps understandable in a German context, where the concern with history and interpretation often has a tendency to preclude serious philosophical
argument. Negotiating a new path between positivism and Romanticism will,
though, require a more adequate relationship between the need to interpret
and contextualize, and the need to argue, than is evident in some of Tugendhat's approaches." Bowie, "Review Essay," 346.
2. Tugendhat, "Language Analysis and the Critique of Ontology," 100.
3. Ibid., 101.
4. Carnap, "The Elimination of Metaphysics," 60–61. Carnap's thesis in this
essay is that Heidegger, in *What Is Metaphysics?* (1929), made logical mistakes in his employment of the word "nothing" as a noun (*Gegenstandsname*),
because it is customary in ordinary language to use it in this form in order
to construct a negative existential statement. Carnap showed that the negative existential statement "it is not the case that there exists something that
has a certain property" is also expressed by the sentence "nothing has this
property." It is through the objectification of this use of "nothing" that the

meaningless talk of "the nothing" comes about. Although Tugendhat partly follows Carnap's objections, as we will see below, in the section "Semantizing Being" in this chapter, he is not in complete agreement with his conclusions. On the dispute between Carnap and Heidegger, see Witherspoon, "Much Ado About the Nothing," 291–322.

5. Tugendhat, "Language Analysis and the Critique of Ontology," 102.

6. Ibid.

7. Quine, "On What There Is," 1–19.

8. "According to Quine's usage," Tugendhat specifies, "a person does not *engage in* ontology, but *has* this or that ontology." Tugendhat, "Language Analysis and the Critique of Ontology," 102.

9. Tugendhat, "Language Analysis and the Critique of Ontology." 102–103.

10. Tugendhat is referring to Strawson, *Individuals* (1959).

11. Russell, "On Denoting," 39–56.

12. *Essentia* in traditional ontology referred to the meanings of real predicates that were to be understood as beings.

13. Tugendhat, "Language Analysis and the Critique of Ontology," 103.

14. Ibid., 104.

15. Ibid., 101.

16. Tugendhat's interest in language can also be found in this comment on philosophy and language in Gadamer: "Philosophy continually finds itself in a state of urgent linguistic need [*Sprachnot*]. This is constitutive of philosophy, and this calamity, this distress, becomes all the more felt, the more boldly the philosophizer is breaking new paths. One generally marks oneself as a dilettante in thinking if one arbitrarily introduces terms and zealously 'defines one's concepts.' Rather, the true philosopher often awakens the intuitive power already resident in language, and every linguistic zeal, or even linguistic violence, can be in place if only this can be accepted into the language of those who would think along with the philosopher, think further with him, and that means if the words are able to push forward, extend, or light up the horizon of communication." Gadamer, "Reflections on My Philosophical Journey," in his *The Philosophy of Hans-Georg Gadamer*, 38.

17. Tugendhat, "Language Analysis and the Critique of Ontology," 106.

18. In the next chapter I will analyze the meaning of formalization in analytic philosophy.

19. Kant, "The Only Possible Argument in Support of a Demonstration of the Existence of God," 107–202.

20. Tugendhat, "Language Analysis and the Critique of Ontology," 107.

21. Ibid., 109.

22. Ibid.

23. Ibid., 110–111.

24. Against this idea that philosophy moves predominantly within systems of propositions, Gadamer gives a very clear explanation that deserves to be recalled here in order to give further validity to my thesis that Gadamer and Tugendhat are Heidegger's most distinctive disciples and continuators, one in hermeneutics and the other in analytical philosophy: "It is unavoidable that philosophy, which never finds its object already at hand but must itself provide it, does not move within systems of propositions whose logical formalization and critical testing for conclusiveness and univocity might somehow deepen its insights. Such a way with language will create from the world no 'revolution,' not even that proclaimed by the analysts of ordinary language. To illustrate this point with an example, if one analyzes with logical methods the arguments in a Platonic dialogue, shows inconsistencies, fills in gaps, unmasks false deductions, and so on, one can achieve a certain gain in clarity. But does one learn to read Plato by proceeding in this way? Does one make his questions one's own? Does one succeed in learning from Plato instead of just confirming one's own superiority? What applies to Plato in this case applies by extension to all philosophy. Plato has in his *Seventh Letter* rightly described this, once and for all: The means one uses for philosophizing are not the same as philosophizing itself. Simple logical rigor is not everything. Not that logic does not have its evident validity. But the thematization in logic restrains the horizon of questioning in order to allow for verification, and in doing so blocks the kind of opening up of the world which takes place in our own experience of that world. This is a hermeneutical finding which I believe in the end converges with what we find in the later Wittgenstein. In his later writings he revised the nominalistic prejudices of his *Tractatus* in favor of leading all speaking back to the context of life-praxis. Of course, the result of this proposed reduction of philosophy to a praxis-context remained for him a negative one. It consisted in a flat rejection of all the undemonstrable questions of metaphysics rather than in a *winning back* of these undemonstrable questions of metaphysics, however undemonstrable they might be, by detecting in them the linguistic constitution of our being-in-the-world [*In-der-Welt-Sein*]. For this, of course, far more can be learned from the word of the poets than from Wittgenstein." Gadamer, "Reflections on My Philosophical Journey," in his *The Philosophy of Hans-Georg Gadamer*, 38–39.

25. This problem is very well analyzed by Carman in chapter 1 of *Heidegger's Analytic*.

26. Tugendhat, "Language Analysis and the Critique of Ontology," 111. An accurate analysis of this important essay can be found in Herman Frank, "La Critique Analytique de L'Ontologie."

27. Habermas, *The Philosophical Discourse of Modernity*, 403.

28. Tugendhat, *Self-Consciousness and Self-Determination*, 147.

29. Ibid., 145.

30. I should point out that at the moment of my research, the amount of Tugendhat's work on Heidegger consists of more than just his direct critiques and analyses (his book on the concept of truth and the ten essays), because he based also his *TI KATA TINOS, Traditional and Analytical Philosophy*, and *Self-Consciousness and Self-Determination* in Heidegger's thought. Although in the dialogue in the epilogue of this book Tugendhat reproaches me for making him too dependent on Heidegger, Heidegger is the author Tugendhat most frequently quotes *and* refers to indirectly.

31. Tugendhat, *Self-Consciousness and Self-Determination*, 220.

32. The "evocative" character that Tugendhat diagnoses in Heidegger's philosophy is well explained in Wolin, *The Politics of Being*.

33. Tugendhat, *Self-Consciousness and Self-Determination*, 150. Carman believes that the problem with Tugendhat's account is that it confines "intelligibility" and "practice" to an exclusively linguistic context: "Tugendhat simply folds the pragmatic notions of acceptance and refusal, or assent and dissent, into the specifically semantic concepts of affirmation and negation, assertion and denial. But, of course, we can reject what someone says by uttering affirmative statements, just as we can embrace what they say using negations. Tugendhat's 'linguistic-analytical' reconstruction of the question of Being therefore tends to suppress the distinction between pragmatic and linguistic intelligibility on which . . . Heidegger insists. For Heidegger, by contrast, Being is not restricted to the intelligibility we can explicitly affirm or deny in linguistic utterances; it is more fundamentally the intelligibility in virtue of which we treat things as they are—as human beings, as environments or practical artifacts, or as mere objects, properties, or relations. Not all practice is linguistic practice, nor does treating things appropriately necessarily involve affirming or denying anything about them." Carman, *Heidegger's Analytic*, 14–15.

34. Tugendhat, *Self-Consciousness and Self-Determination*, 160.

35. Ibid., 161.

36. Ibid., 162. The late philosopher R. Schürmann took Tugendhat's work very seriously and criticized it on several occasions. In his most important book, *On Being and Acting: From Principles to Anarchy*, he notes how "Tugendhat criticizes the later Heidegger for eliminating 'any leeway for various pre-

given possibilities' for action. 'Whereas in *Being and Time* and *The Essence of Ground*, being-there's freedom was thought in such a way that no link was possible to any referent for obligation, [in the later writings] on the contrary, freedom gets lost for the sake of obligation.' It is clear—and he says so—that for Tugendhat the concept of freedom in *Being and Time* is decisionist. It is also obvious that in the transmutation of freedom and truth into economic concepts, Tugendhat sees the elimination of the very possibility of alternatives, of choice. . . . As for Tugendhat, the way he understands the notion of responsibility in Heidegger remains entirely dependent on that of freedom as faculty of choice, which is why he ignores the two terms of the temporal difference—the economic order of presence and the event of presencing—and declares that Heidegger 'posits the manifest [present entities] immediately as measure and thereby as binding.'" Schürmann, *On Being and Acting*, 380–381.

37. Tugendhat, foreword to *Philosophische Aufsätze*, 12. Although Tugendhat does not think Heidegger's philosophy goes very far, according to Bowie he does consider "that the basic (and highly problematic) meaning of Sein in Heidegger is the happening clearing as such (*das . . . Lichtungsgeschehen als Solches*), the temporal disclosure (*Erschlossenheit*) which is the condition of possibility of the manifest world." Bowie, *Schelling and Modern European Philosophy*, 71.

38. Tugendhat, "The Question About Being and Its Foundation in Language," 260.

39. Heidegger, *Being and Time*, xix.

40. Tugendhat, "The Question About Being and its Foundation in Language," 260.

41. Klostermann, ed., *Durchblicke*.

42. "Die Sprachanalytische kritik der Ontologie" (1967), "Das Sein und das Nichts" (1970), and "Die Seinsfrage und ihre sprachliche Grundlage" (1977).

43. Inwood, *A Heidegger Dictionary*, 144.

44. Tugendhat, "Das Sein und das Nichts," in *Philosophische Aufsätze*, 36.

45. Gadamer comments on Tugendhat's criticism by replying to Habermas in the final contribution to a discussion volume addressing *Hermeneutik und Ideologiekritik*: "Hermeneutics makes critical reflection possible, e.g., where intelligible discourse is defended from misguided demands of logics. Such a case occurs when specific standards of the calculus of utterances are brought to bear on philosophical texts. Carnap and Tugendhat attempt to demonstrate

that Heidegger's or Hegel's talk of nothing is meaningless because it fails to fulfill logical conditions. In this case philosophical hermeneutics can critically show that such objections do not correspond to hermeneutic experience, and thus fail to recognize what should be understood. The *'das "nichtende Nichts,"'* 'nothing which nothings,' e.g., does not express, as Carnap contends, a feeling, but rather the way in which a movement of thought is to be valued. In this way hermeneutic reflection seems to me productive— productive, to take an example, in the way in which someone closely examines the logical cogency of Socratic argumentation in Platonic dialogue. Hermeneutic reflection reveals in this that the communicative movement [*Vorgang*] of such Socratically led conversations in a movement of understanding and agreement, something which is completely missed in the epistemological goal of the logical analysis. In all these cases reflective critique plainly refers to an instance represented through hermeneutic experience and its linguistic execution. It elevates to critical consciousness the *'scopus'* of the expression under consideration and the hermeneutic efforts which its claim to truth demands." Gadamer, "Reply to My Critics," 276–278.

46. Bowie, commenting on Tugendhat's "Das Sein und das Nicht," rightly notes that "the difference between the model based on perception and the model based on the proposition form of '*x* as *y*' is a version of what Heidegger will term 'ontological difference.' This is the difference between *what* there is ('entities'), and the always underlying fact *that* there is (the fact of 'being'), which is the condition of predicating anything of anything at all." Bowie, *Introduction to German Philosophy*, 92. The only other English language philosopher to make an accurate analysis of this essay was Rosen, *Hegel's Dialectic and Its Criticism*, 144–146.

47. Tugendhat, "Das Sein und das Nichts," in *Philosophische Aufsätze*, 36.

48. Rosen is absolutely correct in specifying that "although, in the modern epoch, new conceptions of the philosophical enterprise—epistemology and transcendental philosophy—have challenged ontology's central role, what they had *not* done until the advent of Heidegger and analytical philosophy, according to Tugendhat, was to dislodge ontology's distorting orientation towards objects." Rosen, *Hegel's Dialectic and Its Criticism*, 145.

49. The best reconstruction of the linguistic turn is still Rorty, ed., *The Linguistic Turn*.

50. Tugendhat, *Self-Consciousness and Self-Determination*, 30. Tugendhat goes even further in underlining the significance of appealing to the history in order to understand the meaning of Being: "In whatever way we may attempt

a new conception of the fundamental questions of philosophy at present, we will have to take a positive or negative position with respect to the conceptual tradition into which we have been born, a tradition essentially determined by Plato and Aristotle. For them the question about Being (Sein) was the fundamental question of philosophy." Tugendhat, "The Question About Being and Its Foundation in Language," 259.

51. Tugendhat, "Language Analysis and the Critique of Ontology," 108.

52. In chapter 4, I analyze the meaning of the singular term.

53. Tugendhat, *Traditional and Analytical Philosophy*, 42.

54. In a similar way, says Tugendhat, "we can nominalize a sentence and then speak about the meaning of what was previously said. That the meaning is now an object is shown by the fact that the new expression is a possible sentence-subject of which, in turn, we can predicate something." Tugendhat, "Phenomenology and Linguistic Analysis," 329.

55. Tugendhat, "The Question About Being and Its Foundation in Language," 270.

56. Ibid.

57. Ibid.

4. PHILOSOPHIZING ANALYTICALLY

1. Tugendhat, *Traditional and Analytical Philosophy*, ix. R. P. Pippin clearly explains how Tugendhat's purpose in this book is to be understood as post-metaphysical or, as he calls it, "meta-philosophical": "In admittedly still very different ways, recent work by Dummett, Putnam, Cavell, and recent 'back-to-the-roots-in-Wittgenstein' moments have all brought much more into prominence both the nature, and, more importantly, the *point* of 'philosophy of language.' In this context, Tugendhat's massive, ambitious, polemical book [*Traditional and Analytical Philosophy*] is a most interesting attempt to return to some of the earliest dreams of the analytical movement: to sketch a unified, inter-connected project in the philosophy of language as a whole (as well as to differentiate that program from linguistics), and to make use of that program directly to deny the legitimacy of 'traditional' philosophy from Aristotle to Heidegger. Tugendhat has a certain conception of philosophy of language in mind, one whose leading luminaries are (in order of importance) Dummett, Wittgenstein, and Davidson; he has a certain view of philosophy of language he wants to attack, one whose corresponding luminaries are Grice, Searle, and any version of 'ordinary language philosophy'; and he has a specific view

of the core of the 'tradition' he wants to attack, a core he designates as an 'object-centered' point of view, and whose main proponents are Aristotle, Hegel, and Husserl." Pippin, "Traditional and Analytical Philosophy," 165.

2. Dummett, *Frege*. The distinguished linguist Noam Chomsky, in an interview in 1968, also notices this problem in contemporary philosophy and has suggested that philosophers do precisely what Tugendhat has done: "A very healthy thing for philosophy would be to rethink its own historical origins. I think it has been much too unhistorical and has lost a lot of the insights of the past. Fruitful lines of thinking and development have been abandoned partly because of fashion and partly because of what I mentioned earlier, the availability of certain simple, reasonably well-understood problems where you can do technical work that will succeed and will even be rather classy in a way, and elegant. In a way I think philosophy always has to keep going back to its own sources and try to return to the central problems that every generation somehow rethought and reformulated." Chomsky, *Language and Politics*, 68.

3. This same elimination of the metaphorical mode of speaking in philosophy was also employed by contemporaneous colleagues of Tugendhat such as Derrida in *Of Grammatology* (1967), Rorty in *Philosophy and the Mirror of Nature* (1979), Vattimo in *The Adventure of Difference* (1980), and Habermas in *Postmetaphysical Thinking* (1988).

4. Tugendhat, *Self-Consciousness and Self-Determination*, 30.

5. Steven Crowell, commenting on how for Tugendhat a "new conceptuality" can be generated only through "reflection on the weakness and limits of a previous conceptuality," goes on to explain that "on the basis of such reflection, then, he argues that the question 'what is it to understand a sentence?' appropriates the 'language-analytically purified' sense, the 'defensible core,' of traditional questions concerning (e.g.) the *a priori*, being *qua* being, subject and object, intuition, representation, intentionality, and so on. This fills out his *Vorbegriff* of language-analytical philosophy as a 'first philosophy,' as a genuine successor-discipline to classical ontology and modern transcendental philosophy." Crowell, "Traditional and Analytical Philosophy," 96. Mauersberg has also specified how the change of paradigm from philosophy of consciousness to philosophy of language "is one of the central intentions of Habermas and Tugendhat. According to Tugendhat's interpretative scheme western philosophy is articulated in three phases. To the ancient and medieval interrogation on the Being of beings, the question of the conditions of knowledge has been introduced by Descartes, and this last question was finally resolved in the search for the conditions of understanding meanings.

In the history of philosophy two changes of paradigms have happened: from ontology to philosophy of consciousness and from the philosophy of consciousness to philosophy of language." Mauersberg, *Der lange Abschied von der Bewusstseinphilosophie*, 14. On the dissolution of ontology and modern transcendental philosophy, see the great study by Pippin, *Modernism as a Philosophical Problem*. On transcendental philosophy specifically, see Höffe, "Ist die Transzentale Vernunftkritik in der Sprachphilosophie aufgehoben"; Wetzel, "Tugendhat und Apel im Verhältnis zu Kant"; and Peschl, *Transzendentalphilosophie—Sprachanalyse—Neoontologie*, parts 1 and 2.

6. Tugendhat, *Traditional and Analytical Philosophy*, 75.

7. The fact of considering or acknowledging understanding as a linguistic factor does not mean we should think on or against language, but, as Gadamer explains, "with language" (Gadamer, *Gadamer in Conversation*, 68) or as Rorty suggests when he notes that "there is no way of getting behind our descriptive language to the object as it is in itself" (Rorty, "Being That Can Be Understood Is Language," 23).

8. Bubner explains that Tugendhat concludes from this "that it is necessary to get away from the conception of a synthesis as the fundamental structure of the predicative sentence, since in it the independence of the synthesized elements is presupposed. That conception is not adequate to our normal understanding and use of sentences. Like Frege, therefore, one must start from the *sentence as an original unity*. The relation of subject and predicate can then be conceived, along the lines suggested by Strawson and more recent linguistic analysts, as the combination of a referring element, which 'stands for' the object, and an 'ascriptive expression,' which contains what is asserted about the object indicated. The phenomenological notion of 'intending an object' is thus replaced by the semantics of understanding a proposition. Tugendhat explains in this connexion: 'The theory of predication which I have proposed belongs to linguistic analysis in the pregnant sense that it does not merely analyze linguistic expressions, but also has the consequence that our dealings with linguistic signs are not merely means of expression but prove to be the element of understanding itself.'" Bubner, *Modern German Philosophy*, 95.

9. Tugendhat, foreword to the Italian edition of *Traditional and Analytical Philosophy*, 6.

10. Habermas analyzes Tugendhat's conception of semantical rules for employing assertoric sentences in *The Theory of Communicative Action*, vol. 1, *Reason and the Rationalization of Society*, 313–315. And Pelsch observes that from this interpretation it "emerges how Tugendhat when he addresses his criticism

of transcendental philosophy against the idea of a non-linguistic reference to objects, comprehends this idea as an idea which necessarily results from an un-observation of its logical trait. On the other hand, instead, such interpretation also clarifies how logic and linguistic analysis for formal semantics are identical." Pelsch, *Transʒendentalphilosophie—Sprachanalyse—Neoontologie*, 211.

11. Tugendhat, *Traditional and Analytical Philosophy*, 6. Analytical philosophy's presupposition of the linguistic turn, in other words, is that the access to material and mental phenomena does not happen by means of consciousness but by means of language. Later we will see that Tugendhat arrives at a point where he even considers the origin of our same consciousness as a propositional attitude. Language is not only the a priori of the relation between mind and world but also the a priori of the access of the subject with itself. The same consciousness of phenomena is only propositional, until we can talk about the *propositional nature of intentional consciousness*.

12. Tugendhat, *Traditional and Analytical Philosophy*, 8.

13. Ibid., 9–10.

14. Ibid., 24–25.

15. Ibid., 25–26.

16. For a clear investigation and analysis of the theories of propositions in the Middle Ages, see De Libera, *La référence vide*; and de Rijk, *Through Language to Reality*.

17. Tugendhat, *Traditional and Analytical Philosophy*, 30. Rorty explains clearly in his great review of Tugendhat's book that "Tugendhat thinks that the principal false presupposition of 'classical modern philosophy' was that 'the field of givenness reflected upon was conceived as consciousness, a dimension of representation in ideas,' whereas 'in the new conception of philosophy it is conceived as the sphere of the understanding of our linguistic expressions.' He thinks that although 'all the decisive steps of Greek ontology resulted from semantic reflection' the Greeks were unable to describe their thought in terms of semantics because 'every step led to an objectifying reinterpretation which concealed the linguistic dimension of their reflection. For want of other categories the meaning of a linguistic expression was interpreted as an object.' Thus Aristotle's question 'What is being qua being?' was an unfortunately 'objectified' form of the question which Aristotle *should* have posed but which we have only recently got into focus: viz., 'How can one refer to objects with linguistic expressions?' . . . This identification of Aristotelian and Fregean questions will seem less odd when one realizes that Tugendhat is

convinced that philosophy is 'not the explanation of something that is not yet understood, but the clarification of what is already understood.' . . . Philosophy-as-formal-semantics is, in Tugendhat's, eyes, a way of recapturing pre-Platonic innocence by recognizing that 'all that is given to us of something is our speaking about it'—a recognition which the later Heidegger expressed in his claim that language is not a human instrument but rather what 'speaks man.' " Rorty, review of *Traditional and Analytical Philosophy*, 721–722.

18. Tugendhat, *Traditional and Analytical Philosophy*, 29.

19. Ibid., 33–34.

20. Frank has explained how "for the self-understanding of philosophy, such methodical individualism implicates far-reaching consequences. Due to its claim of supreme universality, philosophy since Aristotle has consistently thought of itself as *first* philosophy. This claim of supreme universality arises from the fact that philosophy is not a 'regional ontology' (e.g., as history is concerned with the being of acts and events, or zoology is concerned with the being of living organisms, or geology is concerned with the being of the earth, or philology is concerned with the being of texts), but is instead concerned with being as 'being.' . . . Such thought of being can be called universal, according to Aristotle, to the extent that some capacity of being is thought of in every other known discipline. As long as one can say of each and every thing that it is, some capacity of being is implicated—and it is in this sense that Aristotle understands being. 'Being object' and 'being something' (*tode ti*) are synonymous. . . . Heidegger has reformulated this fundamental Aristotelian question, 'What are the beings *as* beings?' into 'What is the Being *of* Beings?' Heidegger's defense of this reformulation is the claim that we can experience and understand beings 'only if we understand something like *being*.' The priority of understanding Being, before any possible discovery of concrete beings as 'this one or that one'—flower or stone—represents the main conviction of Heidegger's own philosophy. By this conviction, Heidegger thought he stood in solidarity with Aristotle. This conviction may be clarified in the following manner: only through the mediation of meaning can subjects relate to the objects of the world. Therefore, the original intentional relation does not lie between subjects and beings, but between subjects and meanings. Consequently, understanding (that is, the manner by which meanings are made accessible to us) is prior (hence, a priori) to our reference to the world. The fundamental philosophical concept of the a priori can now be given a definite meaning. Philosophy is a priori in the sense that it discloses the universal structures—or, as more frequently preferred by philosophy, the 'forms' of understanding.

Thus, philosophy can be called 'formal semantics': a theory of the formal possibility-conditions of understanding." Frank, "Style in Philosophy," 269.

21. Tugendhat, *Traditional and Analytical Philosophy*, 22.

22. Bowie makes a good point indicating that "non-being cannot just be seen as the polar opposite of being. Ernst Tugendhat . . . has suggested that if we doubt the existence of unicorns we do not go around looking at unicorns to see if they possess the attribute 'existence.' Instead we look at objects in the world to see if they can justifiably be characterized by the predicate 'unicorn.' The structure of our thinking about what we consider to be real is therefore the propositional structure of 'something as something,' not just 'something.' The world cannot adequately be described as the totality of somethings which are defined by their not being other somethings, but has instead to be described as the totality of 'states of affairs' ('x's as something'), because somethings can always be described in an indefinite number of ways. The something which may get in my way can, for example, be described as a table, the table as wood, as an object weighing thirty pounds, as brown, as protection against an earthquake, etc." Bowie, *Introduction to Modern German Philosophy*, 91.

23. Tugendhat, *Traditional and Analytical Philosophy*, 22–23. Brandom specifies that "singular terms are linguistic expressions that refer to, denote, or designate particular objects. The point of having something playing this role in linguistic practice is to make it possible to talk about particular objects, which, together with their properties and relations, make up the world in which the practice is conducted." Brandom, *Making It Explicit*, 360.

24. Tugendhat, *Traditional and Analytical Philosophy*, 31.

25. Ibid., 33. Pelsch writes that anyone "who, as Tugendhat, moves in the terrain of a semantics of truth, for which the relation of language with reality is fundamental, will not be able to simply keep the problem of 'the ontological difference' away from this analysis. If the semantical clarification of the 'totality of our understanding' and of its relation with reality is so important, then, one must also reflect on the following problem: whether the proposition and reality coincide or not, because this problem presupposes the existential inauguration of a sense of Being. This sense of Being precedes any truth of the proposition in the sense of a hermeneutical disclosure of single horizons of meanings." Pelsch, *Transzendentalphilosophie—Sprachanalyse—Neoontologie*, 319–320.

26. Tugendhat, *Traditional and Analytical Philosophy*, 413. On Aristotle's semantics, see de Rijk, *Semantics and Ontology*, vol. 1, *General Introduction: The Works on Logic*, and vol. 2.

27. Tugendhat, *Traditional and Analytical Philosophy*, 50. Tugendhat is referring here to Aquinas *De Veritate* 1.1: "Illud autem quod primum intellectus concipit notissimum et in quo omnes conceptiones resolvit est ens." Duns Scotus, Ord. I, dist. 3, pars. 1, q. 3, no. 137: "Primum objectum intellectus nostril est ens."

28. Tugendhat, *Traditional and Analytical Philosophy*, 62.

29. Ibid., 63.

30. Tugendhat gives a clear explanation of this medieval conception of truth in a passage at the end of *Self-Consciousness and Self-Determination:* "In the Middle Ages a definition came into fashion according to which truth was supposed to consist in the correspondence of thought with the thing, *adaequatio intellectus et rei*. This formulation can be understood to contain a correct though preliminary definition of the word *true*; but it can just as easily be interpreted in a way that results in nonsense. It is only meaningful (1) if both sides are understood propositionally, and (2) if the side of thinking is also interpreted objectively in the sense of what is thought, believed, or asserted." Tugendhat, *Self-Consciousness and Self-Determination*, 284–285. A complete account of this theory can be found in de Rijk, *Through Language to Reality*; and Newman, *The Correspondence Theory of Truth*.

31. Tugendhat, *Traditional and Analytical Philosophy*, 58.

32. Ibid.

33. Ibid., 414.

34. For a semantical analysis of the *Selbstbewusstsein* in Heidegger, see Tugendhat's detailed analyses in lectures 8, 9, and 10 of *Self-Consciousness and Self-Determination*, 144–218.

35. Tugendhat, *Traditional and Analytical Philosophy*, 60.

36. Tugendhat is right when he notes that if Heidegger "had written in English, perhaps he might have chosen the word *awareness*; there is no equivalent for this in German, and its meaning seems to me to come closest to what Heidegger means by *disclosure*." Tugendhat, *Self-Consciousness and Self-Determination*, 151–152.

37. Tugendhat, *Traditional and Analytical Philosophy*, 415.

38. Ibid.

39. Ibid., 66.

40. Ibid.

41. Ibid., 73.

42. Ibid., 380.

43. Ibid., 37.

44. Ibid., 135.

45. Against Tugendhat's interpretation, Barry Smith and Kevin Mulligan have argued that "whenever a sentence is asserted, according to Tugendhat, various rules are followed: for example, verification rules, identification rules, and rules for the application of a predicate. But unfortunately Tugendhat continually avoids dealing in a more than metaphorical fashion with the ontological problem of the nature of the relation between the *events* which are the followings of the respective rules. . . . For even this analysis would involve accepting some sort of ontology of composition amongst events, and this too would transcend the boundaries of 'universal formal semantics.' " Smith and Mulligan, "Traditional Versus Analytical Philosophy," 200. Their criticism of Tugendhat stems from their being what Rorty calls "materialist metaphysicians." See Rorty's definition of nominalism in note 48, below.

46. Tugendhat, *Traditional and Analytical Philosophy*, 139.

47. Ibid., 140.

48. I believe that Tugendhat's understanding of nominalism fits well in the account of nominalism given by Rorty: "Let me define 'nominalism' as the claim that all essences are nominal and all necessities *de dicto*. This amounts to saying that no description of an object is more true to the nature of that object than any other. Nominalists think that Plato's metaphor of cutting nature at the joints should be abandoned once and for all. Proponents of nominalism are often described as 'linguistic idealists' by the materialist metaphysicians. For the latter believe that Dalton and Mendeleev did indeed cut nature at the joints. From this Kripkean perspective, Wittgensteinians are so infatuated with words that they lose touch with the real world, the world modern science has opened up to us. Philosophers of this sort accept the account of the history of philosophy that Gadamer summed up when he wrote that 'the rapid downfall of the Hegelian empire of the Absolute Spirit brought us to the end of metaphysics, and thereby to the promotion of the empirical sciences to the top-most position in the kingdom of the thinking mind.' Nominalism, however, protests against any sort of metaphysics. . . . All consistent nominalists will insist that the predicative and explanatory success of a corpuscularian vocabulary has no bearing on its ontological status, and that the very idea of 'ontological status' should be dropped." Rorty, "Being That Can Be Understood Is Language," 23.

49. Wittgenstein, *Philosophical Investigations*, para. 560.

50. Tugendhat, *Traditional and Analytical Philosophy*, 293.

51. Bubner has observed that this interpretation of ontology "reveals a weakness when, before any intervention of logic, it patterns the manifold forms of living speech on the single mode of a predicative statement of the form 'Fa.' The

Aristotelian introduction of ontology as a new science loses its point, if all sentences are construed in the same way in terms of their form because the logician has already treated them *uniformly*, contrary to the variety of manifold modes of discourse which are precisely not such as to allow any recognition of a single relationship between them. The ontological theme which is latent in language as it is does not need to be further disclosed. The semanticist has already taken command and defines the theme of ontology from his interpretation of the structure of the sentence. In opposition to his starting-point in Heidegger and Aristotle, who first wanted to uncover the problem of Being in language, Tugendhat thus follows by turning in this direction a projection of the professional semanticists. This line of thought proceeds from a schematized preconception of language as a referential system of signs and, in the manner of Quine for instance, allows 'ontological commitment' to follow from this as a second step." Bubner, *Modern German Philosophy*, 98–99.

52. Tugendhat, *Traditional and Analytical Philosophy*, 251.

53. Ibid., 253.

54. Ibid., 254.

55. Ibid.

56. Ibid., 380.

57. Ibid., 385.

58. "We explain the word 'red' through its use, with positive and negative examples. He will have understood the explanation if he is capable of using this example in the same way. For this explanation it is of no use to presuppose the representation of something universal." Tugendhat and Wolf, *Logisch-semantische Propädeutik*, 140.

59. Pelsch notes that Tugendhat's fundamental character of formal semantics consists only of linguistic problems. For this philosophy there is no thematic that does not depend from language. Instead of taking about Being or consciousness as a starting point, language is the radical point of departure, which "is used to examine the problem of the meaning of rationality." Pelsch, *Transzendentalphilosophie—Sprachanalyse—Neoontologie*, 241–242.

60. Tugendhat, *Traditional and Analytical Philosophy*, 392.

61. Ibid.

62. Habermas, "Richard Rorty's Pragmatic Turn," 40. Habermas goes on to rightly specify that this is an "anti-foundational conception of knowledge" and a "holistic conception of justification." A detailed analysis of the concept of truth and meaning in Tugendhat can be found in Wyller, *Wahrheit und Bedeutung bei Tugendhat und Davidson*.

63. Aristotle, *De Interpretatione*, chap. 4.
64. Tugendhat, *Traditional and Analytical Philosophy*, 41. Bubner has rightly seen that if Tugendhat's fundamental question of semantics is "what is it to understand a sentence?" then the traditional analysis of the structure of predicative statements as a synthesis of elements of meaning is to be rejected, because the sentence is treated as an original semantic unity and is related to the problem of truth. In this way, everything will depend on an adequate interpretation of the role of the predicate, as he explains in this passage: "The predicate does not, like the subject of the sentence, stand for an object, but characterizes it in a certain way. The result is that there is an unequal distribution of roles in the predicative sentence between a referring and a characterizing part. The characterization by the predicate consequently presupposes the identification of an object to be characterized. Truth turns out to be a correct characterization of an object in an assertion. Tugendhat's definition of truth is as follows: 'The assertion that *a* is *F* is true if and only if the predicate *F* applies to the object for which the singular term *a* stands.' This conclusion is not particularly startling, if one remembers the oldest account of truth in Plato or Aristotle, who explicated the truth of assertions in terms of the 'existence' (*hyparchein*) of what is asserted. Tugendhat in general makes no secret of this borrowing. However the problem arises of what is denoted by the word 'applies.' Tugendhat falls back for its elucidation fundamentally on the correct use of the predicate, so that the understanding of the predicate and the problem of truth become well-nigh indistinguishable. The rules of verification of a sentence refer to the rules of application of the predicates. But is truth to be nothing other than correct use of words? Is the wide domain of the false, of illusion, of delusion, of error to be narrowed down to a series of violations of rules of language? The problem here is that false sentences do not tell us that they are false because the incorrect use of words does not show. *These sentences look quite correct at first sight, so that it needs a special effort to find out what is wrong* under the surface. How can this critical effort get under way? The intricate and protracted discussions which Tugendhat devotes to this difficulty show that he is conscious of the unsatisfactory nature of his definition, though he is unable entirely to give it up." Bubner, *Modern German Philosophy*, 96–97.
65. Tugendhat, *Traditional and Analytical Philosophy*, 42.
66. Ibid.
67. Ibid., 46.
68. Tugendhat, *Traditional and Analytical Philosophy*, 413. Habermas has pointed out that as "Tugendhat has shown, this program of translating subjective

expressions into situation-independent objective expressions cannot be carried through; singular terms, like performative expressions, are examples of genuinely pragmatic meanings that cannot be explained independently of an intersubjective practice of applying rules." Habermas, *The Philosophical Discourse of Modernity*, 173. And a very detailed and clear account of Tugendhat's theory of "intersubjective practice and validation" is given in Jopling, *Self-Knowledge and the Self*, 142–153.

69. Tugendhat, *Traditional and Analytical Philosophy*, 73. These investigations by Tugendhat have received vast acknowledgment from distinguished philosophers such as Gasché, Rorty, and others. Gasché, for example, in his great work *The Tain of the Mirror*, explains that for Tugendhat and the analytic tradition he represents, knowledge and truth can only be propositional and are thus incommensurable with any form of self-identification because "by eliminating altogether the ontological dimension of self-identity in self-consciousness (and, for that matter, in absolute reflection), one deprives oneself of the possibility of thinking the very foundations of propositional knowledge and truth, as well as of the very idea of epistemic self-consciousness. The very possibility of propositional truth requires that kind of immediate identification Tugendhat rejects as contradictory to all cognitive achievement proper. Without the presupposition of ontological or formal-ontological identity of being and thought, of subject and object, of the knower and what is known, there is no ground for any propositional attribution whatsoever." Gasché, *The Tain of the Mirror*, 77. And Rorty confessed that on "the 'analytic' view I share with Tugendhat and Habermas, the very idea of a 'ground' for 'propositional attribution' is a mistake. The practice of playing sentences off against one another in order to decide what to believe—the practice of argumentation—no more requires a 'ground' than the practice of using one stone to chip pieces off another stone in order to make a spear-point." Rorty, *Essays on Heidegger and Others*, 125.

70. Tugendhat, *Self-Consciousness and Self-Determination*, 220.

71. Ibid., 24–25.

72. A clear account of how Tugendhat criticizes German idealism can be found in Lütterfelds, *Bin ich nur öffentliche Person?* And M. Frank has commented that "both Tugendhat and Derrida take exception to the idea that consciousness is a kind of perception ('*Anschauung*') and that, correspondingly, self-consciousness is a kind of internal perception. The subject-object scheme accounts neither for the fact that the elementary data of consciousness are states of affairs rather than things (i.e., entities that are articulated in propositions), nor for the fact that intentional acts can acquire significance only within a

language. The meaning of an intention is the minimum of what could be conscious to a consciousness, and this meaning only occurs 'interwoven' with an expression, i.e., in the form of a sign that is differentially distinguished from other signs." Frank, *What Is Neostructuralism?*, 229. And Lewis Hinchman has given a clear explanation of how Tugendhat tries to rescue the notion of self-determination through his critical reading of Heidegger in *What Is Enlightenment?*, 502–503.

73. R. B. Pippin in *Hegel's Idealism* comments on Tugendhat's interpretation of the school of Heidelberg, with particular emphasis on the idealist tradition that constitutes it, but it is Gasché who noted that for Tugendhat, not only can these three models not produce self-consciousness but neither can identity be understood as knowledge, because for him knowledge and truth can only be propositional. From all this, Tugendhat concludes, says Gasché, "that 'a structure of the form "I know myself" is in itself impossible and contradicts the very meaning of "knowing."'" Yet it does not follow from all this that self-consciousness itself would be an impossibility. On the contrary, Tugendhat accuses Henrich of disposing of self-consciousness, despite the fact that Henrich's regress from self-consciousness to consciousness is a step toward the deduction of self-consciousness as a secondary phenomenon from what he calls 'selfless consciousness of self.' Instead of relinquishing self-consciousness, Tugendhat intends to give an analytic account of what he calls 'epistemic self-consciousness,' in particular in its immediate form. This form of self-consciousness, the only that Tugendhat concedes, is entirely linguistic. It is grounded in the immediate knowledge one has *of having* certain states. It is a knowledge not of oneself or of one's states in themselves but only a knowledge that one has those states. Tugendhat contends that this kind of self-consciousness can be thought without aporias, since its concept can be elaborated without the three models that inform traditional theories of self-reflection." Gasché, *The Tain of the Mirror*, 77. And although Frank, in *Die Unhintergehbarkeit der Individualität*, disagrees with Tugendhat's criticism of the school of Heidelberg, he gives a very detailed account of the dispute, which was echoed in several studies: Pothast, *In assertorischen Sätzen*; Soldati, *Selbstbewusstsein und unmittelbares Wissen bei Tugendhat*; Heinrich, *Noch einmal in Zirkeln*; Frank, *What Is Neostructuralism?*, lecture 14. On the problem of identity, see Meuter, *Das Problem der personalen Identität*.

74. Tugendhat, *Self-Consciousness and Self-Determination*, 9–10.

75. Ibid., 13. Larmore, after analyzing several theories of self-consciousness in contemporary philosophy, notes that Tugendhat is one of the few philoso-

phers who does not consider the knowledge of oneself to rest or depend on "any process of knowledge outside language." Larmore, *Les pratiques du moi*, 168.

76. Tugendhat, *Self-Consciousness and Self-Determination*, 35.

77. Ibid., 29.

78. Ibid., 71.

79. Ibid., 10. Against Tugendhat's effort to dismantle the epistemologist's point of view by suggesting that "apparently" and "really" should be treated as propositional operators—"*Applied to a proposition, they give rise to a new proposition*"—Descombes argues that "if this analysis were accepted, there would still be a loophole for the epistemologist. He can concede Tugendhat's opposition between the subjective proposition (*It seems to me that* p) and the objective proposition (*Really* p). Prior to this opposition, or profound schism (*Entzweiung*), we had only the simple or immediate proposition, consisting in a statement of the given, still lacking an appropriate determinant. Consequently, the immediate proposition precedes the subjective proposition that precedes the objective proposition. Understanding the subjective proposition is conditional on having understood the immediate proposition, but the latter does not yet bear upon either appearance or reality. It concerns what is given in any case, whether as mere appearance or as confirmed appearance, objective phenomenon. The epistemological argument asks no more than this." Descombes, *Objects of All Sorts*, 94–95.

80. Tugendhat, *Traditional and Analytical Philosophy*, 74. Rorty noticed that although "Frank says 'The linguistic turn consists in the transferal of the philosophical paradigm of consciousness onto that of the sign,' I myself would have said 'the sentence' rather than 'the sign,' in order to exclude the sorts of iconical and indexical signs Peirce included in his semiotic. This would accord with what Frank, following Tugendhat, says about propositional attitudes being 'the basic form of all intentional consciousness.' He there quotes Tugendhat as saying that 'the question of consciousness dissolves into the question of propositional understanding'; I take that dissolution to be the crucial difference between philosophers' talk of 'experience' circa 1900 and their talk of 'language' circa 1990." Rorty, *Truth and Progress*, 293.

81. Tugendhat, *Self-Consciousness and Self-Determination*, 12. Taylor has noticed that "to analytical philosophers in the English-speaking world, demolishing German Idealism with the help of post-Fregean terminology may seem like the day before yesterday's agenda. But as it happens even the destructive part of Tugendhat's book is extremely interesting. It brings us up against the

issue: what kind of awareness is self-awareness in the strong sense, the sense in which we might want to ascribe it to someone as a virtue? Just consciousness of some property that applies to me is not sufficient. I am not self-aware because I know my weight, height, and the colour of my eyes. The obvious suggestion which springs from our tradition is to say that what we're talking about here is knowledge of the self, of the basic core or kernel of our subjectivity or personality. But when we try to say what this is as an object, we run into seemingly insurmountable difficulties, as Hume saw. When do I relate to myself? The essence of Tugendhat's solution seems to be this: I relate to myself, properly speaking, when I consider myself as an agent, a being who has goals and purposes, for whom outcomes can be good or bad, and when I recognize that in some sense the responsibility falls to me to define these goals and purposes, the good and the bad." Taylor, "Ernst Tugendhat," 219–220. See also Taylor, "Theories of Meaning," 248–249.

82. Rorty, commenting on Gasché, *The Tain of Mirror*, says that "Gasché is quite right in saying that to follow Wittgenstein and Tugendhat in this nominalism will reduce what he wants to call 'philosophical reflection' to 'a fluidization (*Verflüssigung*) of all oppositions and particularities by means of objective irony.' Such liquefaction is what I am calling *Aufhebung* and praising Derrida for having done spectacularly well. We nominalists think that all that philosophers of the world-disclosing (as opposed to the problem-solving) sort can do is to fluidize old vocabularies. We cannot make sense of the notion of discovering a 'condition of the possibility of language'—nor, indeed, of the notion of 'language' as something homogeneous enough to have 'conditions.' If, with Wittgenstein, Tugendhat, Quine, and Davidson, one ceases to see language as a medium, one will reject *a fortiori* Gasché's claim that '[language] must, in philosophical terms, be thought of as a totalizing medium.' That is only how a certain antinominalistic philosophical tradition—'the philosophy of reflection'—must think of it." Rorty, *Essays on Heidegger and Others*, 126–127.

83. Tugendhat, *Self-Consciousness and Self-Determination*, 118.

EPILOGUE.
THE LINGUISTIC TURN AS THE END OF METAPHYSICS

1. Tugendhat, *Self-Consciousness and Self-Determination*, 150.
2. Tugendhat, *Traditional and Analytical Philosophy*, 410.
3. Rorty, "Review of *Traditional and Analytical Philosophy*," 727.

4. Rorty, "Being That Can Be Understood Is Language," 28.

5. A. Bowie is one of the few philosophers that have noted (together with Rorty, Gasché, Descombes, Pippin, Grondin, Taylor, Vattimo, Aubenque, Larmore, and D'Agostini) Tugendhat's use of the linguistic turn to overcome metaphysics: "Common to nearly all Tugendhat's arguments—and here he concurs with a widely held nominalist position—is a rejection of any approach to understanding which entails the non-propositional or the sub-propositional: these he associates with a notion of 'intuition'. He regards 'intuition,' in the form, for example, of the idea of the 'mental eye,' as part of a tradition which goes from Plato to Husserl, which the linguistic turn has finally discredited. Tugendhat thinks the modern problem of 'self-consciousness' is generated by philosophers moving away from the rules governing how the term was used in everyday language towards a use that is generated by the relationship between the two terms contained in the concept. Distorting everyday usage in this way leads to the problems of reflective self-identification familiar from Fichte and the Romantics and some contemporary philosophers of mind. These positions are dismissed on the grounds that self-consciousness must be understood propositionally, and thus intersubjectively, via the rules for converting deictic expressions between the 'he' and the 'I' perspectives, which allow us to identify a person, including ourselves, and not via the epistemological problems concerning the 'intuitive' nature of self-knowledge or 'inner evidence.' If Tugendhat is right, then, his version of a Frege-derived semantics of singular terms and general terms is able to obviate a whole series of the problems in Kantian and post-Kantian metaphysics." Bowie, "Review Essay," 348. On Tugendhat's linguistic turn, see note 34 of the introduction, above.

6. Tugendhat, *Philosophische Aufsätze*, 9–10.

7. Tugendhat, *Traditional and Analytical Philosophy*, 107. Rorty has rightly observed that "the connection Tugendhat sees between Gottlob Frege's claim that 'only in the context of a sentence do words have meaning' and analytic philosophy's realization that its 'field of givenness' is the 'sphere of the understanding of our linguistic expressions.' Tugendhat thinks that Frege's claim helps move philosophy from questions like 'What object or quasi-object does this word (e.g., "being" or "consciousness") stand for?' to 'How do we put words together?' and thus moves us out from under the 'objectualist' tradition. We could not think of language as philosophy's sphere until we were no longer held captive by the picture that made us ask 'What are we using this word to represent?' For that picture suggested that, before one could understand our understanding of language, one had to understand the relation be-

tween language and something else (e.g., 'the world'). We are fated to remain 'objectualist' in our philosophizing—i.e., to accept this false suggestion—as long as we think of the relation between subject and predicate in terms of 'composition,' of predicative sentences as forging one bigger meaning out of two smaller meanings. . . . One cannot hope to clarify the meaning of a sentence by recourse to the idea of a 'fact' which the sentence represents, where a fact is a composite object made up of something signified by the subject and something signified by the predicate. For you cannot understand what a fact is except by understanding what a true sentence is, so the former notion can shed no light on the latter. Since 'we can only define the relation between attribute and object by means of the original predicative sentence' we cannot use a compositional relation so defined to tell us what the original sentence means." Rorty, "Review of *Traditional and Analytical Philosophy*," 722–723.

8. Heidegger, letter to O. Pöggeler, January 5, 1973, in Pöggeler, *Heidegger und die Hermeneutische Philosophie*, 395. According to Heinrich Wiegand Petzet, Heidegger "esteemed [Tugendhat] highly." Petzet, *Encounters and Dialogues with Martin Heidegger*, 206. Also, it is interesting to note, as Dahlstrom explains in his "Editor's Afterword" to Heidegger's *Introduction to Phenomenological Research*, that "at the time that Heidegger was planning and preparing his *Gesamtausgabe*, he had asked Professor Ernst Tugendhat, the nephew of Helene Weiss, to make available to him from the surviving papers of his aunt copies of all the notes taken in his lectures. Professor Tugendhat had kindly complied with this wish." Dahlstrom, in Heidegger, *Introduction to Phenomenological Research*, 245–246.

9. Gadamer, "Boundaries of Language," 16. Gadamer goes further: "Lastly, I would like to name as a boundary to language the trans-linguistic [*Übersprachliche*], the boundary to the unsaid and perhaps even the inexpressible. I will approach this from what we call the statement. Its boundary was probably the fate of our western civilization. Following the extreme preference for the 'apophansis,' the statement, our civilization developed a corresponding logic. It is the classical logic of judgment, the logic founded on the concept of judgment." Gadamer, "Boundaries of Language," 15.

10. Lafont believes there are certain limits in Tugendhat's conception of language entailed in his formal semantics because they depend very much on his criticism of Heidegger: "Tugendhat regards Heidegger's reflection on the world-disclosing function of language as 'speculative,' because no propositional form exists that would be able to establish it. But this does not yet mean that a model such as Tugendhat's remains untarnished by the problems raised

in this connection. The difficulties connected with every attempt to seek the smallest unity of meaning in something other than language as a whole, difficulties that are discussed in analytical philosophy under the heading 'meaning holism,' are nothing other than the consequences of the problem that Heidegger addresses here. This is also the very problem considered from the outset by the German tradition of the philosophy of language, which consistently begins with a holistic model of language." Lafont, *Heidegger, Language, and World-Disclosure*, 60.

11. Habermas, "Hans-Georg Gadamer."

12. Although I analyze this debate in chapter 2 by comparing investigations by Pöggeler, Lafont, Aubenque, Wrathall, Schürmann, and Dahlstrom, it is interesting to emphasize how the debate over whether Tugendhat found an "error" (in Heidegger's concept of truth) or just a "confirmation" (of the fact that Heidegger was looking for a new conceptuality beyond truth and falsity) will depend on how one understands Heidegger's relation to the end of metaphysics: as discovery or just as "never ending epoch-ending disclosure of Being." On this matter, Pippin notes that "Heidegger's enterprise is not supposed to be revolutionary, a decisive origination that can make it seem as 'metaphysical' as what it rejects, but a genuine *An-denken*, or re-collection of the metaphysical tradition; essentially a perpetual hermeneutics concerned with 'where,' in Heidegger's unusual sense, truth has happened by not happening." Pippin, *Hegel's Idealism*, 138. Dahlstrom also sees this distinction: "Heidegger's attempt to explain the originality or primordiality of this truth, not only over and against competing claims in the history of philosophy, contradicts the charge that he fails to uphold what Tugendhat understands as the specific and basic sense of truth. Heidegger interprets the original truth as the disclosedness that lies in advance of every proposition and thereby every possibility of propositional truth or falsity. Insofar as the interpretation takes the form of a transcendental argument or a scientific discourse, the original truth is construed in assertions for which there are contraries. Thus, propositional truth or, more precisely, the bivalency criterion of meaningful talk about truth, on which Tugendhat rightly insists, remains in force." Dahlstrom, *Heidegger's Concept of Truth*, 423.

13. Vattimo, foreword to *Analitici e continentali*, xv.

14. Wallace, *A New History of Philosophy from Descartes to Searle*, 473.

15. Rorty, "Analytic and Conversational Philosophy," 120.

16. Tugendhat, foreword to *Philosophische Aufsätze*, 12–13. After 1975, Tugendhat concentrated on ethics, morality, and politics, writing several books, such

as *Probleme der Ethik* [*Problems of Ethics*] (1984), *Ethik und Politik. Vorträge und Stellungnahmen aus den Jahren 1978–1991* [*Ethics and Politics. Lectures and Statements from the Years 1978–1991*] (1992), *Vorlesungen über Ethik* [*Lectures on Ethics*] (1993), *Dialog in Leticia* [*Dialogue in Leticia*] (1997), *Wie sollen wir handeln? Schülergespräche über Moral* [*How Should We Act? Discussions with Students on Morality*] (2000), *Aufsätze 1992–2000* [*Essays, 1992–2000*] (2001), *Egozentrizität und Mystik* [*Egocentricity and Mysticism*] (2003), *Über den Tod* [*On Death*] (2006), and, recently, *Anthropologie statt Metaphysik* [*Anthropology Instead of Metaphysics*] (2007). These books have received many reviews and much commentary, detailed in the bibliography. Habermas analyzes Tugendhat's conception of morality in Habermas, *The Inclusion of the Other*, 20–25.

17. Tugendhat, in his latest books *Egozentrizität und Mystik* (2003), *Über den Tod* (2006), and *Anthropologie statt Metaphysik* (2007), confirms, as Vattimo once emphasized, how many analytical philosophers have ended up dealing with mysticism, following Wittgenstein's call at the end of the *Tractatus Logico-Philosophicus* when he wrote that there are "things that cannot be put into words. They make themselves manifest. They are what is mystical." Wittgenstein, *Tractatus Logico-Philosophicus*, 89.

18. Bubner specified that "Tugendhat, as one of Heidegger's last pupils, is at the same time one of the least subservient to his master. If the lesson which can be learned from Heidegger is, as many proclaim, that the ethos of philosophy is open and relentless questioning, then Tugendhat has taken this lesson to heart and applied it not least against his teacher." Bubner, *Modern German Philosophy*, 93.

19. Schleiermacher, *Hermeneutics and Criticism*, 23.

I. WORKS BY ERNST TUGENDHAT

A. In German and Spanish

"Die Philosophie des Aristoteles." *Gnomon* (1957): 310.

TI KATA TINOS. Eine Untersuchung ʒu Struktur und Ursprung aristotelischer Grundbegriffe. Friburg/Brisgovia: Verlag Karl Alber, 1958, 1988.

"Tarskis semantisches Definition der Wahrheit und ihre Stellung innerhalb der Geschichte des Wahrheitsproblems im logischen Positivismus." *Philosophische Rundschau* 8 (1960): 131–159. Also in Tugendhat, *Philosophische Aufsätʒe*, 179–213. Frankfurt: M. Suhrkamp, 1992.

"Zum Rechtfertigungsproblem in Pindars 7. Nemeischen Gedicht." *Hermes* 88 (1960): 385–409. Also in Tugendhat, *Philosophische Aufsätʒe*, 147–179. Frankfurt: M. Suhrkamp, 1992.

Review of Aristotle, *Metaphysik* (German translation by F. Bassenge). *Gnomon* (1961): 703–706.

Review of W. Wieland, *Die aristotelische Physik*. *Gnomon* (1963): 543–555. Also in Tugendhat, *Philosophische Aufsätʒe*, 385–401. Frankfurt: M. Suhrkamp, 1992.

"Ciencia y Verdad." *Memorias del XIII Congresso Internacional de Filosofía* 5 (1964): 635–645.

"Zum Verhältnis von Wissenschaft und Wahrheit." In *Collegium Philosophicum. Festschrift für J. Ritter*, 389–402. Basel, 1965. Also in Tugendhat, *Philosophische Aufsätʒe*, 214–229. Frankfurt: M. Suhrkamp, 1992.

"Der Wahrheitsbegriff bei Aristoteles" (1966). In Tugendhat, *Philosophische Aufsätʒe*, 251–260. Frankfurt: M. Suhrkamp, 1992.

Review of K. Oehler, *Die Lehre vom noetischen und dianoetischen Denken bei Platon und Aristoteles. Gnomon* (1966): 752–760. Also in Tugendhat, *Philosophische Aufsätze*, 402–413. Frankfurt: M. Suhrkamp, 1992.

Der Wahrheitsbegriff bei Husserl und Heidegger. Berlin: Walter de Gruyter, 1967, 1970, 1983.

"Die Sprachanalytische Kritik der Ontologie." In *Das Problem der Sprache*, edited by H.-G. Gadamer, 483–493. München: W. Fink Verlag, 1967. Also in Tugendhat, *Philosophische Aufsätze*, 21–35. Frankfurt: M. Suhrkamp, 1992.

"Heideggers Idee von Wahrheit, Heidegger." In *Perspektiven zur Deutung seines Werkes*, edited by O. Pöggeler, 286–297. Köln-Berlin: Kiepenheuer & Witsch, 1969.

"Das Sein und das Nichts." In *Durchblicke. Festschrift für Martin Heidegger*, edited by Vittorio Klostermann, 132–162. Frankfurt: Klostermann, 1970. Also in Tugendhat, *Philosophische Aufsätze*, 36–66. Frankfurt: M. Suhrkamp, 1992.

"Phänomenologie und Sprachanalyse." In *Hermeneutik und Dialektik*, 2 vols., edited by R. Bubner, K. Cramer, and R. Wiehl, 2:3–23. Tübingen: Mohr Siebeck, 1970.

Vorlesungen zur Einführung in die Sprachanalytische Philosophie. Frankfurt: M. Suhrkamp, 1976, 1990.

Review of Charles H. Kahn, *The Verb "Be" in Ancient Greek*. "Die Seinsfrage und ihre sprachliche Grundlage." *Philosophische Rundschau* 24 (1977): 161–176. Also in Tugendhat, *Philosophische Aufsätze*, 90–107. Frankfurt: M. Suhrkamp, 1992.

Korreferat zu Charles Taylor, *What Is Human Agency?* Text of a conference that took place in a congress at the Starnberger Max Planck-Institut in June 1977. In Tugendhat, *Philosophische Aufsätze*, 441–425. Frankfurt: M. Suhrkamp, 1992.

"Gegen die autoritäre Pädagogik. Streitschrift gegen die Thesen 'Mut zur Erziehung.'" *Die Zeit*, June 2, 1978. Also in Tugendhat, *Ethik und Politik. Vorträge und Stellungnahmen aus den Jahren 1978–1991*, 17–26. Frankfurt: M. Suhrkamp, 1992.

"Zigeuner und Juden." Foreword to *In Auschwitz vergast, bis heute verfolgt. Zur Situation der Roma und Sinti in Deutschland und Europa*, edited by T. Zülch, 9–11. Reinbeck, 1979. Also in Tugendhat, *Ethik und Politik. Vorträge und Stellungnahmen aus den Jahren 1978–1991*, 27–31. Frankfurt: M. Suhrkamp, 1992.

Selbstbewusstsein und Selbstbestimmung. Sprachanalytische Interpretationen. Frankfurt: M. Suhrkamp, 1979, 1989.

"Zur Entwicklung von moralischen Begründungsstrukturen im Modernen Recht." *Archiv für Recht- und Sozialphilosophie*, Beiheft 14 (1980): 1–20.

"Antike und Moderne Ethik." In *Die Antike Philosophie in ihrer Bedeutung für die Gegenwart*, edited by Reiner Wiehl, 55–73. Heidelberg, 1981. Also in Tugendhat, *Probleme der Ethik*. Stuttgart: Reclam, 1984.

"Langage et Etique." *Critique* 37, no. 413 (October 1981). German version, *Sprache und Ethik*, in Tugendhat, *Philosophische Aufsätze*, 275–314. Frankfurt: M. Suhrkamp, 1992.

Review of John Rawls, *Eine Theorie der Gerechtigkeit. Die Zeit* 38, no. 10 (April 1983): 46. Also in *ZEIT-Bibliothek der 100 Sachbücher*, 360–363. Frankfurt: M. Suhrkamp, 1984.

"Über den Sinn der vierfachen Unterscheidung des Seins bei Aristoteles." In *Spiegel und Gleichnis*, edited by N. W. Bolz and W. Hübner, 49–54. Würzburg, 1983. Also in Tugendhat, *Philosophische Aufsätze*, 136–144. Frankfurt: M. Suhrkamp, 1992.

"Die Bundesrepublik ist ein fremdenfeindliches Land geworden." Foreword to *Die kurdischen Yezidi. Ein Volk auf dem Weg in den Untergang*, edited by R. Schneider, 9–11. Kassel. Also in Tugendhat, *Ethik und Politik. Vorträge und Stellungnahmen aus den Jahren 1978–1991*, 62–65. Frankfurt: M. Suhrkamp, 1992.

Probleme der Ethik. Stuttgart: Reclam, 1984.

"Panorama de conceptos de filosofía." *Cuadernos de filosofía y letras*, 5–17, VII, nos. 1 and 2 (1984).

"El método analítico." *Cuadernos de filosofía y letras*, 49–60, VII, nos. 1 and 2 (1984).

"Über die Notwendigkeit einer Zusammenarbeit zwischen philosophischer und empirischer Forschung bei der Klärung der Bedeutung des moralischen Sollens." In *Zur Bestimmung der Moral. Philosophische und sozialwissenschaftliche Beiträge zur Moralforschung*, edited by W. Edelstein and G. Nummer-Winkler, 25–36. Frankfurt: M. Suhrkamp, 1986.

"Asyl: Gnade oder Menschenrecht?" In *Kursbuch*, 172–176, n. 86, 1986. Also in Tugendhat, *Ethik und Politik. Vorträge und Stellungnahmen aus den Jahren 1978–1991*, 66–75. Frankfurt: M. Suhrkamp, 1992.

"Gegen die Abschiebung in den Libanon." In *Kirche aktuell*, 27–29, February 1987. Also in Tugendhat, *Ethik und Politik. Vorträge und Stellungnahmen aus den Jahren 1978–1991*, 76–79. Frankfurt: M. Suhrkamp, 1992.

"Als Jude in der Bundesrepublik Deutschland." In *Geschichte–Schuld–Zukunft, Loccumer Protokolle*, n. 66, 1987. Also in Tugendhat, *Ethik und Politik. Vorträge und Stellungnahmen aus den Jahren 1978–1991*, 80–93. Frankfurt: M. Suhrkamp, 1992.

"Der Begriff der Willensfreiheit." In *Theorie der Subjektivität*, edited by K. Cramer, 373–393. Frankfurt: M. Suhrkamp, 1987. Also in Tugendhat, *Philosophische Aufsätze*, 334–351. Frankfurt: M. Suhrkamp, 1992.

Nachdenken über die Atomkriegsgefahr und warum man sie nicht sieht. Berlin: Rotbuch Verlag, 1987.

"Die Geisteswissenschaften als Aufklärungswissenschaften. Auseinandersetzung mit Odo Marquard" (1988). In Tugendhat, *Philosophische Aufsätze*, 453–463. Frankfurt: M. Suhrkamp, 1992.

"Die Hilflosigkeit der Philosophen angesichts der moralischen Schwierigkeiten von heute." In *Frankfurter Hefte* (October 1989): 927–935. Also in Tugendhat, *Philosophische Aufsätze*, 371–382. Frankfurt: M. Suhrkamp, 1992.

"Überlegungen zur Methode der Philosophie aus analytischer Sicht." In *Zwischenbetrachtungen. Im Prozess der Aufklärung. Jürgen Habermas zum 60. Geburtstag*, edited by A. Honneth et al., 305–317. Frankfurt: M. Suhrkamp, 1989. Also in Tugendhat, *Philosophische Aufsätze*, 261–272. Frankfurt: M. Suhrkamp, 1992.

"Die Hilflosigkeit der Philosophie angesichts der moralischen Herausforderungen unserer Zeit." In *Information Philosophie*, 5–15, Herf 2 (1990).

"Zum Begriff und zur Begründung von Moral." In *Mensch und Moderne. Festschrift für Helmut Fahrenbach*, edited by C. Bellert and N. Müller-Scholl. Würzburg, 1989. Also in Tugendhat, *Philosophische Aufsätze*, 315–333. Frankfurt: M. Suhrkamp, 1992.

"Die Rolle der Identität in der Konstitution der Moral" (1990). In *Moral und Person*, edited by W. Edelstein and G. Nunner-Winkler, 33–47. Frankfurt: M. Suhrkamp, 1993.

"Das Euthanasieproblem und die Redefreihiet." *Die Tageszeitung*, June 6, 1990. Also in Tugendhat, *Ethik und Politik. Vorträge und Stellungnahmen aus den Jahren 1978–1991*, 94–97. Frankfurt: M. Suhrkamp, 1992.

"Korreferat zu Harry Frankfurt, 'On the Necessity of Ideals'" (1990). In Tugendhat, *Philosophische Aufsätze*, 462–467. Frankfurt: M. Suhrkamp, 1992.

"Heideggers Seinsfrage" (1991). In Tugendhat, *Philosophische Aufsätze*, 108–135. Frankfurt: M. Suhrkamp, 1992.

"Der Golfkrieg, Deutschland und Israel." *Die Zeit*, February 22, 1991. Also in Tugendhat, *Ethik und Politik. Vorträge und Stellungnahmen aus den Jahren 1978–1991*, 98–115. Frankfurt: M. Suhrkamp, 1992.

"Das Friedensproblem heute." In *Kursbuch*, 1–12, n. 105 (1991). Also in Tugendhat, *Ethik und Politik. Vorträge und Stellungnahmen aus den Jahren 1978–1991*, 116–132. Frankfurt: M. Suhrkamp, 1992.

"Die Singer-Debate. Zu Rainer Hegselmann und Reinhard Merkel (Hrsg.): Zur Debatte über Euthanasie, Frankfurt 1991." *Die Zeit*, October 18, 1991. Also in Tugendhat, *Ethik und Politik. Vorträge und Stellungnahmen aus den Jahren 1978–1991*, 133–138. Frankfurt: M. Suhrkamp, 1992.

"Rückblick im Herbst 1991." In Tugendhat, *Ethik und Politik. Vorträge und Stellungnahmen aus den Jahren 1978–1991*, 7–16. Frankfurt: M. Suhrkamp, 1992.

"Una nueva concepción de la filosofía moral." In *El derecho, la política y la ética*, edited by D. Sobrevilla. Mexico City: Siglo XXI, 1991.

"Der aufgescheuchte Normativist." In *Dialektischer Normativismus. Michael Theunissen zum 60. Geburtstag*, edited by E. Angehern, 368–371. Frankfurt: M. Suhrkamp, 1992.

Ethik und Politik. Vorträge und Stellungnahmen aus den Jahren 1978–1991. Frankfurt: M. Suhrkamp, 1992.

"Heidegger und Bergson über die Zeit." *Das Argument* 194 (1992): 573–584. Also in Tugendhat, *Aufsätze 1992–2000*, 11–26. Frankfurt: M. Suhrkamp, 2001.

"Identidad: Personal, nacional y universal." In Tugendhat, *Justicia y derechos humanos*. Barcelona: Publicaciones de la Universidad de Barcelona, 1992. Also in Tugendhat, *Problemas*, 15–31. Barcelona: Gedisa, 2002.

Philosophische Aufsätze, Frankfurt: M. Suhrkamp, 1992.

"Das Euthanasieproblem in philosophischer Sicht." *Logos* 1 (1993): H. 2, 123, 138. Also in Tugendhat, *Aufsätze 1992–2000*, 40–56. Frankfurt: M. Suhrkamp, 2001.

"Die Kontroverse über die Menschenrechte." *Analyse und Kritik* 15 (1993): 101–110. In English in *Norms, Values, and Society*, edited by H. Pauer-Studer, 33–41. Dordrecht: Kluwer, 1994. Also in Tugendhat, *Aufsätze 1992–2000*, 27–39. Frankfurt: M. Suhrkamp, 2001.

"El 'yo.'" In *Revista Latinoamericana de Filosofía*, 3–16. Buenos Aires, 1993.

Vorlesungen über Ethik. Frankfurt: M. Suhrkamp, 1993.

"Partikularismus und Universalismus." In *Frieden machen*, edited by D. Senghaas, 324–333. Frankfurt: M. Suhrkamp, 1995. Also in Tugendhat, *Aufsätze 1992–2000*, 57–66. Frankfurt: M. Suhrkamp, 2001.

"Überreden und Begründen." *Deutsche Zeitschrift für Philosophie* 44 (1996): 245–247.

"Gibt es eine moderne Moral?" *Zeitschrift für philosophische Forschung* 50 (1996): 323–338.

Dialog in Leticia. Frankfurt: M. Suhrkamp, 1997.

"Gleichheit und Universalität in der Moral." In *Ernst Tugendhat: Moralbegründung und Gerechtigkeit*, edited by M. Willaschek, 3–25. Münster: LIT-Verlag, 1997.

"Erwiderungen." In *Ernst Tugendhat: Moralbegründung und Gerechtigkeit*, edited by M. Willaschek, 95–93. Münster: LIT-Verlag, 1997.

"Wer sind alle?" In *Naturethik. Grund-texte der gegenwärtigen Tier- und ökoethischen Diskussion*, edited by A. Krebs, 100–110. Frankfurt: M. Suhrkamp, 1997.

"Über den Tod." In *Philosophie in synthetischer Absicht*, edited by M. Stamm, 487–512. Stuttgart: Klett-Cotta, 1998. Also in Tugendhat, *Aufsätze 1992–2000*, 67–90. Frankfurt: M. Suhrkamp, 2001.

"Wissenschaft und Wolken." In *Einladung zum Denken. Ein kleiner Streifzug durch die analytische Philosophie*, edited by D. Borchers et al., 47–52. Vienna, 1998.

"Es gibt keine Gene für die Moral. Sloterdijk stellt das Verhältnis von Ethik und Gentechnik schlicht auf den Kopf." *Die Zeit*, September 23, 1999.

"Was heisst es, moralische Urteile zu begründen?" In Tugendhat, *Aufsätze 1992–2000*, 91–108. Frankfurt: M. Suhrkamp, 2001.

"Schwierigkeiten in Heideggers Umweltanalyse." In *Zwischen Literatur und Philosophie. Festschrift zum 60. Geburtstag von Víctor Farías*, edited by Davis Schidlowsky, Olaf Gaudig, and Peter Veit, 109–137. Berlin: Wissenschaftlicher Verlag Berlin, 2000. Also in Tugendhat, *Aufsätze 1992–2000*, 109–137. Frankfurt: M. Suhrkamp, 2001.

"Wie sollen wir Moral verstehen?" In Tugendhat, *Aufsätze 1992–2000*, 163–185. Frankfurt: M. Suhrkamp, 2001.

"Wir sind nicht fest verdrahtet: Heideggers 'Man' und die Tiefendimensionen der Gründe." In *Anthropologie, Ethik und Gesellschaft*, edited by R. Brunner, 77–100. Frankfurt: M. Suhrkamp, 2000. Also in Tugendhat, *Aufsätze 1992–2000*, 137–162. Frankfurt: M. Suhrkamp, 2001.

"Las raíces antropológicas de la religion y de la mística." In Tugendhat, *Problemas*, 215–228. Barcelona: Gedisa, 2002.

"Macht und Antiegalitarismus bei Nietzsche und Hitler." *Die Zeit* 38 (September 2000). Expanded edition in Tugendhat, *Aufsätze 1992–2000*, 225–261. Frankfurt: M. Suhrkamp, 2001.

"Moral in evolutionstheoretischer Sicht." In Tugendhat, *Aufsätze 1992–2000*, 199–224. Frankfurt: M. Suhrkamp, 2001.

"Nietzsche y la antropología filosófica: el problema de la trascendencia inmanente" (2000). In Tugendhat, *Problemas*, 199–214. Barcelona: Gedisa, 2002.

"Zeit und Sein in Heideggers 'Sein und Zeit.'" *Sats-Nordic Journal of Philosophy* 1 (2000): 13–25. Also in Tugendhat, *Aufsätze 1992–2000*, 185–199. Frankfurt: M. Suhrkamp, 2001.

Aufsätze 1992–2000. Frankfurt: M. Suhrkamp, 2001.

Problemas. Barcelona: Gedisa, 2002. (Spanish translation of *Aufsätze 1992–2000*. Contains three essays not included in the German edition).

Egozentrizität und Mystik. Eine anthropologische Studie. München: Verlag C. H. Beck, 2003.

"Gibt es eine Moral ohne Gefühle?" In *Erwägen, Wissen, Ethik*, 653–655, n. 14 (2003).

"Nachwort zur fünften Auflage" and "Anhang: Wie kam Aristoteles zu seiner Auffassung vom eidos als energeia." In Tugendhat, *TI KATA TINOS*. 5th ed. Friburg/Brisgovia: Verlag Karl Alber, 2003.

"Das Problem einer aufgekläten Moral." In *Aufgeklärten im 21. Jahrhundert*, edited by H. Schmidt-Glintzer, 41–66. Memminged: Herrassowitz Verlag, 2004.

"Unsere Angst vor dem Tod." In *Der Tod im Leben*, edited by F. W. Graf and H. Meier, 47–62. Munich/Zurich (2004).

"Immanente Transzendenz." In *Tübinger Universitätsreden, Neue Folge*, edited by E. Schaich, 43–64, vol. 40. Tübingen, 2004.

"Über SelbstBewusstsein: Einige Missverständnisse." In *Anatomie der Subjektivität. Bewusstsein, Selbstbewusstsein und Selbstgefühl*, edited by T. Grundmann et al., 247–254. Frankfurt: M. Suhrkamp, 2005.

"Sobre mística." *Diálogo Científico* 14, no. 1/2 (2005): 11–21.

"Spiritualität, Religion und Mystik." In *Spiritualität und Wissenschaft*, edited by S. Leutwyler and M. Nägeli, 95–106. Zurich, 2005.

"Das Problem einer autonomen Moral." In *Ernst Tugendhats Ethik. Einwaende und Erwiderungen*, ed. Nico Scarano and Mauricio Suárez, 13–30. München: C. H. Beck, 2006.

"Erwiderungen." In *Ernst Tugendhats Ethik. Einwände und Erwiderungen*, edited by Nico Scarano and Mauricio Suárez, 273–312. München: C. H. Beck, 2006.

Über den Tod. Frankfurt: M. Suhrkamp, 2006.

"Über west-östliche Mystik und höhere Traurigkeit." *Le monde diplomatique*, January 2006.

Anthropologie statt Metaphysik. München: Verlag C. H. Beck, 2007.

E. Tugendhat and Ursula Wolf. *Logisch-semantische Propädeutik*. Stuttgart: Reclam, 1983.

E. Tugendhat, Celso López, and Ana María Vicuña. *Wie sollen wir handeln? Schülergespräche über Moral*. Translated from the Spanish edition. Stuttgart: Reclam, 2000.

B. In English Translation

"The Meaning of 'Bedeutung' in Frege." *Analysis* 30 (1970): 177–189.

"Description as the Method of Philosophy: A Reply to Mr. Pettit." In *Linguistic Analysis and Phenomenology*, edited by W. Mays and S. C. Brown, 256–266. London: MacMillan, 1972.

"Existence in Space and Time." *Neue Hefte für Philosophie* 8 (1975): 14–33.

"Phenomenology and Linguistic Analysis." In *Husserl: Expositions and Appraisals*, edited and translated by F. Elliston and P. McCormick. Notre Dame, Ind.: University of Notre Dame Press, 1977.

"The Fusion of Horizons: Review of Hans-Georg Gadamer, *Truth and Method* and *Philosophical Hermeneutics*." *Times Literary Supplement*, May 19, 1978. Also in Tugendhat, *Philosophische Aufsätze*, 426–432. Frankfurt: M. Suhrkamp, 1992.

"Comments on Some Methodological Aspects of Rawl's 'Theory of Justice.'" *Analyse und Kritik* 1 (1979): 77–89.

Traditional and Analytical Philosophy: Lectures on the Philosophy of Language. Translated by P. A. Gorner. Cambridge: Cambridge University Press, 1982.

"Language Analysis and the Critique of Ontology." In *Contemporary German Philosophy*, edited by Darrel E. Christensen, translated by J. S. Fulton and K. Kolenda, 2:100–111. State College: Pennsylvania State University Press, 1983.

"The Question About Being and Its Foundation in Language (on Charles H. Kahn, "The Verb 'Be' In Ancient Greek")." In *Contemporary German Philosophy*, edited by Darrel E. Christensen, translated by David Mallon, 3:259–370. State College: Pennsylvania State University Press, 1983.

"Ancient and Modern Ethics." In *Contemporary German Philosophy*, edited by Darrel E. Christensen, translated by Martin Livingston, 4:32–48. State College: Pennsylvania State University Press, 1984.

"Habermas' Concept of Communicative Action." In *Social Action*, edited by G. Seebass and R. Tuomela, 179–186. Dordrecht: D. Reidel, 1985. Also in Tugendhat, *Philosophische Aufsätze*, 433–440. Frankfurt: M. Suhrkamp, 1992.

Self-Consciousness and Self-Determination. Translated by Paul Stern. Cambridge, Mass.: MIT Press, 1986.

"The Necessity for Cooperation Between Philosophical and Empirical Research." In *The Moral Domain: Essays in the Ongoing Discussion Between Philosophy and Social Sciences*, edited by Thomas E. Wren, 3–14. Cambridge, Mass.: MIT Press, 1990.

"Mead: Symbolic Interaction and the Self." In *Philosophy, Social Theory, and the Thought of George Herbert Mead*, edited by Mitchell Aboulafia, 169–200. Albany: State University of New York Press, 1991. (Lectures 11 and 12 of *Self-Consciousness and Self-Determination*.)

"Reflections on Philosophical Method from an Analytic Point of View." In *Philosophical Interventions in the Unfinished Project of Enlightenment*, edited by Axel Honneth, 113–124. Cambridge, Mass.: MIT Press, 1992.

"Liberalism, Liberty, and the Issue of Economic Human Rights." In Tugendhat, *Philosophische Aufsätze*, 352–370. Frankfurt: M. Suhrkamp, 1992.

"Topic and Method of Philosophy in Wittgenstein." In *A Wittgenstein Symposium*, edited by Josep-Maria Terricabras, 9–14. Amsterdam: Rodopi, 1993.

"The Role of Identity in the Constitution of Morality." In *Moral Self: Building a Better Paradigm*, edited by Gil G. Noam and Thomas Wren, 3–15. Cambridge, Mass.: MIT Press, 1993.

"Justice." In *Norms, Values, and Society*, edited by H. Pauder-Studer, 1–12. Dordrecht: Kluwer, 1994.

"The Controversy About Human Rights." *Norms, Values, and Society*, ed. H. Pauer-Studer, 33–41. Dordrecht: Kluwer, 1994.

"Notes on Some Methodological Aspects of Rawls' Theory of Justice." *Filozoficky Casopis* 42 (1994): 966–980.

"The Moral Dilemma in the Rescue of Refugees." *Social Research* 62, no. 1 (Spring 1995): 129–142.

"Heidegger's Idea of Truth." In *Hermeneutics and Truth*, edited by Brice Wachterhauser, translated by Christopher Macann, 83–97. Evanston, Ill.: Northwestern University Press, 1994. This essay was also appears in *Critical Heidegger*, edited and translated by C. Macann, 227–240. London: Routledge, 1996.

"Heidegger on the Relation of Oneself to Oneself: Choosing Oneself." In *Heidegger Reexamined: Dasein, Authenticity, and Death*, edited by Hubert Dreyfus and Mark Wrathall, 248–266. New York: Routledge, 2002. (Lectures 8, 9, and 10 of *Self-Consciousness and Self-Determination*.)

"Habermas on Communicative Action." In *Jürgen Habermas*, edited by David Rasmussen and James Swindal, 216–222. London: SAGE, 2002.

"Justification in Bernard Gert's Moral Theory." In *Rationality, Rules, and Ideals. Critical Essays on Bernard Gert's Moral Theory*, edited by W. Sinnott-Armstrong and R. Audi, 17–29. Lanham, Md.: Rowman & Littlefield, 2003.

"Universalistically Approved Intersubjective Attitudes: Adam Smith." Translated by Bernard Schriebl. *The Adam Smith Review* 1 (2004): 88–104.

2. OTHER WORKS

Ackrill, J. L. "E. Tugendhat. *TI KATA TINOS*." *Gnomon* 32 (1960): 774–775.

Allan, D. J. "E. Tugendhat, *TI KATA TINOS*." *The Classical Review* 75 (1961): 221–222.

Allen, Barry. *Truth in Philosophy*. Cambridge, Mass.: Harvard University Press, 1993.

Apel, Karl-Otto. *Toward a Transformation of Philosophy*. Translated by Glyn Adey and David Frisby. Boston: Routledge and Kegan Paul, 1980.

———. "Comments on Professor Pöggeler's Paper." In *Phenomenology: Dialogues and Bridges*, edited by R. Bruzina and B. Wilshire, 99–106. Albany: State University of New York Press, 1982.

———. "Wittgenstein and Heidegger: Language Games and Life Forms." In *Critical Heidegger*, edited by C. Macann, 241–274. London. Routledge, 1996.

———. "Regulative Ideas or Truth-Happening? An Attempt to Answer the Question of the Conditions of the Possibility of Valid Understanding." In *The Philosophy of Hans-Georg Gadamer*, edited by Lewis Edwin Hahn, translated by Ralf Sommermeier, 67–94. Chicago: Open Court, 1997.

Aubenque, Pierre. "Review of E. Tugendhat, *TI KATA TINOS*." *Revue des etudes Grecques* 73 (1960): 300–301.

———. *Le problème de l'être chez Aristote*. Paris: Press Universitaires de France, 1962.

Bäck, T. Allan. *Aristotle's Theory of Predication*. Leiden: Brill, 2000.

Badiou, Alain. *Being and Event*. 1988. Translated by Oliver Feltham. New York: Continuum, 2005.

———. *Manifesto for Philosophy*. Edited by Norman Madarasz. New York: State University of New York Press, 1999.

———. *Theoretical Writings*. Edited by Ray Brassier and Alberto Toscano. New York: Continuum, 2004.

Barth, Hans-Martin. "Egozentrizität, Mystik und christlicher Glaube: Eine Auseinandersetzung mit Ernst Tugendhat." *Neue Zeitschrift für Systematische Theologie und Religionsphilosophie* 4, no. 46 (2004): 467–482.

Barthes, Roland. *Elements of Semiology*. New York: Hill and Wang, 1977.

Beaney, M., ed. *The Frege Reader*. London: Blackwell, 1997.

Benoist, Jocelyn. *Représentations sans objet. Aux origines de la phénoménologie et de la philosophie analytique*. Paris: Press Universitaires de France, 2001.

Bleicher, Joseph. *Contemporary Hermeneutics: Hermeneutics as Method, Philosophy, and Critique*. London: Routledge and Kegan Paul, 1980.

Borcher, D., O. Brill, and U. Czaniera, eds. *Einladung zum Denken. Eine Kleiner Streifzug durch die Analytische Philosophie.* Vienna: Verlag Hölder-Pichler-Tempsky, 1998.

Bouveresse, Jacques. "L'autonomie de la conscience, Ernst Tugendhat: SelbstBewusstsein und Selbsbestimmung." *Critique* 38 (1982): 861–865.

———. *Herméneutique et linguistique. Suivi de 'Wittgenstein et la philosophie du langage.'* Combas: Éditions de Éclat, 1991.

Bowie, Andrew. "Review Essay: 'Ernst Tugendhat, Philosophische Aufsätze.'" *European Journal of Philosophy* 2/3 (1994): 345–351.

———. *Schelling and Modern European Philosophy: An Introduction.* London: Routledge, 1994.

———. "German Philosophy Today: Between Idealism, Romanticism, and Pragmatism." In *German Philosophy Since Kant,* edited by Anthony O'Hear, 375–398. Cambridge: Cambridge University Press, 1999.

———. *Introduction to German Philosophy: From Kant to Habermas.* London: Polity Press, 2003.

Brand, G. "E. Tugendhat. *Der Wahrheitsbegriff bei Husserl und Heidegger.*" *Philosophische Rundschau* 17 (1970): 77–94.

Brandom, Robert. *Making It Explicit.* Cambridge, Mass.: Harvard University Press, 1994.

———. *Articulating Reasons: An Introduction to Inferentialism.* Cambridge, Mass.: Harvard University Press, 2000.

———, ed. *Rorty and His Critics.* Oxford: Blackwell, 2000.

———. *Tales of the Mighty Dead: Historical Essays in the Metaphysics of Intentionality.* Cambridge, Mass.: Harvard University Press, 2002.

———. "Hegelian Pragmatism and Social Emancipation." An interview with Robert Brandom by Italo Testa. *Constellations* 10, no. 4 (December 2003): 554–570.

———. "Interview with R. Brandom by Carlo Penco." *Epistemologia* 22 (1999): 143–150.

Braum, E. "E. Tugendhat *TI KATA TINOS.*" *Archives de Philosophie* 23 (1959): 624–626.

Brenner, W. "Traditional and Analytical Philosophy: Lectures on the Philosophy of Language, E. Tugendhat." *International Studies in Philosophy* 18, no. 3 (1986): 105–106.

Brezina, F. *Die Achtung. Ethik und Moral der Achtung und Unterwerfung bei Immanuel Kant, Ernst Tugendhat, Ursula Wolf und Peter Singer.* Frankfurt: Peter Lang Europäischer Verlag der Wissenschaften, 1999.

Brinkmann, K. "Tugendhat on Fichte and Self-Consciousness." In *Fichte: Historical Contexts/Contemporary Controversies*, edited by D. Breazeale and T. Rockmore, 220–233. Atlantic Highlands, N.J.: Humanities Press, 1994.

Brogan, W. *Heidegger and Aristotle: The Twofoldness of Being*. New York: State University of New York Press, 2005.

Brogan, W., and J. Risser, eds. *American Continental Philosophy: A Reader*. Bloomington: Indiana University Press, 2000.

Bruns, Gerald L. *Hermeneutics: Ancient and Modern*. New Haven, Conn.: Yale University Press, 1992.

Brunschwig, J. "E. Tugendhat, *TI KATA TINOS*." *Revue Philosophique de la France et del'Etranger* 88 (1963): 286–289.

Bruzina, R., and B. Wilshire, eds. *Phenomenology: Dialogues and Bridges*. Albany: State University of New York Press, 1982.

Bubner, Rüdiger. *Modern German Philosophy*. Cambridge: Cambridge University Press, 1981.

———. *Essays in Hermeneutics and Critical Theory*. Translated by Eric Matthews. New York: Columbia University Press, 1988.

———. *Zur Wirkung der analytischen Philosophie in Deutschland*. In *Die sog. Geisteswissenschaften*, edited by W. Prinz and P. Weingart, 448–458. Frankfurt: M. Suhrkamp, 1990.

Bubner, Rüdiger, K. Cramer, and R. Weihl, eds. *Hermeneutik und Dialektik*. 2 vols. Tübingen: J. C. B. Mohr, 1970.

Carman, Taylor. *Heidegger's Analytic: Interpretation, Discourse, and Authenticity in* Being and Time. Cambridge: Cambridge University Press, 2003.

Carnap, R. "The Elimination of Metaphysics Through Logical Analysis of Language." 1932. In *Logical Positivism*, edited by A. J. Ayer, 60–81. New York: Free Press, 1959.

Cavell, Stanley. *Philosophical Passages: Wittgestein, Emerson, Austin, Derrida*. Cambridge, Mass.: Blackwell, 1995.

Chomsky, Noam. *Cartesian Linguistics: A Chapter in the History of Rationalist Thought*. New York: Harper and Row, 1966.

———. *Language and Politics*. Edited by C. P. Otero. Oakland, Calif.: AK Press, 2004.

———. *Rules and Representations*. New York: Columbia University Press, 2005.

Cobb-Stevens, R. *Husserl and Analytic Philosophy*. Dordrecht: Kluwer, 1990.

Coltman, Rod. *The Language of Hermeneutics: Gadamer and Heidegger in Dialogue*. Albany: State University of New York Press, 1998.

Constantineau, P. "L'éthique par-delà la sémantique et la pragmatique." *Critique* 42 (1986): 1210–1224.

Critchley, Simon. *Continental Philosophy: A Very Short Introduction.* Oxford: Oxford University Press, 2001.

Crothers, Maurucio Suárez. "La odisea del filósofo Ernst Tugendhat." *Diálogo Científico* 14, no. 1/2 (2005): 32–36.

Crowell, Steven. "Traditional and Analytical Philosophy: Lectures on the Philosophy of Language. Ernst Tugendhat." *International Philosophical Quarterly* 24 (1984): 95–97.

Crowell, Steven, and J. Malpas, eds. *Transcendental Heidegger.* Stanford, Calif.: Stanford University Press, 2007.

D'Agostini, Franca. *Analitici e continentali. Guida alla filosofia degli ultimi trent'anni.* Milan: Cortina, 1997.

————. *Breve storia della filosofia nel Novecento. L'anomalia paradigmatica.* Turin: Einaudi Editore, 1999.

————. *Logica del nichilismo. Dialettica, differenza, ricorsività.* Rome-Bari: Laterza, 2000.

————. "From a Continental Point of View." *International Journal of Philosophical Studies* 3, no. 9 (2001): 349–367.

————. *Disavventure della verità.* Turin: Einaudi Editore, 2002.

————. "Redefining Human Beings—Where Politics Meets Metaphysics." In *International Intervention in the Post-Cold-War: Moral Responsibility and Power Policies,* edited by M. C. Davies et al., 145–159. New York: M. E. Sharpe, 2003.

————. "The Epistemological Liar: The Many Ways in Which It Is Not True That There Is Not Truth." *Croatian Journal of Philosophy* 3, no. 8 (2003): 125–144.

Dahlstrom, Daniel O. *Das logische Vorurteil. Untersuchengen zur Wahrheitstheorie des frühen Heidegger.* Vienna: Passagen Verlag, 1994.

————. *Heidegger's Concept of Truth.* Cambridge: Cambridge University Press, 2001.

————. "The Clearing and Its Truth: Reflections on Tugendhat's Criticisms and Heidegger's Concessions." *Études Phénoménologiques* 37–38 (2003): 3–25.

————. "Editor's Afterword." In M. Heidegger, *Introduction to Phenomenological Research,* 245–252. Bloomington: Indiana University Press, 2005.

D'Amico, R. *Contemporary Continental Philosophy.* Boulder, Colo.: Westview Press, 1999.

Davidson, Donald. *Truth and Predication.* Cambridge, Mass.: Harvard University Press, 2005.

De Libera, Alan. *La référence vide. Théories de la proposition.* Paris: Presses Universitaires de France, 2002.

Delius, Harald. *Self-Awareness: A Semantical Inquiry.* München: C. H. Beck, 1981.

Demmerling, C. "Richtiges Handeln, Identität und Glück. Zur Moralphilosophie Ernst Tugendhat." *Philosophische Rundschau* 42 (1995): 137–146.

Derrida, Jacques. *Of Grammatology.* 1967. Translated by G. Chakravorty Spivak. Baltimore, Md.: The Johns Hopkins University Press, 1997.

———. *Dissemination.* 1972. Translated by B. Johnson. Chicago: University of Chicago Press, 1981.

———. *Writing and Difference.* Translated by Alan Bass. Chicago: University of Chicago Press; London: Routledge and Kegan Paul, 1978.

———. *Edmund Husserl's Origin of Geometry: An Introduction.* Translated by John P. Leavey Jr. Lincoln: University of Nebraska Press, 1989.

De Rijk, L. M. *Through Language to Reality: Studies on Mediaeval Semantics and Metaphysics.* Edited by E. P. Bos. Northampton, Mass.: Variorum, 1989.

———. *Semantics and Ontology.* Vol. 1, *General Introduction: The Works on Logic.* Vol. 2, *The Metaphysics: Semantics in Aristotle's Strategy of Argument.* Leiden: E. J. Brill, 1994.

Descombes, Vincent. "La Philosophie comme science rigoureusement descriptive." *Critique* 37 (1981): 351–375.

———. *Objects of All Sorts.* Translated by Lorna Scott-Fox and Jeremy Harding. Baltimore, Md.: The Johns Hopkins University Press, 1986.

———. *Le complément de sujet.* Paris: Gallimard, 2004.

Dostal, R. J. "The Experience of Truth for Gadamer and Heidegger: Taking Time and Sudden Lightning." In *Hermeneutics and Truth,* edited by Brice Wachterhauser, 49–50. Evanston, Ill.: Northwestern University Press, 1994.

———, ed. *The Cambridge Companion to Gadamer.* Cambridge: Cambridge University Press, 2002.

Dreyfus, Hubert L. *Being-in-the-World: A Commentary on Heidegger's Being and Time, Division 1.* Cambridge, Mass.: MIT Press, 1991.

Dummett, Michael. *Frege: Philosophy of Language.* London: Duckworth, 1973.

———. *Truth and Other Enigmas.* London: Duckworth, 1978.

———. *Origins of Analytical Philosophy.* Cambridge, Mass.: Harvard University Press, 1993.

Elliott, Brian. *Phenomenology and Imagination in Husserl and Heidegger.* London: Routledge, 2004.

Elliston, F., and P. McCormick, eds. *Husserl: Expositions and Appraisals.* South Bend, Ind.: University of Notre Dame Press, 1977.

Engel, Pascal. *La dispute. Une introduction à la philosophie analytique.* Paris: Éditions de Minuit, 1997.

———, ed. "Philosophy and the Analytic-Continental Divide." *Stanford French Review,* special number (1994).

Enskat, R. "Von der Semantik zur Seinsfrage E. Tugendhat (review of E. Tugendhat, *Philosophische Aufsätze*)" *Philosophische Rundschau* 2 (1994): 101–115.

Esfeld, Michael. "What Heidegger's *Being and Time* Tells Today's Analytic Philosophy." *Philosophical Explorations* 4 (2001): 46–62.

Faulconer, James E., and Mark A. Wrathall, eds. *Appropriating Heidegger.* Cambridge: Cambridge University Press, 2000.

Frank, Herman. "La Critique Analytique de l'Ontologie." In *Essays in Semiotics,* edited by J. Kristeva, 28–30. The Hague: Mouton & Co, 1971.

Frank, Manfred. *Die Unhintergehbarkeit der Individualität. Reflexionen über Subjekt, Person und Individuum aus Anlass ihrer "postmodernen" Toterklärung.* Frankfurt: M. Suhrkamp, 1986.

———. *What Is Neostructuralism?* Translated by S. Wilke and R. Gray. Minneapolis: University of Minnesota Press, 1989.

———, ed. *Analytische Theorien des Selbstbewusstseins.* Frankfurt: M. Suhrkamp, 1994.

———. *The Subject and the Text: Essays on Literary Theory and Philosophy.* Edited by A. Bowie. Translated by Helen Atkins. Cambridge: Cambridge University Press, 1998.

———. "Style in Philosophy." Translated by J. Jansen and M. K. Shim. *Metaphilosophy* 30, no. 4 (1999): 265–301.

———. "Against Apriori Intersubjectivism. An Alternative Inspired by Sartre." In *Critical Theory After Habermas: Encounters and Departures,* edited by Dieter Freundlieb, Wayne Hudson, and John Rundell, 259–279. Leiden: Brill Academic Publishers, 2004.

Gadamer, H.-G. *Truth and Method.* 1960. Translated by Joel Weinsheimer and Donald G. Marshall. London: Continuum, 2004.

———. *Philosophical Hermeneutics.* Translated by David E. Linge. Berkeley: University of California Press, 1976.

———. "Boundaries of Language." 1985. In *Language and Linguisticality in Gadamer's Hermeneutics,* edited by Lawrence K. Schmidt, 9–17. Lanham, Mass.: Lexington Books, 2000.

―――. "Ethos und Ethik (MacIntyre u. a)." *Philosophische Rundschau* 32 (1985): 1–26.

―――. "Reply to My Critics." In *Hermeneutic Tradition: From Ast to Ricoeur*, edited by Gayle L. Ormiston and Alan D. Schrift, translated by G. H. Leiner, 273–297. Albany: State University of New York Press, 1990.

―――. *Hans-Georg Gadamer on Education, Poetry, and History: Applied Hermeneutics.* Edited by Dieter Misgeld and Graeme Nicholson. Translated by Lawrence Schmidt and Monica Reuss. Albany: State University of New York Press, 1992.

―――. *The Philosophy of Hans-Georg Gadamer.* Edited by Lewis Edwin Hahn. Library of Living Philosophers 24. Chicago: Open Court Press, 1997.

―――. *Gadamer in Conversation: Reflections and Commentary.* Edited by Richard Palmer. New Haven, Conn.: Yale University Press, 2003.

Gasché, Rodolphe. *The Tain of the Mirror: Derrida and the Philosophy of Reflection.* Cambridge, Mass.: Harvard University Press, 1986.

―――. *Views and Interviews: On 'Deconstruction' in America.* Aurora, Colo.: Davies Group, 2007.

Gethmann, C. F. "Heideggers Wahreitskonzeption in seinen Marburger Vorlesungen." In *Forum für Philosophie Bad Homburg. Martin Heidegger: Innen- und Aussenansichten*, 101–130. Frankfurt: Suhrkamp, 1989.

Gipper, Helmut. *Das Sprachapriori: Sprache als Voraussetzung menschlichen Denkens und Erkennens.* Stuttgart: Frommann-Holzboog, 1987.

―――. "Zu Heideggers Wahrheitsbegriff." *Kant-Studien* 65 (1974): 186–200.

Glock, H.-J. "The Object of Philosophy: Tugendhat's Semantical Transformation of Ontology." *Cogito* 3, no. 8 (1994): 234–241.

Gómez-Lobo, Alfonso. "E. Tugendhat, *TI KATA TINOS*, Eine Untersuchung zu Struktur und Ursprung aristotelischer Grundbegriffe." Freiburg, 1958. *Revista de Filosofía* (Chile) 8 (1961): 129–130.

Gosepath, S. "Ernst Tugendhat." In *Philosophie der Gegenwart in Einzeldarstellungen von Adorno bis v. Wright*, edited by J. Nida-Rümelin, 752–754. Stuttgart: Kröner Verlag, 1999.

Greve, Jens. "Heideggers Wahrheitskonzeption in Sein und Zeit: Die Interpretation von Ernst Tugendhat und Carl Friedrich Gethmann." *Zeitschrift für philosophische Forschung* 54, no. 2 (April–June 2000): 263.

Grondin, Jean. *Le tournant dans la pensée de Martin Heidegger.* Paris: Presses Universitaires de France, 1987.

―――. "Hermeneutical Truth and Its Historical Presuppositions. A Possible Bridge Between Analysis and Hermeneutics." In *Anti-Foundationalism and*

Practical Reasoning, edited by Evan Simpson, 45–58. Edmonton: Academic Printing and Publishing, 1987.

———. "La contribution silencieuse de Husserl à l'hermeneutique." *Philosophiques* 22 (1993): 383–393.

———. *Der Sinn der Hermeneutik.* Darmstadt: Wissenschaftliche Buchgesellschaft, 1994.

———. *Introduction to Philosophical Hermeneutics.* Translated by Joel Weinsheimer. New Haven, Conn.: Yale University Press, 1994.

———. *Sources of Hermeneutics.* Albany: State University of New York Press, 1995.

———. "Continental or Hermeneutical Philosophy: The Tragedies of Understanding in the Analytic and Continental Perspectives." In *Interrogating the Tradition: Hermeneutics and the History of Philosophy*, edited by J. Sallis and J. Scott, 75–83. Albany: State University of New York Press, 2000.

———. *Hans-Georg Gadamer. A Biography.* Translated by Joel Weinsheimer. New Haven, Conn.: Yale University Press, 2003.

———. *The Philosophy of Gadamer.* Montreal: McGill-Queen's University Press, 2003.

Guess, R. *Morality, Culture, and History: Essays on German Philosophy.* Cambridge: Cambridge University Press, 1999.

Guzzoni, G. "Ernst Tugendhat, *TI KATA TINOS.*" *Il Pensiero* 6, no. 1 (1961): 216–220.

———. "Ernst Tugendhat Der Wahrheitsbegriff bei Husserl und Heidegger." *Il Pensiero* 16, no. 1 (1971): 91–93.

Habermas, Jürgen. "Hans-Georg Gadamer: Urbanizing the Heideggerian Province." In *Philosophical-Political Profiles*, translated by Frederick Lawrence. Cambridge, Mass.: MIT Press, 1983.

———. *The Theory of Communicative Action.* Vol. 2, *Lifeword and System: A Critique of Functionalist Reason.* Translated by Thomas McCarthy. Boston: Beacon Press, 1985.

———. *The Philosophical Discourse of Modernity: Twelve Lectures.* Translated by Frederick G. Lawrence. Cambridge, Mass.: MIT Press, 1987.

———. *Moral Consciousness and Communicative Action.* Translated by Thomas McCarthy. Cambridge: Polity Press, 1992.

———. *Postmetaphysical Thinking.* Translated by William M. Hohengarten. Cambridge, Mass.: MIT Press, 1994.

———. *The Inclusion of the Other: Studies in Political Theory.* 1996. Cambridge, Mass.: MIT Press, 1998.

————. "Richard Rorty's Pragmatic Turn." In *Rorty and His Critics*, edited by R. Brandom, 31–55. Oxford: Blackwell, 2000.

————. *Pragmatics of Social Interaction*. Cambridge, Mass.: MIT Press, 2002.

————. *The Theory of Communicative Action*. Vol. 1, *Reason and the Rationalization of Society*. Translated by Thomas McCarthy. Cambridge: Polity Press, 2004.

————. "After Historicism, Is Metaphysics Still Possible? On Hans-Georg Gadamer's 100th Birthday." In *Gadamer's Repercussions: Reconsidering Philosophical Hermeneutics*, edited by Bruce Krajewski, 15–20. Berkeley: University of California Press, 2004.

Haeffner, G. "Grammatik des Geistes. Zu Tugendhats Analyse des Selbsbewusstsein und der Selbsbestimmung." *Teologie und Philosophie* 55 (1980): 250–259.

Harman, Graham. *Tool-Being: Heidegger and the Metaphysical of Objects*. Chicago: Open Court, 2002.

Harries, Karsten. "On the Power and Limit of Transcendental Reflection." In *From Kant to Davidson: Philosophy and the Idea of the Transcendental*, edited by J. Malpas, 139–161. London: Routledge, 2002.

Harrington, A. *Hermeneutical Dialogue and Social Science: A Critique of Gadamer and Habermas*. London: Routledge, 2001.

Hegel, G. W. F. *Science of Logic*. Translated by A. V. Miller. Oxford: Oxford University Press, 1969.

Heidegger, Martin. *Being and Time*. 1927. Translated by Joan Stambaugh. New York: State University of New York Press, 1996.

————. *Off the Beaten Track*. 1950. Translated by Julian Young and Kenneth Haynes. Cambridge: Cambridge University Press, 2002.

————. *Introduction to Metaphysics*. 1953. Translated by Gregory Fried and Richard Polt. New Haven, Conn.: Yale University Press, 2000.

————. *Identity and Difference*. 1957. Translated by Joan Stambaugh. Chicago: University of Chicago Press, 2002.

————. *On the Way to Language*. 1959. Translated by Peter D. Hertz. New York: Harper and Row, 1982.

————. "Preface." 1962. In *Heidegger: Through Phenomenology to Thought*, edited by William Richardson, xiii–xxiii. New York: Fordham University Press, 2003.

————. *Pathmarks*. 1967. Edited by William McNeill. Cambridge, Mass.: MIT Press, 2002.

————. *On Time and Being*. 1969. Translated by B. Johnson. Chicago: University of Chicago Press, 2002.

————. *The Basic Problems of Phenomenology*. Translated by Albert Hofstadter. Bloomington: Indiana University Press, 1982.

————. *Logic: The Question of Truth*. Edited by Thomas Sheehan and Corinne Painter. Bloomington: Indiana University Press, forthcoming.

Heintel, E. "Ernst Tugendhat Der Wahrheitsbegriff bei Husserl und Heidegger." *Wiener Jahrbuch für Philosophie* 2 (1969): 300–303.

Henrich, D. "Noch einmal in Zirkeln. Eine Kritik von Ernst Tugendhat semantischer Erklärung von SelbsBewusstsein." In *Mensch und Moderne*, edited by C. Bellut and U. Müller-Schöll, 93–132. Würzburg: Königshausen y Neuman, 1989.

Hermann, F. von. *Der Begriff der Phänomenologie in Heidegger und Husserl*. Frankfurt: Vittorio Klostermann Verlag, 1981.

————. "Way and Method: Hermeneutic Phenomenology in Thinking the History of Being." In *Critical Heidegger*, edited by C. Macann, 171–190. London: Routledge, 1996.

Hinchman, Lewis. "Autonomy, Individuality, and Self-Determination." In *What Is Enlightenment? Eighteenth-Century Answers and Twentieth-Century Questions*, edited by James Schmidt, 488–516. Berkeley: University of California Press, 1996.

Hodge, Joanna. *Heidegger and Ethics*. London: Routledge, 1995.

Höffe, O. "Ist die Transzentale Vernunftkritik in der Sprachphilosophie aufgehoben? Eine programmatische Auseinandersetzung mit Ernst Tugendhat und Karl-Otto Apel." *Philosophische Jahrbuch* 91 (1984): 250–272.

Honderich, Ted. "Tugendhat, Ernst." In *The Oxford Companion to Philosophy*, 883. New York: Oxford University Press.

Horn, P. R. *Gadamer and Wittgenstein on the Unity of Language: Reality and Discourse Without Metaphysics*. London: Ashgate, 2005.

Hrachovec, Herbert. "Unterwegs zur Sprachanalyse. Über Jacques Derrida zu Ernst Tugendhat." In *Zur philosophischen Aktualität Heidegger's*, vol. 2, *Im Gespräch der Zeit*, edited by D. Papenfuss and O. Pöggeler, 284–295. Frankfurt: 1990–1991.

————. "Deletion or Deployment: Is That Any Way to Treat a Sign?" In *Questioning Foundations. Truth/Subjectivity/Culture*, edited by H. Silverman, 61–78. London: Routledge, 1993.

Husserl, Edmund. *Ideas Pertaining to a Pure Phenomenology and to a Phenomenological Philosophy: First Book: General Introduction to a Pure Phenomenology*. 1913. Translated by F. Kersten. New York: Sprinter, 1983.

————. *Logical Investigations.* Translated by J. N. Findlay. 2 vols. New York: Humanities Press, 1977.

Inwood, Michael J. *A Heidegger Dictionary.* Oxford: Blackwell, 1999.

Jopling, David A. *Self-Knowledge and the Self.* New York: Routledge, 2000.

Kant, Immanuel. "The Only Possible Argument in Support of a Demonstration of the Existence of God." 1763. In Kant, *Theoretical Philosophy, 1755–1770,* 107–202. Cambridge: Cambridge University Press, 1992.

Keller, Pierre. *Husserl and Heidegger on Human Experience.* Cambridge: Cambridge University Press, 1999.

Kisiel, Theodore. *The Genesis of Heidegger's* Being and Time. Berkeley: University of California Press, 1993.

Klostermann, Vittorio. *Durchblicke. Festschrift für Martin Heidegger.* Frankfurt: Klostermann, 1970.

Kolenda, Konstantin. "Ernst Tugendhat, Vorlesungen zur Einfuehrung in die sprachanalytische Philosophie." In *Contemporary German Philosophy,* edited by Darrel E. Christensen, 1:253–262. University Park: The Pennsylvania State University Press, 1982.

Krajewski, Bruce, ed. *Gadamer's Repercussions: Reconsidering Philosophical Hermeneutics.* Berkeley: University of California Press, 2004.

Kramer, H. "E. Tugendhat Probleme der Ethik." *Allgemeine Zeitschrift für Philosophie* 11 (1986): 31–35.

Krebs, A. "Moral und Gemeinschaft. Eine Kritik an Tugendhat." *Zeitschrift für Philosophische Forschung* 1 (1997): 93–102.

Krusch, Martin. *Language as Calculus Versus Language as Universal Medium: A Study in Husserl, Heidegger, and Gadamer.* Dordrecht: Kluwer, 1989.

Lafont, Cristina. *The Linguistic Turn in Hermeneutic Philosophy.* Cambridge, Mass.: MIT Press, 1999.

————. *Heidegger, Language, and World-Disclosure.* Cambridge, Mass.: MIT Press, 2000.

Lange, E. M. "Quasprädikate die Verständlichkeit der Bezugnahme auf Gegenstände bei Tugendhat." *Zeitschrift für Philosophische Forschung* 34 (1980): 79–87.

Larmore, Charles. *Les practiques du moi.* Paris: Presses Universitaires de France, 2004.

————. "*Self-Consciousness and Self-Determination,* E. Tugendhat." *The Philosophical Review* 1 (January 1989): 104–107.

Lawn, C. *Wittgenstein and Gadamer: Towards a Post-Analytic Philosophy of Language.* London: Continuum, 2005.

Lemaigre, B.-M. "Ernst Tugendhat. Der Wahrheitsbegriff bei Husserl und Heidegger." *Revue des Sciences Philosophiques et Theologiques* 52 (1968): 293–396.

Long, C. P. *The Ethics of Ontology: Rethinking an Aristotelian Legacy*. New York: State University of New York Press, 2004.

Lütterfelds, W. *Bin ich nur öffentliche Person? E. Tugendhats Idealismuskritik (Fiche)—ein Anstoss zur transzendentalen Sprachanalyse (Wittgenstein)*. Forum Academicum in der Verlagsgruppe Athenäum. Hain: Scriptor, Hanstein, 1982.

Malowitz, K. "Ernst Tugendhat und die Diskursethik—Notizen zu einem Widerlegungsprogramm." *Zeitschrift für Philosophische Forschung* 4 (1995): 595–604.

Malpas, J. *Heidegger's Topology: Being, Place, World*. Cambridge, Mass.: MIT Press, 2007.

Malpas, J., U. Arnswald, and J. Kertscher, eds. *Gadamer's Century*. Cambridge, Mass.: MIT Press, 2002.

Marconi, Diego. "Ernst Tugendhat, Introduzione alla filosofia analitica." *L'indice* 10 (1989).

————. *Lexical Competence (Language, Speech, and Communication)*. Cambridge, Mass.: MIT Press, 1997.

Marion, Jean-Luc. *Reduction and Givenness: Investigations of Husserl, Heidegger, and Phenomenology*. Translated by T. O. Carlson. Evanston, Ill.: Northwestern University Press, 1998.

Marrati, P. *Genesis and Trace: Derrida Reading Husserl and Heidegger*. Stanford, Calif.: Stanford University Press, 2005.

Mauersberg, B. *Der lange Abschied von der Bewusstseinsphilosophie. Theorie der Subjektivität bei Habermas und Tugendhat nach dem Paradigmenwechsel zur Sprache*. Frankfurt: Peter Lang Europäischer Verlag der Wissenschaften, 2000.

McNeill, William. *The Glance of the Eye: Heidegger, Aristotle, and the Ends of Theory*. Albany: State University of New York Press, 1999.

Meuter, N. *Das Problem der personalen Identität im Anschluss an Ernst Tugendhat, Niklas Luhmann und Paul Ricoeur*. Stuttgart: M. and P. Verlag für Wissenschaft und Forschung, 1995.

Moran, Dermot. *Introduction to Phenomenology*. London: Routledge, 2000.

————. Introduction to *Logical Investigations*, by E. Husserl, 1:xxi–lxxiii. London: Routledge, 2001.

Morard, M.-S. "E. Tugendhat, *TI KATA TINOS*." *Zeitschrift für Philosophie und Teologie* 6 (1959): 321–324.

Mulligan, Kevin. "Continental and Analytic Philosophy." Letter to the editor, *Times Literary Supplement*, July 24, 1998.

Nagel, Thomas. *The View from Nowhere*. New York: Oxford University Press, 1986.

Newman, Andrew. *The Correspondence Theory of Truth: An Essay on the Metaphysics of Predication*. Cambridge: Cambridge University Press, 2002.

Nink, S. J. "E. Tugendhat, *TI KATA TINOS*." *Scholastik* 34 (1959): 435–436.

Niznik, J., and J. T. Sanders, eds. *Debating the State of Philosophy: Habermas, Rorty, and Kolakowski*. Westport, Conn.: Praeger Publishers, 1996.

Obermeier, O.-P. "Ernst Tugendhats Kritik an Heidegger." In *Martin Heidegger Unterwegs im Denken*, edited by R. Wisser, 293–326. Freiburg/Munich: Alber, 1987.

Ormiston, Gayle L., and Alan D. Schrift, eds. *Transforming the Hermeneutic Context: From Nietzsche to Nancy*. Albany: State University of New York Press, 1990.

————. *The Hermeneutic Tradition: From Ast to Ricoeur*. Albany: State University of New York Press, 1990.

Pagnini, A. "Tugendhat: Dall'ontologia alla semantica formale." In *La filosofia*, edited by Paolo Rossi, 1:146–187. Rome-Bari: Laterza, 1985.

Palmer, Richard. *Hermeneutics: Interpretation Theory in Schleiermacher, Dilthey, Heidegger, and Gadamer*. Evanston, Ill.: Northwestern University Press, 1969.

Passmore, John Arthur. *Recent Philosophers*. Chicago: Open Court, 1985.

Peschl, A. *Transzendentalphilosophie—Sprachanalyse—Neoontologie. Zum Problem ihrer Vermittlung in exemplarischer Auseinandersetzung mit Heinrich Rickert, Ernst Tugendhat und Karl-Otto Apel*. Frankfurt: Peter Lang Europäischer Verlag der Wissenschaften, 1992.

Petzet, Heinrich Wiegand. *Encounters and Dialogues with Martin Heidegger, 1929–1976*. Translated by Parvis Emad and Kenneth Maly. Chicago: University Of Chicago Press, 1993.

Pippin, R. P. "Traditional and Analytical Philosophy: E. Tugendhat." *Independent Journal of Philosophy* 5/6 (1988): 165–168.

————. *Hegel's Idealism: The Satisfactions of Self-Consciousness*. Cambridge: Cambridge University Press, 1989.

————. *Modernism as a Philosophical Problem: On the Dissatisfactions of European High Culture*. Cambridge, Mass.: Blackwell, 1991.

Platzeck, E.-W. "E. Tugendhat, *TI KATA TINOS*." *Franziskanische Studien* 42 (1960): 210–212.

Pöggeler, Otto. "Ernst Tugendhat 'Der Wahrheitsbegriff bei Husserl und Heidegger.'" *Philosophisches Jarhbuch* 76 (1969): 376–386.

————, ed. *Heidegger: Perspektiven zur Deutung seines Werkes*. Köln/Berlin, 1969.

————. "Selbst Bewusstsein und Identität, Ernst Tugendhats 'SelbstBewusstsein und Selbsbestimmung.'" *Hegel-Studien* 16 (1981): 198–207.

————. *Heidegger und die Hermeneutische Philosophie*. Freiburg: Alber, 1983.

————. "Heideggers logische Untersuchungen." In *Martin Heidegger: Innen- und Aussenansichten*, 75–100. Forum für Philosophie Bad Hamburg. Frankfurt: M. Suhrkamp, 1989.

————. *Martin Heidegger's Path of Thinking*. Translated by Dan Magurshak and Sigmund Barber. New York: Humanity Books, 1994.

————. "Heidegger's Topology of Being." In *On Heidegger and Language*, edited by Joseph J. Kockelmans, 107–146. Evanston, Ill.: Northwestern University Press, 1972.

Pothast, U. "In assertorischen Sätzen wahrnehmen und in praktischen Sätzen überlegen, wie zu reagieren ist, Ernst Tugendhat, SelbstBewusstsein und Selbstbestimmung." *Philosophische Rundschau* 28 (1981): 26–43.

Prado, C. G. *A House Divided: Comparing Analytic and Continental Philosophy*. New York: Humanity Books, 2003.

Prange, C. "Heidegger und die sprachanalytische Philosophie." *Philosophische Jahrbuch* 79 (1972): 39–51.

Preyer, G. "Referenz—Gegenstand—Erste-person. Zu Ernst Tugendhats 'formaler' Semantik." *Prima philosophia* 6 (1993): 285–298.

Puntel, L. B. "Idee und Problematik einer Formalen Semantik. Zu E. Tugendhat 'Vorlesusgen zur Einführung in die sprachanalytische Philosophie.'" In *Zeitschrift für Philosophische Forschung* 31 (1977): 413–427.

Quine, Willard V. O. "On What There Is." 1948. In *From a Logical Point of View. Nine Logico-Philosophical Essays*. Cambridge, Mass.: Harvard University Press, 1953.

Rajchman, John, and Cornel West, eds. *Post-Analytic Philosophy*. New York: Columbia University Press, 1985.

Rasmussen, Anders Moe. "Heidegger sproganalytisk fortolket: Ernst Tugendhats sproganalytiske videreförsel af Heideggers faenomenologi." *Philosophia: Tidsskrift for filosofi* 20 (1991): 139–149.

Raulet, Gérard. *La philosophie allemande depuis 1945*. Paris: Armand Colin, 2006.

Reemtsma, Jan Philipp. "Laudatio en la concesión del Premio 'Meister Eckhart' a Ernst Tugendhat." *Diálogo Científico* 14, no. 1/2 (2005): 22–31.

Richardson, William. *Heidegger: Through Phenomenology to Thought*. New York: Fordham University Press, 2003.

Richter, M. "Heideggers These vom 'Überspringen der Welt' in traditionellen Wahrheitstheorien und die Fortführung der Wahrheitfrage nach Sein und Zeit." *Heidegger Studies* 5 (1989): 47–78.

Ricoeur, Paul. Forward to *Husserl: Expositions and Appraisals*, by Ernst Tugendhat, edited and translated by F. Elliston and P. McCormick. Notre Dame, Ind.: University of Notre Dame Press, 1977.

———. *The Conflict of Interpretations*. Edited by Don Ihde. Translated by Kathleen McLaughlin. London: Continuum, 2004.

Ricoeur, Paul, and Hans-Georg Gadamer. "The Conflict of Interpretations." In *Phenomenology: Dialogues and Bridges*, edited by Ronald Bruzina and Bruce Wilshire, 299–320. Albany: State University of New York Press, 1982.

Risser, James. *Hermeneutics and the Voice of the Other. Re-reading Gadamer's Philosophical Hermeneutics*. Albany: State University of New York Press, 1997.

Rochlitz, R. "Un échec instructif, Ernst Tugendhat SelbstBewusstsein und Selbsbestimmung." *Critique* 44 (1988): 370–383.

Römpp, Georg. "Wesen der Wahrheit und Wahrheit des Wesens. Über den Zusammenhang von Wahrheit und Unverborgenheit im Denken Heideggers." *Zeitschrift für philosophische Forschung* 40 (1986): 193.

Rorty, Richard, ed. *The Linguistic Turn*. Chicago: The University of Chicago Press, 1967.

———. *Philosophy and the Mirror of Nature*. Princeton, N.J.: Princeton University Press, 1979.

———. *Consequences of Pragmatism*. Minneapolis: University of Minnesota Press, 1982.

———. "Review of *Traditional and Analytical Philosophy: Lectures on the Philosophy of Language* by Ernst Tugendhat." *The Journal of Philosophy* 82 (1985): 720–729.

———. *Objectivity, Relativism, and Truth*. Cambridge, Mass.: Cambridge University Press, 1991.

———. *Essays on Heidegger and Others*. Cambridge, Mass.: Cambridge University Press, 1991.

———. *Truth and Progress*. Cambridge, Mass.: Cambridge University Press, 1998.

———. "Being That Can Be Understood Is Language." In *Gadamer's Repercussions: Reconsidering Philosophical Hermeneutics*, edited by Bruce Krajewski, 21–29. Berkeley: University of California Press, 2004.

————. "Analytic and Conversational Philosophy." In *Philosophy as Cultural Politics*, by Richard Rorty, 120–130. Cambridge, Mass.: Cambridge University Press, 2007.

Rorty, Richard, and Gianni Vattimo. *The Future of Religion*. Edited by Santiago Zabala. New York: Columbia University Press, 2005.

Rosen, Michael. *Hegel's Dialectic and Its Criticism*. Cambridge: Cambridge University Press, 1985.

Runggaldier, E. *Zeichen und Bezeichnetes: sprachphilosophische Untersuchungen zum Problem der Referenz*. Berlin: de Gruyter, 1985.

Russell, Bertrand. "On Denoting." *Mind* 14 (1905): 479–493.

Rutten, C. "E. Tugendhat, *TI KATA TINOS*." *Revue Philosophique de Louvain* 55 (1959): 451–452.

Sabada, Javier. *La filosofía moral analítica de Wittgenstein a Tugendhat*. Madrid: Mondadori, 1989.

Sallis, John. *Delimitations: Phenomenology and the End of Metaphysics*. 1986. Bloomington: Indiana University Press, 1995.

Scarano, Nico, and Suárez Mauricio, eds. *Ernst Tugendhats Ethik. Einwaende und Erwiderungen*. Munich: C. H. Beck, 2006.

Schleiermacher, Friedrich. *Hermeneutics and Criticism and Other Writings*. Edited and translated by Andrew Bowie. Cambridge, Mass.: Cambridge University Press, 1998.

Schmitz, H. E. "Tugendhat, *TI KATA TINOS*." *Revue Internationale de Philosophie* 14 (1960): 101–102.

Schönrich, G. "Innere Autonomie oder Zurechnungsfähigkeit? Eine Auseinandersetzung mit E. Tugendhats 'Der Begriff der Willensfreiheit.'" *Zeitschrift für Philosophische Forschung* 2 (1990): 278–291.

Schürmann, Reiner. *Heidegger on Being and Acting: From Principles to Anarchy*. Translated by C.-M. Gros. Bloomington: University of Indiana Press, 1990.

————. *Broken Hegemonies*. Translated by R. Lilly. Bloomington: University of Indiana Press, 2003.

Sheehan, Thomas. "Husserl and Heidegger: The Making and Unmaking of a Relationship." In *Psychological and Transcendental Phenomenology and the Confrontation with Heidegger, 1927–1931*, by E. Husserl, edited and translated by T. Sheehan and R. Palmer, 1–32. Dordrecht: Kluwer, 1997.

————. "Heidegger." In *The Shorter Routledge Encyclopedia of Philosophy*, edited by Edward Craig, 359. London: Routledge, 2005.

Siep, L. "Kehraus mit Hegel? Zu Ernst Tugendhats Hegelkritik." *Zeitschrift für Philosophische Forschung* 35 (1981): 518–531.

Silverman, Hugh J., ed. "Phenomenology: From Hermeneutics to Deconstruction." *Research in Phenomenology* 14 (1984): 19–34.

———. *Inscriptions: Between Phenomenology and Structuralism.* New York: Routledge and Kegan Paul, 1987.

———. *Continental Philosophy: Gadamer and Hermeneutics.* London: Routledge, 1991.

———, ed. *Questioning Foundations. Truth/Subjectivity/Culture.* London: Routledge, 1993.

Skirbekk, G., ed. *Wahrheitstheorien. Eine Auswahl aus den Diskussionen über Wahrheit im 20. Jahrhundert.* Frankfurt: M. Suhrkamp, 1992.

Skirke, Christian. "Egozentizität und Mystik: Eine anthropologische Studie, by Ernst Tugendhat." *European Journal of Philosophy* 13 (2005): 306–311.

Smith, Barry. "Frege and Husserl: The Ontology of Reference." *Journal of the British Society for Phenomenology* 9 (May 1978): 111–125.

Smith, Barry, and Kevin Mulligan. "Traditional Versus Analytic Philosophy: Lectures on the Philosophy of Language: E. Tugendhat." *Grazer Philosophische Studien* 21 (1984): 193–201.

Soldati, G. "Selbsbewusstsein und unmittelbares Wissen bei Tugendhat." In *Die Frage nach dem Subjekt,* edited by M. Frank, G. Raulet, and W. v. Reijen, 85–100. Frankfurt: M. Suhrkamp, 1988.

———. *Bedeutung und psychischer Gehalt: eine Untersuchung zur sprachanalytischen Kritik von Husserls früher Phänomenologie.* Paderborn: Ferdinand Schöningh, 1994.

———. "Bedeutungen und Gegenständlichkeiten. Zu Tugendhat's sprachanalytischer Kritik von Husserls früher Phänomenologie." *Zeitschrift für Philosophische Forschung* 50 (1996): 410–441.

Somek, Alexander. "Die Moralisierung der Menschenrechte. Eine Auseinandersetzung mit Ernst Tugendhat." In *Die Gegenwart der Gerechtigkeit. Diskurse zwischen Recht, praktischer Philosophie und Politik,* edited by Christoph Demmerling and Thomas Rentsch, 48–49. Berlin: Akademie Verlag, 1995.

Stallmach, J. "E. Tugendhat, *TI KATA TINOS.*" *Theologische Revue* 55 (1959): 165–168.

Starr, David E. *Entity and Existence: An Ontological Investigation of Aristotle and Heidegger.* New York: Burt Franklin & Co., 1975.

Staten, H. *Wittgenstein and Derrida.* Oxford: Blackwell, 1985.

Steinfath, Holmer. "Heidegger und Ernst Tugendhat. Die sprachanalytische Transformation der Philosophie Heideggers." In *Heidegger-Handbuch.*

Leben—Werk—Wirkung, edited by Dieter Thomä, 408–410. Stuttgart: Metzler, 2003.

Steinvorth, U. "Tugendhat und die Sprachanalytische Philosophie." *Zeitschrift für Philosophische Forschung* 34 (1980): 59–69.

Stenstad, Gail. *Transformations: Thinking After Heidegger*. Madison: University of Wisconsin Press, 2005.

Stern, David S. "A Hegelian Critique of Reflection." In *Hegel and His Critics: Philosophy in the Aftermath of Hegel*, edited by William Desmond, 179–190. Albany: State University of New York Press, 1989.

Strawson, P. F. *Individuals*. 1959. London: Routledge, 1990.

Suhrkamp. *Sein, das verstanden werden kann, ist Sprache. Hommage an Hans-Georg Gadamer*. Frankfurt: M. Suhrkamp, 2001.

Taylor, C. "Ernst Tugendhat, SelbstBewusstsein und Selbstbestimmung." *The Journal of Philosophy* 79 (1982): 218–222.

———. "Theories of Meaning." In *Philosophical Papers 1*, 248–249. Cambridge, Mass.: Cambridge University Press, 1985.

Tegtmeier, E. *Grundzüge einer kategorialen Ontologie: Dinge, Eigenschaften, Beziehungen, Sachverhalte*. Munich: Verlag Karl Alber, 1992.

Theunissen, Michael. *Sein und Schein. Die kritische Funktion der Hegelschen Logik*. Frankfurt: M. Suhrkamp, 1978.

———. *The Other: Studies in the Social Ontology of Husserl, Heidegger, Sartre, and Bubner*. Cambridge, Mass.: MIT Press, 1986.

———. *Kierkegaard's Concept of Despair*. Princeton, N.J.: Princeton University Press, 2005.

Thomä, D. "Tugendhat, der Prinz und die Moral." *Deutsche Zeitschrift für Philosophie* 1 (1994): 35–58.

Tichy, M. "Ernst Tugendhat, Philosophische Aufsätze." *Zeitschrift für Philosophische Forschung* 47 (1993): 656–660.

———. "Ernst Tugendhat, 'Vorlesungen über Ethik.'" *Zeitschrift für didaktik der Philosophie und Ethik* 4 (1994): 286–290.

Tietz, U. *Sprache und Verstehen in analytischer und hermeneutischer Sicht*. Berlin: Akademie Verlag, 1995.

Tomasello, P. "Introduzione alla filosofia analitica. E. Tugendhat." *Iride* 3 (1989): 329–330.

———. "La svolta linguistica nell'ermeneutica tedesca contemporanea." *Iride* 8 (1992): 52–81.

Vattimo, Gianni. *The End of Modernity: Nihilism and Hermeneutics in Postmodern Culture.* Translated by J. R. Snyder. Baltimore, Md.: John Hopkins University Press, 1988.

———. *Essere, storia e linguaggio in Heidegger.* Genoa: Marietti, 1989.

———. *The Adventure of Difference: Philosophy After Nietzsche and Heidegger.* Translated by C. P. Blamires and T. Harrison. Cambridge: Polity Press, 1993.

———. "Diritto all'argomentazione." In *Filosofia '92,* edited by G. Vattimo, 59–70. Rome-Bari: Laterza, 1993.

———. *Beyond Interpretation: The Meaning of Hermeneutics for Philosophy.* Translated by D. Webb. Cambridge: Polity Press, 1997.

———. "Pensiamo in compagnia." *L'espresso* 45 (November 8, 2001): 193.

———. *After Christianity.* Translated by L. D'Isanto. New York: Columbia University Press, 2002.

———. "Gadamer and the Problem of Ontology." In *Gadamer's Century,* edited by J. Malpas, U. Arnswald, and J. Kertscher, 299–306. Cambridge, Mass.: MIT Press, 2002.

———. *Nihilism and Emancipation: Ethics, Politics, and Law.* Edited by Santiago Zabala. Translated by William McCuaig. New York: Columbia University Press, 2004.

Vattimo, Gianni, and Pier Aldo Rovatti, eds. *Il pensiero debole.* Milan: Feltrinelli, 1983.

Vieth, Andreas. *Richard Rorty: His Philosophy Under Discussion.* Frankfurt: Ontos Verlag, 2005.

Volpi, Franco. *Heidegger e Aristotele.* Padua: Daphne, 1984.

———. "Dasein as Praxis: The Heideggerian Assimilation and Radicalization of the Practical Philosophy of Aristotle." In *Critical Heidegger,* edited by C. Macann, 27–66. London: Routledge, 1996.

Voss, Christiane. *Narrative Emotionen: Eine Untersuchung Uber Moglichkeiten Und Grenzen Philosophischer Emotionstherorien.* Berlin: de Gruyter, 2004.

Vries, S. J. De. "Ernst Tugendhat, Der Wahrheitsbegriff bei Husserl und Heidegger." *Teologie und Philosophie* 44 (1969): 395–397.

Wachterhauser, Brice, ed. *Hermeneutics and Modern Philosophy.* Albany: State University of New York Press, 1986.

———. *Hermeneutics and Truth.* Evanston, Ill.: Northwestern University Press, 1994.

Wallace, Matson. *A New History of Philosophy from Descartes to Searle.* New York: Harcourt Brace, 2000.

Welsch, Wolfgang. *Unsere postmoderne Moderne.* Berlin: Akademie Verlag, 1997.

Wetzel, M. "Tugendhat und Apel im Verhältnis zu Kant. Zu: Höffe O, Ist die Transzentale Vernunftkritik in der Sprachphilosophie aufgehoben? Eine programmatische Auseinandersetzung mit Ernst Tugendhat und Karl-Otto Apel." *Philosophische Jarhbuch* 94 (1987): 387–394.

Wheeler, Samuel C. *Deconstruction as Analytic Philosophy*. Stanford, Calif.: Stanford University Press, 2000.

Wildt, A. "Gefühle in Tugendhats Konzeption von Moralbegründung." *Deutsche Zeitschrift für Philosophie* 1 (1997): 119–136.

Willaschek, M., ed. *Ernst Tugendhat. Moralbegründung und Gerechtigkeit, Vortrag und Kolloquium in Münster 1997*. Münster: Lit Verlag, 1997.

Williams, John. "Traditional and Analytical Philosophy: Lectures on the Philosophy of Language: Ernst Tugendhat." *The Heythrop Journal* 26 (1985): 346–348.

Williams, Michael. *Unnatural Doubts: Epistemological Realism and the Basic of Scepticism*. Princeton, N.J.: Princeton University Press, 1996.

———. *Groundless Belief: An Essay on the Possibility of Epistemology*. Princeton, N.J.: Princeton University Press, 1999.

———. *Problems of Knowledge. A Critical Introduction to Epistemology*. New York: Oxford University Press, 2001.

Wingert, L. "Unter nicht-transzendenten Prämissen begründen und sich fragen, was mit der Moral sonst noch verlorenginge." *Philosophische Rundschau* 42 (1995): 286–296.

———. "Gott naturalisieren? Anscombes Problem und Tugendhats Lösung." *Deutsche Zeitschrift für Philosophie* 4 (1997): 501–528.

Wischke, M. "Ernst Tugendhat, Philosophische Aufsätze." *Deutsche Zeitschrift für Philosophie* 41 (1993): 597–598.

Wittgenstein, L. *Tractatus Logico-Philosophicus*. 1922. Translated by D. F. Pears and B. F. McGuinness. London: Routledge, 2001.

———. *Philosophical Investigations*. Translated by G. E. M. Ascombe. Oxford: Basil Blackwell, 1953.

Wolf, Ursula. *Das Problem des moralischen Sollens*. Berlin: de Gruyter, 1984.

Wolin, Richard. *The Heidegger Controversy: A Critical Reader*. New York: Columbia University Press, 1991. (2nd ed., Cambridge, Mass.: MIT Press, 1993.)

———. *The Politics of Being: The Political Thought of Martin Heidegger*. New York: Columbia University Press, 1992.

Wrathall, Mark. "Heidegger and Truth as Correspondence." *International Journal of Philosophical Studies* 7 (1999): 79–88.

————. "Unconcealment." In *A Companion to Heidegger*, edited by Mark A. Wrathall and Hubert L. Dreyfus, 337–357. London: Blackwell, 2005.

Wright, Kathleen, ed. *Festivals of Interpretation: Essays on Hans-Georg Gadamer's Work*. New York: State University of New York Press, 1990.

Wyller, T. "Wahrheit und Bedeutung bei Tugendhat und Davidson." *Synthesis Philosophica Zagreb* 5 (1988): 177–195.

Zabala, Santiago. "Che cosa significa pensare dopo la svolta linguistica? La filosofia di Ernst Tugendhat." *Eidos* 1 (2003): 39–53.

————. "Pharmakons of Onto-theology." In *Weakening Philosophy: Essays in Honour of Gianni Vattimo*, edited by S. Zabala, 231–249. Montreal: McGill-Queen's University Press, 2007.

————, ed. *Weakening Philosophy: Essays in Honour of Gianni Vattimo*. Montreal: McGill-Queen's University Press, 2007.

Zambelli, P. "Ernst Tugendhat: Filosofia e impegno antinucleare." *Quaderni Piacentini* 13 (1984): 25–45.

INDEX